Eye Contact

Luke Sharrett

ISBN: 978-0-578-32416-6

DEDICATION

To my sons

CONTENTS

1. AIR FORCE ONE

I walked down the airplane aisle like a new kid on his first day of school, craning my neck and looking for my assigned seat. To my relief, the small cabin was only four aisles long. I soon found my spot. A white notecard emblazoned with the Presidential seal lay at my seat. Beneath the seal was a line of cursive script: "Welcome Aboard Air Force One."

Settling into my row, I looked around the press cabin of the Presidential aircraft. The cushy first class-style accommodations were reserved for the White House travel pool, of which I was a part. The travel pool is comprised of a rotating network news camera crew (videographer, sound tech, and producer) a radio reporter, three reporters from various newswires and papers, and four still photographers. Journalists are confined to the press cabin unless invited to the front of the plane by a White House staff member. No one was being invited anywhere at the moment, because the President wasn't even on the plane. An announcement from the flight deck came over the plane's public address system:

"The president has departed the White House with a flight time of ten minutes."

A group of my colleagues—fellow news photographers like myself—stood up and began filing out of the cabin. I followed their lead and exited Air Force One down onto the tarmac at Andrews Air Force Base. We gathered under one of the plane's massive wings to photograph the arrival of Marine One, the presidential helicopter, with President Obama aboard.

A short time later, the distinct sound of helicopter rotor blades caught my attention. I turned and watched as President Obama's highly modified Sikorsky Sea King helicopter landed on the runway. The glistening green and white chopper taxied off the landing strip and past the bulging blue nose of the Air Force One. Once its rotor blades had stopped spinning a sharply dressed US Marine disembarked Marine One, lowering the front staircase of the helicopter as he descended to the tarmac. He did an about-face with his back to Marine One, stood at attention, and snapped into a crisp salute. A moment later President Obama emerged in the doorway of the helicopter, trotted down the stairs and returned the Marine's gesture of respect with a salute of his own.

Part of me couldn't believe I was there.

So, what exactly was a twenty-year-old photography intern with a bad haircut ~~and a poor sense of style~~ doing in the shadow of Air Force One? It's a long story. I was born in Charlottesville, Virginia, in March of 1989. The middle of three siblings, I spent my first years playing in the woods behind my family's home nestled in the foothills of the Blue Ridge Mountains. My father worked as a church planter who founded new congregations for the Presbyterian Church in America. My mother was a stay-at-home mom turned schoolteacher. Around age three, my family packed up and moved to Fort Worth, Texas, to start another church. For the next twelve years I spent my time playing little league sports, camping with my Boy Scout troop, and setting up folding chairs at church on Sundays. Midway through my freshman year of high school my older brother, younger sister, and I received the news from mom and dad. We were moving back to Virginia.

Upon returning to the Old Dominion, I was quickly bested by the challenge of integrating myself into a new high school. I left behind my best friends, the girls I had crushes on, my Boy Scout troop, and my school sports teams. I left behind everything that gave me a sense of belonging. A sense of loneliness and fear settled upon me like a suffocating wet blanket, stifling my joy and blunting my normally optimistic disposition toward life. I backed down from the hard work of making new friends and retreated into the basement of my new house. I was downright terrified by the prospect of social rejection at my new school. For two years I wasted away in the glow of a hand-me-down television set. I stayed up late watching MTV reality shows devoid of any shred of cultural, intellectual, or even comedic value. Hours upon hours of precious time were wasted playing video games. I squandered away my mental and physical health on a ratty old couch, emerging from the basement only to resupply myself with microwaved Hot Pockets and Bagel Bites upon which I would binge late into the night. I was aimless. I had no mission. There was no reason to even get out of bed in the morning.

I shuddered as I reflected upon my generally useless high school self. There was no going back to a life ruled by depression and anxiety, if I could help it. I had wasted too many years flirting with cowardice, isolating myself, and avoiding of responsibility. The only direction was forward.

Thankfully I had come a long way in two years. I knew I had to make the most of this golden opportunity. This was my chance to make my family, friends, editors, and myself proud.

My plum internship with the *New York Times* had more or less fallen in my lap. I was studying photojournalism at Western Kentucky University when one of my professors sent out a department-wide email during my sophomore year. The *Times* was looking for candidates with political photography experience to apply for an internship in Washington, D.C. I was far from being the most-experienced photo student on campus. Nonetheless, I threw my name into the hat. Months passed by without any word from the *Times*. I started to lose hope that I was still in the running for the gig. Upon the conclusion of my final exams in May, I emailed the paper inquiring about the status of my application. I heard back almost immediately. The *New York Times* had picked me.

"How soon can you be in Washington?" The editor asked.

A week later I arrived for my first day on the job.

It was Saturday, September 12, 2009, the day of my first trip on Air Force One. Earlier that morning, I woke up and donned a button-down shirt and tie that I had laid out in anticipation the night before. After getting dressed I looked down at every camera lens, spare camera battery, and memory card that I owned. The thought of being without *exactly* the right lens on my first Air Force One trip meant I committed a classic newbie mistake: I packed too much gear. *Better safe than sorry, I guess.* Over the course of my next year traveling on Air Force One, I would adopt a more minimalist philosophy when it came to camera equipment: Less is more, more or less. But I couldn't know that now, on my first day. Instead, I walked out the door brimming with camera lenses and nervous energy to drive the 35 minutes from where I was staying in Arlington, Virginia, to the rear gate at Joint Base Andrews.

Originally built in 1942 as Camp Springs Air Base, Andrews is now home to several military units, including the US Air Force's 89th Airlift Wing, Special Air Mission Squadron responsible for transporting high-ranking government and military leaders across the United States and across the globe. In 1948, the base became Andrews Air Force Base. In 2009, the base's official designation switched from Andrews Air Force Base to Joint Base Andrews. Andrews' new title properly reflected the presence of various military units other than those under the command of the US Air Force. These units include the Army's Priority Air Transport Squadron, The Navy's 10th Fleet Cyber Command, and the Marine Corp's 4th Marine Airlift Wing to name a few.

My 23-mile commute from Arlington to Andrews seemed to take forever. The anticipation I felt somehow stretched the otherwise uneventful half hour drive into an eternity. Finally, I pulled into a line of cars outside the rear gate. SUV's, late model sedans, and number of shiny black luxury town cars hired by the cable news networks idled in a line in front of me. The vehicle in front of mine belonged to one of my photographer colleagues whom I recognized from the White House. Seeing me pull in line behind him, he hopped out of his car and walked over to my window.

"You're late! We were starting to get worried about you," he quipped.

I glanced at my watch and saw that I was a whole five minutes early. *Note to self, arrive earlier next time.*

An Air Force officer made his way down the line of cars checking driver's licenses and press credentials against his own access list. I handed him a lanyard containing my US Senate/House of Representatives press pass which would suffice to confirm my identity as a journalist working for the *New York Times* in Washington.

Everyone else in line flashed their coveted White House credentials. Infamously hard to come by and surprisingly modest in appearance, a White House hard pass guaranteed its bearer speedy access through the northwest gate and onto White House grounds. It also granted the bearer instant clout among the social circles of journalists in Washington. By most appearances, it was little more than a red plastic card bearing one's name and news outlet beneath the all-caps word *PRESS* in a serifed font. In fairness, the credential does look like something a student might design in photoshop for their high school and on more than one occasion, I have seen law enforcement officers from outside the DC metro area eye a colleague's White House hard pass with suspicion. Nonetheless, in order to possess such a mythical credential one had to endure a thorough vetting from both the White House Press Office and the US Secret Service. The process took months for even the most respected Associated Press reporter or well-known cable news anchor to successfully navigate.

Maybe someday I would have one of my own.

Having passed the first of multiple redundant security checks, I put my turquoise, hand-me-down Nissan Altima in gear and followed the line of cars in front of me toward Andrews' rear gate, stopping at the guard shack to meet the gaze of a foreboding Air Force Security Forces Airman. Dressed in camouflage fatigues and cradling an M-16 assault rifle, the guard was an intimidating sight. A black beret sat cocked at an angle on his buzzed head. As we made eye contact, he nodded ever so slightly and waved me through.

I brought up the rear as the line as press vehicles snaked toward the base passenger terminal at an agonizingly slow 25mph. Along the way we passed modest neighborhoods of on-base housing for military families. Occasionally the column of cars slowed for a golf cart to scoot across the road to their next tee box. Joint Base Andrews is home to an 18-hole golf course that is a favorite of Air Force retirees. Presidents stretching back to Ronald Reagan have utilized the course on their weekends as well.

Leaving the golf course behind, our caravan passed building after nondescript building used by the tenant commands housed on site. Eventually, I pulled into a parking spot outside the modest passenger terminal and gathered my equipment for the trip. As I walked toward the single-story tan-bricked building, the hair stood up on the back of my neck. The distinctive hump of Air Force One's upper-level flight deck protruded above the roofline of the terminal.

"Wow!" I whispered under my breath. "This is so cool." It was a refrain I would repeat more than once that day.

Inside the terminal my colleagues and I assembled in a single file line and passed through a pair of sliding glass doors that lead outside to the tarmac. Stepping outside, the pungent odor of aviation exhaust met my nostrils. The fumes came from Joint Base Andrews's collection of jets parked up and down the airfield.

I first became fascinated by military aircraft growing up in Fort Worth. The city is home to one of Lockheed Martin's most prolific aircraft assembly lines. Unsurprisingly the airspace above West Fort Worth was constantly abuzz with fighter jets and all manner of U.S. military airplanes. My love for the subject was pervasive. As a youngster, the walls of my bedroom were practically papered over with posters of helicopters and jets, both modern and historic. At school I was reprimanded for drawing airplane doodles in the margins of my composition notebooks. Even the field where I played little league soccer was situated at the end of the runway belonging to the local Naval Air Station. During one particularly memorable soccer match, a massive B-2 Spirit nuclear bomber passed low over the field as it came in for a landing at the base. As if on cue the other team, my teammates, and I stopped playing and stared upward at the gargantuan flying wing descending low over our heads. Even the referees stared in disbelief.

Back at Andrews, I surveyed the impressive row of aircraft that had just come into view. A number of dark grey C-17 cargo jets, the backbone of The US Air Force's transport fleet, sat nearest to us on the tarmac. Beside them were multiple blue and white painted 757 VIP passenger jets (designated C27's by the Air Force) Next came a handful of small Learjets painted in a similar blue and white scheme. Toward the end of the eclectic lineup were a couple USAF Bell Huey helicopters used to ferry high-ranking officers and generals back and forth between Andrews and the Pentagon.

Also present on the flight line that day was the Air Force's E4-B, more commonly known as the "Doomsday Plane." Painted in a stark white livery with a single blue stripe tracing its window line, this unique Boeing 747 was designed to be an airborne command post in the event of a nuclear war. Thanks to an airframe hardened against the effects of an atomic blast as well as in-flight refueling capability, the E4-B could theoretically stay airborne indefinitely in the unpleasant event of a nuclear apocalypse. A mysterious white and black dome rising from the roof of the plane caught my eye. No other 747 that I was aware of possessed something similar. I could only guess what manner of top-secret communications equipment was housed inside the strange tumor-like bulge that protruded from the top of the flight deck. Such an imposing aircraft looked like something ripped from the pages of a Tom Clancy novel.

The only thing that stood a chance of pulling my gaze away from the fascinating collection of jets off to my left was the queen herself: Air Force One. Gleaming in the morning sun, the legendary Boeing 747 commanded the attention of everyone on the flight line. Sporting its classic white, blue, and sea foam paint job, Air Force One is an unmistakable symbol of American diplomatic and military dominance. Just looking at it made the hair stand up on the back of my neck.

As we made our way toward the magnificent airplane, reporters pulled out their iPhones to snap a quick photo for their social media feeds. Veteran CBS Radio White House correspondent Mark Knoller is known to say that "Air Force One never takes a bad picture." He's right.

I stepped out of line to take a couple photos for myself. A fellow photographer told me to turn around so he could get a picture of me with the plane in the background. The photo he took would become a cherished memento commemorating my first flight on Air Force One. The wide grin on my clean-shaven face betrayed how I felt about achieving such an incredible milestone. I couldn't believe it was happening.

The red carpeted staircase parked at the front of the plane is reserved only for the President and his guests. The press gets to sneak in the back door. As our group drew near, a hatch began to protrude from the reflective chrome underbelly of Air Force One's fuselage. A mechanical staircase started to unfold like the giant outstretched arm of a transformer robot. Rear entrance or not, it doesn't matter how you get on Air Force One. Just stepping onboard is the honor of a lifetime.

One by one, my colleagues ahead of me paused at the foot of the retractable staircase to speak with a formidable looking Air Force Officer. I waited in line until it was my turn to check-in with him. Sporting more than a couple stripes on his sleeve, the square-jawed officer looked at me through a pair of gold rimmed Ray Ban aviator sunglasses.

"Name." The officer's tone communicated that this was more of a demand than a question.

"Sharrett, Luke. Luke Sharrett," I blurted in response.

He glanced down at a small piece of paper in the palm of his hand and scratched through a line of text with a ballpoint pen.

"Welcome aboard," he said as he moved aside to let me pass.

As I stepped into the belly of the plane, I realized I was standing right where the intense gunfight between Harrison Ford and that group of Eastern European terrorists broke out in the movie *Air Force One*. The 1997 action thriller was the first R-rated movie I'd ever seen as a kid.

"Get off my plane", I thought to myself, hearing Ford's famous one-liner in my head.

The movie incorporates fictional elements like escape pods into its Hollywood imagining of the Presidential Aircraft, and while many of the plane's features and capabilities remain highly classified, this myth has been disappointingly debunked. The real Air Force One has no escape pods and no parachute ramp.

I watched through my camera's viewfinder between shutter clicks as the President walked from Marine One toward Air Force One. He chatted casually with an Air Force Officer who was acting as his escort between aircraft. Upon reaching Air Force One, the President bid his escort farewell and gave another salute to two more Air Force Officers standing guard at the bottom of the red-carpeted staircase. After a quick jog up the steps, he turned and waved goodbye.

As soon as he disappeared from sight, the entire press corps made a mad dash back to the rear staircase. The same Air Force officer from earlier checked our names against his list once again. I dashed back up the stairs to the press cabin. President Obama was already aboard which meant the clock was ticking. While Air Force One is equipped with satellite internet, secure telephone lines, and advanced communications equipment, none of these privileges are extended to those of us hitching a ride in the press cabin. For security reasons, Wi-Fi access is restricted, so the travel pool's photographers must rely on cellular connections to send our photos before we reach altitude and lose service. If I wanted to send any photos to New York, I would have to do so while we were still on the ground. Before long I would no longer have the ability to send photos to my editors in New York.

Every photo transmitted to the *New York Times* photo desk requires an embedded caption explaining the who, what, when, where, and why of each photo. While a truly successful news photo will clearly communicate the story of a given moment to the reader without the help of the printed word, photojournalists nonetheless caption every photo they send from the field. On a tip from my boss Doug, I had already crafted captions for each of the possible photos I might take throughout the course of the day.

As soon as I reached my seat, I hurriedly removed my memory cards from my cameras and started searching for my best photos. I dropped my best 3 or 4 frames into Photoshop for a quick levels adjustment and felt the plane lurch slowly forward.

We were on the move.

With my heart beating and fingers trembling, I saved my photos and applied my captions. I could feel the plane begin to turn onto the runway as the pilot lined us up for take-off. I connected to my Wi-Fi card and dropped the photos onto *the New York Times* photo server. "Come on, come on! Go baby, go!" I uttered under my breath as I watched the photos start to transmit. We begin to pick up speed. The grass growing alongside the runway became a green blur as our landing gear lifted off the ground. In a matter of seconds, we would reach an altitude above the umbrella of cellular coverage. I glanced back and forth between my computer and the view outside the window trying to gauge if my photos would make it in time. Success! The last of my photos zoomed off to New York City just as my Verizon hotspot lost connectivity.

I let out a sigh of relief and finally took a breath.

With my heart still pounding, I closed my laptop and tried to settle in for the hour and forty-minute flight to Minneapolis. I looked around the press cabin and was able to take in the scene for the first time since that morning. Comfortable first class-style seats configured in rows of two by two filled the press cabin. CNN was playing on a pair of flat-screen TVs that were mounted to the front bulkhead of the cabin. In the rear stood a small bathroom stocked with toothpaste, mouthwash, and washcloths. Nearby, a basket of complimentary fresh fruit, nuts, and candy bars was displayed for the taking. Copies of the *New York Times* and *Washington Post* sat beside the basket of snacks. We had all the comforts of home. These amenities, plus a gauntlet of Secret Service agents sitting in the next cabin in front of ours, were discouragement enough against any attempts to explore the rest of the plane.

Shortly after takeoff an Air Force flight attendant came through our cabin passing out hot towels. He returned a few minutes later to take each person's drink order. Dressed in a sharp Navy-blue vest with a high-and-tight haircut, the attendant worked his way to the back of the cabin.

"Welcome aboard, Mr. Sharrett," he said upon reaching me. "I hear this is your first time aboard Air Force One. Can I get you anything to drink?" Caught off-guard, I asked for the first thing that came to mind.

"Do you have cran-apple?"

As soon as the words came out of my mouth, I regretted it. *Luke, you're on Air Force One, not Southwest Airlines!* I thought to myself.

"Cran…apple?" The attendant replied with a puzzled tone. "I'm sorry sir I don't think we have that onboard."

I apologized for the oddball request and settled for a water instead.

"Absolutely, Mr. Sharrett," he replied. "One water coming right up." A few minutes later the attendant returned with a crystal glass full of red liquid. "Mr. Sharrett," he began, "I got to thinking and combined a bit of cranberry juice with some apple juice and Sierra Mist. Give this a try."

I took a sip of the ice-cold cocktail. It was a superb take on a traditional Minute Maid cran-apple. "Wow, that's incredible! Thank you!"

I sat in my seat, sipping my sparkling juice and taking in the scene around the posh press cabin. We were certainly not in economy class anymore.

In order to board Air Force One, my colleagues and I had to pass through multiple layers of security. Back at the terminal we passed through a security checkpoint not unlike those found in commercial airports. We were then directed to a private waiting area. There, a member of the White House press team was waiting to provide us with White House credentials and a pocket-sized trip schedule detailing each of the events to which we would be accompanying the President. These press schedules, usually made from copy paper of varying colors, acted as a helpful logistical guide for the day.

Next, our Secret Service agent for the day introduced himself and handed each of us a White House pool pass. The P-pass is a hexagon of thin plastic about the size of a drink coaster that acts as a signal to the Secret Service that the bearer belongs in the White House entourage. P-passes come in every color of the rainbow and sport a Secret Service sticker of varying tones and numerals. The three variables at play (P-pass color, sticker color, and sticker number) help guarantee that it would be virtually impossible for any bad-actor to successfully forge a pass and slip into the White House press pool unnoticed. My pass for the day would be maroon in color. It would be the first of hundreds that I would receive over the course of the next twelve months. The agent filled out a blank space on the back of the P-pass with my name, outlet (*New York Times*) and the date: Sept 12, 2009. After scribbling down my info he handed me the completed credential. The P-pass would act as my ticket to board both Air Force One and the Presidential motorcade that was already assembled and waiting for us in Minneapolis.

In order to travel aboard Air Force One, the travel pool would be subject to thorough screening. A member of the Secret Service Uniformed Division arrived with a metal detecting wand and began to frisk each member of the press. When it was my turn, I stepped forward and made eye contact with the agent.

"Arms out," he ordered.

I assumed the pose of Davinci's Vitruvian Man with legs spread and arms extended out. The metal clip on my lanyard and my belt buckle evoked a high-pitched squawk from the wand as it passed over them.

"Turn around" the UD officer ordered.

I complied and listened tensely for any more squawks. A few seconds later the officer finished his sweep.

"You're good to go, sir,"

About that time a military Explosive Ordnance Disposal team had arrived. Aside from their short, military-style haircuts and clear plastic earpieces, there was little to give them away as members of the US military. Dressed uniformly in a sharp civilian ensemble of neatly tucked-in forest green polo shirts, wrinkle-free khakis, and brown leather Merrell hiking boots, two of the EOD techs began combing meticulously through our laptop bags and personal effects. No zipper was left unzipped. No pocket left unchecked. Each laptop was powered up and examined to make sure it was, in fact, a working laptop. Similarly, each of our cameras would be used to take multiple test photos in the hands of these focused military bomb techs. As they examined our equipment a third member of the EOD team made the rounds with a K-9 detection unit, aka a bomb-sniffing dog. In this case, an amped-up Belgian Malinois scrambled between our bags and camera equipment and sniffed wildly, its tongue protruding from the side of its long, pointed snout.

Content that none of us were trying to sneak weapons or explosives onboard Air Force One, EOD and the Secret Service gave us all the all-clear to collect our equipment and wipe off the Malinois drool, if necessary. With my previously sparse *New York Times* lanyard now bursting with the colorful credentials necessary for the day's trip, I settled into a terminal chair and began to craft my image captions for the day ahead.

By the time my first Air Force One trip rolled around I had been on the job as the *New York Times*' Washington photo intern for about a month. My first four weeks covering the White House and Capitol Hill had absolutely flown by. I thought I could not possibly have been happier. That is, until I got an email from my boss Doug. "AF1 Trip Saturday" was the subject line of the email. "Luke," the email began, "would you like to cover the President's trip to Minneapolis this weekend?"

My heart skipped a beat. Time stood still. *A White House trip? On Air Force One? YES!* I replied to the email immediately.

"Sure thing, Doug. I would be glad to."

Plans called for President Obama to travel from the White House to Minneapolis, Minnesota to build public support for The Affordable Care act, or Obamacare as it is known in common parlance. The few days leading up to the trip absolutely dragged by. I could not wait to experience my first taste of White House travel.

It had been just over two years since I moved out of my parents' house in Central Virginia and started my first semester at Western Kentucky University. Immediately after arriving on campus, I became possessed by a singular vision for my future. Whatever it took, I was going to work as a newspaper photojournalist. This much I knew. And here I was. Flying aboard Air Force One on behalf of perhaps the most well-respected newspaper in the world: the *New York Times.* A million pairs of eyeballs could potentially see my photos in the following day's Sunday print edition.

While I reveled in the euphoric sense of accomplishment that accompanied me as I sat on Air Force One, I knew that my success had never been guaranteed. Had I not found my personal mission, I would likely still be languishing in my parent's basement back in Central Virginia. Despite all the excitement college and internships had to afford me, my high school years still haunted me. I could not return to that life.

Looking around the press cabin I realized that I was the most inexperienced journalist in the press pool by far. As a twenty-year-old I was undoubtedly the youngest and most green person on the entire plane. Feelings of insecurity started to bubble up inside me. What if I mess this whole thing up? What if I miss a key moment or finish the trip without making any good photos? What if I screw up so badly that I miss my big shot and never fly on Air Force One again? I shuddered at the thought of failure and fished a couple "fun-size" Almond Joy candy bars from my pocket. Before we left Andrews, I had liberated them from the press cabin's wicker snack basket. Stuffing them in my mouth, I sought comfort from their milk chocolate sugar rush. As excited as I was to be here, did I really belong?

It had been quite some time since I last felt this elusive feeling of belonging. My family's move from, Texas to Virginia five years prior had shattered my teenage world. I no longer operated in circles where my presence was accepted, welcomed, and even celebrated. First and foremost, I missed my Boy Scout troop immensely. Upon arriving in Virginia, I plugged in with another Troop, but it just wasn't the same. In addition to scouts, I left behind a close-knit group of friends from the small classical school that I attended. Together the six of us learned Latin and read classics like *The Iliad* and *The Odyssey.* On the weekends we went to the movies, went swimming, and ate out together. Leaving them behind was painful. Ever since then I had been asking myself where I truly belonged. That nagging sense of being "alone" and an "other" still followed me. Even the fact that I was currently seated aboard the single most exclusive airplane in the world wasn't enough to assuage those feelings.

A couple hours after takeoff we began our descent into Minneapolis/St. Paul International Airport. As we approached the ground, the Press Cabin came alive. Reporters finished scribbling in their notebooks and stuffed laptops into backpacks. A cable news producer typed away furiously on her Blackberry as we picked up cell service for the first time since departing Andrews. My colleagues began hanging their cameras from their shoulders and adjusting their exposures to match the atmospheric conditions outside the plane. Some of the more eager members of the press pool rose from their seats and congregated in the aisle before we had even touched down. As I would come to experience over the course of the next 11 months, takeoff and landing with seatbacks reclined, tray tables un-stowed, and electronic devices in use is a common occurrence on Air Force One. The presidential aircraft touched down gently on the runway and was immediately joined on the ground by an SUV containing members of the US Secret Service Counter-Assault Team, or CAT team for short.

Shortly after John Hinkley's unsuccessful assassination attempt against President Ronald Reagan outside the Washington Hilton in 1981, the Secret Service began to re-evaluate the level of protection they were providing to the President. One of the changes they instituted was the formation of the CAT team. Clad in the latest Kevlar helmets and body armor the federal government could procure, members of this elite squad act as an armed deterrent against any plot to capture or harm the President of the United States. As I peered through the window at the SUV pacing alongside us, I caught a glimpse of the agents inside. Dressed in all-black and armed to the teeth with short-barreled assault rifles, sidearms, and flash-bang grenades, this highly trained tactical squad accompanies the President wherever he goes.

Turning my attention back inside the press cabin, I donned my backpack, grabbed my cameras, and joined my colleagues queuing in the aisle. Air Force One taxied off the runway and pulled up to a pre-determined spot in a remote corner of the airport. Once the hulking 747 came to a stop, the aft door opened, and an airport stair car gingerly approached the plane. We followed a group of Secret Service Agents down the rear staircase and onto the airport tarmac as the Presidential motorcade pulled into place alongside the Presidential Aircraft. The whine of Air Force One's four jet engines filled the air. The smell of aviation exhaust wafted the through air above the tarmac.

A few minutes passed before President Obama emerged from Air Force One with a wave. He descended the stairs briskly and shook hands with a waiting group of local officials who were on hand to witness the arrival of the President of the United States (POTUS)

Any time the President travels outside the perimeter of the White House a massive entourage moves with him. White House staff, members of the Secret Service's Presidential Protective Detail (PPD), White House Military Office personnel, paramedics, and members of the press are included in these movements. The White House motorcade, much like the seating chart onboard Air Force One, is arranged in order of importance. The President's limousines lead the way. The press brings up the rear.

With POTUS safely inside his limo I dashed toward the rear of the motorcade toward the press vans. I clambered into a white 12 passenger van and buckled my seat belt. Looking through the windshield, I noticed the vehicles at the front of the motorcade begin to roll forward. It was time to leave, whether those of us at the rear were ready, or not. The last of the press pool mounted up in our white vans and our driver accelerated to catch up with the rest of the convoy in front of us. The motorcade snaked its way past Air Force Once and to my surprise turned out onto the runway upon which we had just landed. Even something as impressive as the Presidential motorcade was dwarfed by the massive landing strip that we were now barreling down. We passed over a collection of gigantic rubber skid marks left behind by the countless jetliners whose runway we were borrowing temporarily.

As the motorcade exited airport property, a swarm of Minneapolis Police motorcycles encompassed us on all sides. They zipped around the motorcade in order to block traffic from entering our pre-determined route. Each motorcycle officer would choose a cross-street to block off, halting traffic until the motorcade had passed. Once the last vehicle of the Presidential movement sped by, they would leapfrog ahead of their fellow officers to block the next cross street or highway on-ramp. This frenzy continued until we reached the site of the rally where POTUS was scheduled to appear. The motorcade pulled into an underground entrance at the Target Arena downtown and came to a stop. The travel pool hurriedly spilled out of the press vans.

"Press, this way" a White House advance staffer called out. We followed his lead through a maze of backstage corridors until we emerged into the packed arena. The crowd was already buzzing with energy at the prospect of seeing the 44th president in the flesh. The crowd let out a cheer as we filed into the cavernous basketball stadium, correctly assuming the start of the event must be close at hand.

It was a new experience to suddenly find myself the focal point of so many eyeballs. I felt a flash of self-consciousness and began to do a personal inventory. How does my hair look? Is my necktie crooked? Can they tell I voted for John McCain in 2008?

The traveling press pool split into two groups. The reporters made their way toward a tiered press riser that had been set up in the back of the room while the photographers and network camera crew remained behind in the buffer. Lined with crowd control barricades, the buffer was a roughly ten-foot-wide space between the stage and the audience that was utilized by the Secret Service, the press, and sometimes the president himself. Audience members who arrived early enough to snag a standing room spot on the floor were often treated to a presidential handshake and maybe a selfie if they were lucky. Those who were persistent enough might even score an autograph from the man himself. Shortly after we settled into the buffer, a White House Communications Agency staffer dressed in navy blue suit walked out to the podium and delivered a black leather binder containing the President's remarks for the evening. The audience let out an even bigger cheer than before. It wouldn't be long now.

When officials in the West Wing hatch an idea for a White House trip, the Secret Service and US military begin their work initiating security protocols. Planning sessions involving law enforcement agencies, state authorities, and local government officials take place long before such a trip is even announced to the public, much less shared in confidence with members of the White House press corps. As the Secret Service begins to draw up contingency plans for the trip, White House advance staffers start planning the event itself. What configuration the stage will take, where the press riser will be set up, and what will be in the background behind the presidential podium are all questions that are taken into consideration. For campaign style events, the use of a catwalk is often employed. The event in Minneapolis was no different. On cue, President Obama would emerge from backstage and walk between throngs of adoring fans toward the podium. A massive American Flag was displayed alongside the catwalk which we photographers would have no choice but to include in our photos. An experienced advance team is often the only thing standing between a downright ugly event and one where each photo has the potential to radiate a dramatic patriotic vibe for those tuning in.

Though I had little else to compare it to at the time, this event was well-organized and well-lit. Not every political event is as well-crafted or fine-tuned as this one was. During the primaries you were more likely to find yourself jostling for a good position inside a barber shop in Iowa or a ham house in South Carolina. And there were few worse places_to photograph a candidate than the dark hotel ballrooms that they seemed to frequent. In contrast, the basketball arena I found myself in could not have been a more ideal place to photograph a presidential rally. The minutes dragged by. I noticed the butterflies in my stomach beating their wings full force. While this wasn't the first political rally I had photographed, nor was this my first time in close proximity to POTUS, I realized that I was about to accomplish a goal and live-out a dream that was some four years in the making. A booming voice interrupted my train of thought.

"Ladies and Gentlemen. The President of the United States."

The room roared to life as the crowd exploded with cheers, screams, and wild applause. President Obama emerged from between a set of black curtains and into the spotlight with a big grin on his face. Supporters lining the walkway strained with all their might to try and touch the hem of his suit pants as he made his way down the catwalk past the large American flag. Middle-aged women burst into tears and chanted "O-BA-MA! O-BA-MA!" The roar was akin to standing behind the jet engines of a fighter jet during takeoff. It was all consuming and downright disorienting if you weren't expecting it.

The release of emotional energy was unlike anything I had ever witnessed. For a moment I stood partially shell-shocked as a I tried to take in the wild scene. Then I remembered what I was doing there. *Dammit Luke, focus! You're here to take photos for the New York Times.*

Ah yes. That's right. *I had better do my job.*

I moved through the buffer to various vantage points as I photographed the President's speech. Doing my best to stay low and avoid blocking the view of the crowd and the television cameras at the back of the room, I went through a mental checklist in my head governing what kind of photos I needed to make. I repeated a mantra my college newspaper editor Evan Sisley had taught me two years before. "Tight, medium, wide," I recited to myself. Images of varying scale would help the page designers for the *New York Times* print edition lay everything out just right for the next day's paper. "Context, emotion, detail," I reminded myself. Images of varying subject matter would help increase the chances of my photos reaching more eyeballs in print and online.

A few minutes into the speech I noticed the veteran political photographers with whom I was traveling that day begin to transition from shooting photos to editing them. One by one they took a seat cross-legged in the buffer and plugged the memory cards from their cameras into their laptops. It was time to transmit photos back to New York. I followed the lead of my colleagues and took a seat near the feet of steely-eyed Secret Service Agent. Looking up, I met a stern downward glance and interpreted this to mean I had picked a bad place to sit. I shuffled a few extra feet away and began trying to sort through the hundreds of photos I had just taken rapid-fire in the minutes before.

There is a friendly competition between colleagues in the White House press pool and in Washington, D.C. at large. Just about everyone covering the White House and Capitol Hill wants to make the best photo of the group. Yet considering our now 24/7 news cycle, simply making the best photo of the day isn't enough. Not only is a news photographer expected to capture the best picture, they are also expected to transmit their photos onto the wire before their competition.

I shuffled quickly through my take and selected a half dozen photos representative of what I had witnessed at the event thus far. As I started dropping my pictures into Photoshop to make minor adjustments, I noticed my colleagues begin to shut their laptops and pack up. *Crap!* I was already falling behind. With my minor tweaks finished, I slapped pre-written captions on my images and dropped them into the *New York Times*' image server. Having made a few photos available to my editors, I was now able to shoot the rest of the event without worry about my deadline. There would be plenty of time for editing later, but only a precious few more minutes to capture POTUS onstage at this event.

Iconic, eloquent, and charismatic, Obama was a natural public speaker. He could command the attention of a school gymnasium and a pro-sports arena alike. It was hard to take a crummy photo of the man. Thanks in large part to a top-notch White House advance team, his events largely shot themselves. I clicked away trying my best to make photos that were a little different from my colleagues were shooting for the newswires. The men and women who photographed for these wires were absolute professionals. Many had been on the White House beat since at least the Clinton administration, if not before. As a rookie intern, I had no hope of matching them head-on technically or visually. Thankfully, my bosses at the Times encouraged me to try and think outside the box. It took me a few months to settle into my new role and become comfortable enough with my surroundings to really start making smart, refined, visually interesting photographs. While I can have the tendency to be hard on myself, I was resolute to make the most of such an amazing opportunity and be the very best *New York Times* intern I could be.

The tempo of President Obama's speech began to quicken as the applause lines built to a crescendo. Our press wrangler signaled to us with a twirl of her finger that the speech was wrapping up. President Obama read the last lines of his remarks from the teleprompter, waved to the TV cameras on the press riser, and walked down a set of stairs from the stage to buffer. As the President descended, we ascended a different flight of stairs to take over his spot onstage. Flanked by multiple Secret Service agents on both sides, President Obama worked his way along the rope line greeting supporters. The press pool shot photos of the back of the President's head framed by the crowd of ecstatic supporters straining for an autograph or handshake with the leader of the free world. Plenty of contrasts presented themselves. From the ever-present, always-adoring, African American women dressed in their Sunday best, to the rather seedy-looking guys with armfuls of memorabilia that would likely find their way to eBay by the next morning, the crowd was diverse. Sometimes the odd baby would even be passed through the crowd in the President's direction. The holy grail of rope line photos, and one I always looked out for, would be the president holding a crying baby. I don't recall ever being lucky enough to snag one for myself.

As the President finished the frenzied meet and greet, the press pool vacated the stage and rushed toward the motorcade. Piling back into the same twelve passenger van that I rode over in from the airport, I opened my laptop to try and sent a few more photos to New York before the paper's last evening deadline passed. Trying to edit, tone, and caption photos in a bouncy van speeding along at the rear of a presidential motorcade is no easy task. By the time we made it back to Air Force One, I was thoroughly car-sick (or maybe more technically van-sick) and hadn't accomplished as much as I had hoped. Before the press van had come to a complete stop, I flung the open the doors, jumped out onto the tarmac, and took off running full speed toward the Presidential aircraft. I made it over to the plane just in time to fire off a few frames of the President jogging up the stairs toward Air Force One. Before disappearing inside the plane, President Obama turned to wave goodbye to the handful of local media who had gathered to cover his departure from the Twin Cities. On my way to re-board the plane I watched as the "nuclear football," a briefcase containing the launch codes for America's nuclear arsenal, changed hands between two US military officers. While I climbed back onboard Air Force One, I felt the Boeing 747's powerful jet engines begin to spool up. It was time to head home.

Onboard Air Force One I noticed a savory aroma wafting through the press cabin. While most of the plane's passengers had disembarked and accompanied President Obama to the rally, a handful of Air Force crew members remained behind in order to prepare meals for the flight home. Shortly after takeoff they served a dinner of fettuccini alfredo and grilled chicken breast garnished with a Caesar salad and warm garlic breadstick. A slice of chocolate-drizzled cheesecake served on Air Force One china rounded out the three-course meal. The flavor was rivaled only by the elegant presentation of the freshly prepared meal. It was quite an upgrade from your typical airline fare. Over the course of my many flights aboard Air Force One I never once had a bad meal, nor was I served the same meal twice.

After every trip, each journalist's respective news organizations were billed by the Air Force for their accommodations onboard. It wouldn't be right for the taxpayers to foot the bill. The sum charged by the Air Force was always the price of a comparable commercial first-class ticket, plus a dollar. If you ever get the chance to upgrade from first class to Air Force One for a buck, take it. On the flight home I edited the rest of my photos and tried to relax on the heels of such a whirlwind trip. Somehow the experience of the day had been simultaneously exhilarating and exhausting all at once.

Soon enough we landed back at Andrews and filed off the plane once more. Wasting no time, President Obama descended the red-carpeted VIP staircase at Andrews and made a beeline for Marine One. It was now the responsibility of the U.S. Marine Corps to safely transport POTUS back to the White House for the evening. As the president's helicopter disappeared over the horizon, the press pool dispersed back to our own personal vehicles.

"See you tomorrow," I called to my fellow photographers. It may have only been my first flight, but I could already see myself getting used to this lifestyle. I might belong in the White House travel pool after all.

My roots in photography stretch back to the years I spent in Boy Scouts as a teenager. The troop I belonged to was composed of a dedicated group of Scouts and adult leaders who made it a point to get outdoors as often as possible. We summited 13,000-foot peaks in Colorado and canoed through the Boundary Waters of northern Minnesota and Canada. We manned a sailboat and cruised down US1 in the Florida Keys, feasting on lobster that we caught while snorkeling on shallow coral reefs. At night we slept above deck under the stars. One summer we spent eight days bushwhacking through the New Mexico desert relying on windmill-powered wells to supply us with precious water in the arid climate. On each trip I brought a small digital camera with me to capture the memories we made as we camped far off the grid. Whether it be a stunning vista atop the snow-capped Rockies, or a breathtaking sunset in the sky above our campsite, I wanted to be to be able to share photos of my experiences with my friends and family back home.

From there my interest in photo-taking grew into a hobby. I followed in the footsteps of my dad and merged the activity with my love of railroads. Together we spent many hours trackside amongst the kudzu-choked Central-Virginia countryside waiting for freight trains to rumble past. We kept watch over the 100-year-old railroad signal that up until a few years ago still governed a siding on the former Norfolk and Western line that ran near our house. We tossed the football, listened to oldies, and wrestled with theology to pass the time until a train would finally show up for us to photograph.

With my senior year of high school fast approaching, my parents encouraged me to start thinking about where I might attend college. My mom and I visited a few liberal arts colleges in the Mid-Atlantic. Due to their small size, most offered only a few photography classes rather than a dedicated degree program. I begrudgingly began to accept the fact that I would likely end up at a school about which I was not all that excited. None of the campuses I had toured were appealing. To make matters worse, time was running out for me to submit my college applications. I had all but abandoned my search for the perfect university when my mom had a chance encounter with a woman at church. It turned out that her son was studying photojournalism at Western Kentucky University. She assured my mom that if we visited, he would be happy to show us around campus.

A few weekends later my mom and I drove eight hours out to Bowling Green, Kentucky to take a tour of the university. The tour guide led our group of prospective students and parents all over Western's picturesque campus. The impressive student activities center and lush green space throughout stood in stark contrast to the other campuses I had toured. The all-you-can-eat pizza buffet and bottomless soft-serve ice cream machine in the expansive dining hall were motivation enough for me to become a Hilltopper. During lunch my mom snuck off to the campus admissions office to fill out an application on my behalf. She returned with good news. Without writing so much as a single essay I had been accepted into Western Kentucky University.

Toward the end of the tour my mom and I split off from the group. We had an afternoon appointment at Western's Mass Media and Technology Hall with the head of the photojournalism department. The bottom third of the building was dedicated to the photojournalism major. I marveled at the dozens of brand-new Apple computers that filled the program's two computer labs. Across the hall from the main lab stood the department's fully equipped dark room. I stepped inside and waited for my eyes to adjust to the dim red glow of the darkroom light. The foreign scent of film developing chemistry, stop bath, and fixer wafted up my nose as I surveyed the negative enlargers that lined the rectangular room. Back outside the darkroom, prize-winning photographs shot by the program's faculty and staff hung in the fluorescent lit hallways.

A gear checkout counter stood adjacent to one of the lab's common spaces. It was stocked with a drool-worthy collection of Nikon and Canon digital cameras, lenses, and lighting equipment. Nearby, a group of photo students had gathered to critique each other's work. A structural support column wrapped in cork served as the photo lab's bulletin board. Nicknamed the *Washington Post,* Photo contest flyers, internship announcements, and job postings covered the concrete cylinder.

That evening I went out to eat with a group of students from the photo program. I took mental notes as I devoured my meal of fried chicken and French fries. The upperclassmen at the table discussed topics ranging from their favorite conflict photographers to the latest camera gear they wanted to purchase. As I looked around the table at the college kids who I hoped would soon be my peers I began noticing an unmistakable feeling developing in my gut. *This could be what I've been looking for. This could be where*

I belong. Little did I know at the time, choosing to enroll at Western would drastically alter the course of my life for the better.

As third man on the NYT photography totem pole in DC, I rarely had the chance to travel internationally with the White House. All things considered however, there was nothing for me to complain about. The amount of domestic travel I was assigned was above and beyond my wildest of dreams as intern.

When the chance to travel internationally with the White House arose, I jumped on it. I would be accompanying President Obama to a pair of international summits in Canada in 2010. The G20, in particular, took place in downtown Toronto. Plans called for us to chopper to a landing zone in the heart of downtown Toronto. With Marine One in the lead our column of Marine Corps helicopters threaded the needle between towering condominium buildings and other skyscrapers. I sat near the rear of the press helicopter and watched through the open ramp as two other helos tailed closely behind us. We flew so close between some of the high-rises that it felt as if I could reach out and touch the apartment building balconies that blurred by us on either side of the bird. Upon reaching the landing zone downtown, I watched as Marine One descended directly overhead and touched down at the base of the iconic CN tower. A ring of water vapor hung suspended in the air with each revolution of the helicopter's main rotor blades.

The next day was spent running, quite literally, in and out of bilateral meetings between President Obama and other world leaders. Often, we were only allowed inside for lightning-fast grip-and-grin photo opportunities, or "sprays." Like usual, a U.S. Secret Service Agent escorted the press pool everywhere we went. Because we were on foreign soil a Canadian diplomatic security agent also followed the travel pool wherever went at the G20. Unlike most of the agents at the summit, she was a woman. Her slender frame and long brown hair immediately caught my eye. The feminine energy that radiated out from her compelled me to introduce myself. I searched unsuccessfully for the proper moment to strike up a conversation with her. Just when I had worked up enough courage to muster a friendly "bonjour," we were hustled off to our first event of the morning. That day we photographed meetings between President Obama and heads of state from South Korea, Japan, and others that escape memory. Interacting with members of foreign press corps during these summits was an eye-opening experience. Photographers who followed the British Prime Minister were not at all bashful about shouting out to the political figures involved in their photo-op.

"Mr. Prime Minister, over here! Look over here please! You're looking marvelous today." Some of them seemed to employ tactics more akin to the paparazzi than professional journalists. Still, most of our colleagues from overseas were amicable enough.

In Toronto the plan called for us to briefly photograph a meeting between President Obama and the Chinese head of state, Hu Jintao. As the White House travel pool began to try and enter the room where the meeting was underway, a Communist Party official from the Chinese delegation blocked our progress in the middle of the hallway outside the meeting room.

"It is forbidden!" he yelled in English again and again.

One of our crack White House advance staffers, a tall, handsome fellow named Brandon Lepow, charged to the front of the line for a showdown with the insistent Chinese official.

"No," he countered firmly. "The American press is coming in, whether you like it or not."

The Chinese official repeated even louder, "It is forbidden!"

After a few seconds of struggle, Lepow maneuvered past the one-man blockade and pinned him against the wall of the narrow hallway. This maneuver created a gap just large enough for us to squeeze through one at a time.

"Let's go, pool!" Lepow yelled.

I charged through the slender opening and ran to catch up with my colleagues at the entrance to the meeting room. A staccato refrain of "It is forbidden" continued to echo down the hall as we joined the bilateral meeting already in progress between the US and Chinese Presidents.

Inside the room members of state-run Chinese media outlets did their best to try and block us from photographing the scene. President Obama sat across a long table from Chinese President Hu Jintao. Various aides and deputies sat on either side of the two leaders, facing their counterparts. As the White House pool maneuvered into position elbows were thrown, bodies were slammed, and many angry shouts emanated from the Chinese press pool. The Chinese press were not exactly in a collegial mood. One of their photographers slid in beside me and raised both his elbows in an attempt to block my view and take up as much space as possible. He shifted his weight onto his right foot and rammed his shoulder up against my body. In the heat of the moment, I decided that his attempt to bully me out of my rightfully held spot should not go unanswered. As the mayhem continued unabated I may, or may not, have returned the favor on behalf of the good old US of A.

Our time at the summit concluded with a large press conference where President Obama took questions from a group of international press. What exactly had been accomplished at the massive gathering of presidents, prime ministers, and princes was unclear to me. But everyone who spoke in front of the cameras insisted that a great deal had been accomplished to bring the world even closer to a long-lasting, meaningful, humanitarian utopia. As the presser concluded, I bid "au revoir" to the French-Canadian diplomatic security agent on whom I had developed a crush over the course of our two days in Toronto. I never did learn her name, partly due to the language barrier, but mostly due to a lack of courage on my part.

Stepping outside the convention center in downtown Toronto was like walking into the exercise yard at a maximum-security penitentiary. Twelve-foot steel security fencing lined the sidewalks in every direction. An anarchist protest had turned violent a few blocks away earlier in the summit. Shop windows were broken, stores looted, and a police car torched to its frame. Before climbing into the motorcade, I paused in the middle of that deserted street in downtown Toronto and listened to the eerie wail of police sirens echoing off the downtown skyscrapers that towered overhead. While I loved my job, home felt very far away.

In no time, the motorcade was loaded and we were speeding toward the airport. When we arrived earlier in the week, then Prime Minister Stephen Harper had greeted President Obama at the foot of the steps beside Air Force One. A pair of Royal Mounted Police officers stood at attention each holding a Canadian and US flag. Since then, the entirety of the tarmac at Toronto International Airport had filled to capacity with aircraft belonging to heads of state from the world's major economies. An Air China 747 towered above smaller aircraft belonging to countries such as the Republic of Italy, Colombia, and Algeria. A shiny British Airways jet had ferried members of the UK delegation from across the pond. Other countries such as Ethiopia followed suit with use of chartered commercial airliners from their home countries. A massive jetliner emblazoned with the words "Saudi Arabia" shimmered despite the overcast skies. One journalist in our press van spoke up and said it was rumored to have a solid gold toilet onboard for use by the Saudi Royal family. Judging by the plane's pristine exterior alone, I did not have a hard time believing that. A Russian-built Ilyushin aircraft that transported Russian Prime Minister Dmitry Medvedev sat nearby looking quite underwhelming in comparison to the Saudi's airborne palace.

The seemingly endless parade of jetliners ended abruptly as the motorcade approached the queen of them all.

Though I had photographed Air Force One's distinctive paint scheme countless times before, goosebumps appeared on my forearms. The plane's paint scheme alone put every other aircraft to shame, even the Saudis with their golden commode. Perhaps it was my exhaustion or a bit of homesickness but seeing Air Force One come into view was one of the most beautiful sights I had ever seen. I read the words painted above the window line: "United States of America". I thought of home. I thought of the country whose opportunity had allowed me to go from my parents' basement as a depressed high schooler to the President of the United States' motorcade on international soil in less than three years' time. What a country. What a life. It made little sense apart from God's scandalous goodness to me. Shortly after takeoff I drifted to sleep in my seat. I awoke just as we touched down back at Joint Base Andrews. I descended the rear staircase and stepped foot back on US soil for the first time in almost a week. Man, it was good to be home.

The final Air Force One trip of my internship took place on July 28, 2010. President Obama took a quick flight up to New York City to attend fundraisers for the Democratic Party. The November midterm elections were only a few short months away and POTUS was called upon to harness the considerable fundraising power that a sitting president possesses for his party. The bill for transporting the President of the United States in the course of his official duties is one normally footed by the US taxpayer. On the other hand, Presidential campaigns are expected to pick up the tab for travel related to re-election campaigning or fundraising. In order to defray the enormous costs associated with operating Air Force One, the Obama administration adopted a practice employed by previous administrations and scheduled a non-political stop during the fundraising trip.

We boarded Air Force One at Andrews and jetted up the East Coast en route to Newark International Airport. Only 240 miles lay between Andrews and Newark. The time passed quickly. After arriving in New Jersey, we loaded into the motorcade and drive a short distance away to the *Tastee Sub Shop* in Edison, N.J. We waited outside the small restaurant until our White House press wrangler led the pool inside. Fourth in line behind AP, Reuters, and AFP, I scrambled through the doorway and found an open spot inside the cramped sandwich shop. President Obama was dressed in a crisp white dress shirt that paired nicely with his sky-blue silk tie. He sat with his back to a refrigerated case stocked full of Snapple brand iced tea. Nearby shelves overflowed with potato chips of various flavors. I took a few photos as the President spoke with three or four local entrepreneurs. They chatted away about the challenges facing small business owners like themselves.

A few short minutes after we were allowed inside our press wrangler signaled the end of the photo op with a passive aggressive "thank you, pool." I filed back outside feeling content to have made a handful photos that would work for the next day's paper.

Jumping back in the press van, I pulled out my laptop and immediately began working on transmitting pictures to the National desk. I was usually miles away from the *New York Times* Manhattan bureau. In this case, however, I imagined my photos sailing the short distance through the air across the nearby Hudson River and up to the sixth-floor picture desk.

My colleagues and I waited in the press vans until President Obama had finished inside. The motorcade retraced its steps back to whichever remote corner of Newark International that air traffic control had directed Air Force One to park during its short stay. Back at the airport President Obama walked from his limousine toward Marine One for the short lift into Manhattan. With my laptop strapped to my back and cameras hanging from my shoulders I sprinted across the tarmac toward our usual ride, Nighthawk 4. Ducking my head, I ran up the rear ramp of the double rotor Vietnam era CH-46 "Phrog." I snagged my favorite seat near the window and jammed a pair of foam ear plugs into my ears in anticipation of our noisy hop over the Hudson Bay to the Big Apple. During the flight I craned my neck to shoot pictures of the majestic Statue of Liberty as we passed by.

The Manhattan skyline soon towered over us as our helo came in for a landing at the Wall Street heliport. Normally filled with touristy sightseeing helicopters, the landing zone was empty in anticipation of our arrival. We touched down on the small landing pad that floated in the East River and hustled over to shore. As soon as we cleared the LZ, Marine One landed on the pad closest to the shore. An additional pair of Presidential limousines that had been pre-positioned in New York City rolled out onto the floating pier to pick up President Obama. We again made our way to the motorcade and began our journey to our next scheduled stop: ABC's midtown television studios. President Obama was scheduled to make an appearance on the long-running daytime talk show, *The View*. The motorcade made record time traversing the normally gridlocked streets of downtown Manhattan. Miles of crowd control fencing lined Park Avenue as hordes of New Yorkers, tourists, and passersby watched us speed down the motorcade route. Arriving at the TV studio, the President's limo turned into an alley that had been secured by the Secret Service. Before our press vans had come to a complete stop, I opened the sliding door and hopped out onto the blocked-off street. Clutching my cameras close to my torso, I raced on foot to catch up with the other pool photographers who were already on their way inside the building. Hundreds of gawkers stared at me from the behind the fences that lined both sides of the street. There was no time to feel self-conscious. I had a job to do.

Inside the building our press wrangler herded the travel pool into a freight elevator that quickly transported us up to the floor where *The View* was filmed. The President had arrived just before the TV cameras started rolling. Our one shot at photographing POTUS on the set would come during the first commercial break. We stepped off the freight elevator into a cramped backstage area. Real estate in Manhattan does not come cheap, so naturally ABC had taken advantage of every square foot of their studio space. Stage lighting, electrical wiring, and other production equipment was crammed into every available nook and cranny around the soundstage. A producer met us at the elevator and guided use through the darkness. She was straight out of central casting dressed head to toe in black, wearing a headset and carrying a clipboard. Our press wrangler held an index finger up to her lip, motioning to us to keep quiet. Wasting no time, the cameras began rolling as soon as President Obama had been mic'd up by a production assistant.

The President's muffled voice met my ears as we tip-toed toward a back entrance to the set. It was hard to make out exactly what he was saying, but his familiar cadence was punctuated by laughter and applause from the audience. We stopped just shy of the set door to wait for the first commercial break. A single emerald-green lamp lit the skinny corridor where we stood waiting. As my eyes adjusted in the darkness, I started to make out the faint outline of the Secret Service CAT team. Bathed in the faint green glow of the light, the agents wore night vision goggles mounted to their ballistic helmets. Infrared US flags Velcroed to their body armor glinted in the dim light as the square-jawed men stood at the ready for the first sign of trouble. My eyes met the steely gaze of one the agents. Intimidated, I decided against raising my camera and snapping a photo. I tried to rationalize my decision. These men meant business. Their sole mission was to protect the leader of the free world. They belonged here. I, on the other hand, did not. To this day I regret not taking that photo.

Our producer returned and gave us a two-minute warning for the commercial break. I double-checked my camera settings. A short time later I followed my colleagues onto the set. My eyes squinted as we emerged from the dim backstage are into the aura of the brightly lit studio. It was like stepping into a different world. I knelt in front of the stage and shot away as the President made small talk with the ladies of *The View*. Mirroring our experience in the sandwich shop earlier in the day, our wrangler pulled us out after just a few short minutes. We made our way back down the freight elevator to the motorcade as President Obama wrapped up filming the rest of the episode.

The next item on The President's schedule called for him to attend a private fundraiser at the Manhattan home of socialite and fashion icon Ana Wintour. The *Vogue* magazine editor hosted the President and various donors from New York's high society at a ritzy fundraiser in the East Village. It's not common for the press to be allowed inside such fundraisers, and this event was no exception. I passed the time hanging out in the press van editing photos from our previous stop at ABC. One of the White House advance team members came by with boxed lunches for dinner. Opening my box I found a cold roast beef sandwich, chocolate chip cookie, and side of bowtie pasta salad. The food disappeared in no time.

A dinner I wandered around the outside of the motorcade in the cramped alley where we had relocated for the fundraiser. A group of officers from the NYPD's Emergency Service Unit stood milling about outside their tactical vehicle. As I approached, they turned to give me a collective cold stare.

"Howdy, gentlemen," I opened with a friendly wave. Although none of the officers returned my salutation, I continued trying to make small talk. "Hey, I've got a question for you guys. Do you all get to play yourselves in the movies and on shows like *Law and Order*?" The highly trained tactical officers stared expressionless at me. Just then, our White House press wrangler came to my rescue.

"Luke, the motorcade is about to leave, it's time to go," she called to me. I turned once more to the anti-social group of officers and offered a farewell.

"Stay safe, gentlemen," I said as started to jog back to the vans.

With the fundraiser complete, we returned to the Wall Street Helipad for our quick hop back to Newark International. Darkness had fallen over Manhattan and our long day was nearly finished. The pool held at the edge of landing zone as Marine One lifted off into the night sky. A Secret Service agent stood with his back to the helicopter as the rotor wash tossed his necktie every which way. I made a few photos as the President's helicopter lifted off and blurred through air. With POTUS airborne, it was our turn to load back onto our twin-rotor CH-46. Once aboard, we hurriedly took off and tailed Marine One back to New Jersey. I repeated my earlier ritual aboard Nighthawk 4 and again sat in my favored spot by the crew chief's open window. I took photos as he peered through a pair of night vision goggles at the New York City skyline. Every few seconds he was bathed in a flash of red from a strobe light mounted on the underbelly of our helicopter. I managed to time my shutter perfectly and caught the Marine illuminated by crimson at just the right moment.

The Statue of Liberty passed by outside my window once again. I took a few deep breaths and tried to savor what I knew might be my last time ever flying with HMX-1 on a Presidential trip. God had been so good to me over the course of the past year. I could only pray that I had made the most of the opportunities that He had given me. Before too long we touched back down at Newark and raced back toward the rear staircase of Air Force One. The beautiful jet gleamed under the yellow sodium lamps that skirted the perimeter of the vast airport. She stopped me in my tracks.

"I'm really going to miss this," I thought nostalgically to myself. I climbed the retractable stairs one last time and settled into my comfy leather seat in the press cabin.

No sooner had I pulled out my laptop to edit my photos from the helicopter ride, was I startled by a familiar voice calling my name.

"Mr. Sharrett, you are wanted at the front of the plane," announced Deputy Press Secretary Josh Earnest. I glanced up with a confused look on my face.

"Wait, what?" I replied baffled. From time to time, Earnest traveled about Air Force One in place of his boss, Press Secretary Robert Gibbs. Earnest usually sat toward the front of the 747 with the rest of the senior White House staff. It was rare to see him back in the press cabin unless he was giving a short press briefing, or "gaggle" as the pool calls them. I stood up at my seat, still confused as to what exactly was going on. I looked toward my colleagues seated nearby for clues. Just then it dawned on me. Someone must have tipped off the White House that this was my last trip on Air Force One as an intern.

"Go! Hurry up!" urged one of the other wire photographers. I stepped into the aisle and started to follow in the footsteps of the Deputy Press Secretary.

Passing the rear staircase that I was plenty familiar with, I took my first steps into a previously unexplored portion of the Presidential aircraft. Members of the travel pool were never allowed outside the press cabin unless we were entering or exiting the plane via the rear staircase. Feeling rather out of place, I turned the corner and began walking down the long aisle that runs along the port side of the jumbo jet. My eyes met those of a stocky Air Force One crew member who sat adjacent to the corner that I had just turned. Unlike the chairs in the press cabin, he sat with his back to the windows facing inward toward the middle of the plane. This vantage point afforded him a view up and down the entirety of the lengthy aisle.

I hurried toward the front of the plane trying to soak in the scenery as best I could. I was again reminded of Air Force One's portrayal in the 1997 Harrison Ford action flick of the same name. The interior of the jet looked almost exactly like it did in the movie. As I neared the front of the aircraft, it dawned on me that I should spiff up my appearance while I still had the chance. A day full of running in and out of buildings, jumping out of motorcade vans, and boarding helicopters and had taken its toll on my hairdo. My shirt was partially un-tucked and my necktie hung loose. Thankfully, I managed to correct these issues just as I arrived at the front of the airplane. A few feet before the aisle ended was an open door that led into Air Force One's miniature oval office. As I stepped toward the entryway, none other than President Obama himself popped his head out into the hallway.

"Luke!" He exclaimed. "Step into my office."

"Yes sir, Mr. President," I replied as I followed him into the modest airborne office space.

A wooden desk complete with a telephone, notepad, and cushy swivel chair jutted out from the starboard wall at a 45-degree angle. A small presidential seal hung above one of the window shades along the fuselage wall, as if any of us needed a reminder whose plane we were on. I was struck by how few Americans had stood in the spot I was currently occupying. I felt the strange sensation of time slowing down. My palms began to sweat. I was finally meeting the man whom I had photographed almost every day for the past year. The President leaned against the front of his desk with arms crossed.

"So, I hear you're leaving us to go back to school?" he queried.

"That's right sir," I replied. "I'm heading back to Western Kentucky University to finish up my degree in photojournalism."

"I don't understand why you have to go back to school when you're already here in Washington." The President studied me with a furrowed brow.

I shared his sentiment. Much to my disappointment, my editors in New York had determined that it was time for me to turn in my press pass and head back to the classroom.

"I don't understand it either," I replied. "But my editors in New York have said that's what I need to do." Apparently bewildered by the decision of the *New York Times'* managing editors, President Obama pressed the issued further.

"But why don't you just show them your portfolio?"

"Mr. President," I responded, "I guess it's just something I have to do."

President Obama nodded and motioned me over for a photo. Air Force One started accelerating down the runway for takeoff as I joined the President by his side. Pete Souza, the official White House photographer, stepped into the office with his camera. His shutter clicked and his camera's flash went off a handful times as I stood next the President of the United States with a big grin on my face. I turned to shake the hands with the leader of the free world as the Presidential aircraft become airborne over Newark.

"We will see you when you get back to DC," he said.

"Yes sir, Mr. President. See you then."

Walking back to my seat at the rear of the aircraft, I tried the best I could to contain my smile. In my mind I was just a 21-year-old college kid from Kentucky. But from this exchange, I was beginning to realize that other people—even the President of the United States—might see me as more.

Over the course of my last week in Washington, I bid farewell to my friends and colleagues with whom I covered Capitol Hill and the White House. The past thirteen months had been a dream come true. I grew leaps and bounds as a photographer and gained valuable experience in the field. My byline appeared above the fold on the front page of the *New York Times* more than a dozen times. I had been afforded a front row seat to history as it unfolded. The magnitude of the opportunity I was given was hard for me to wrap my mind around. I wasn't the best photographer the *New York Times* could have hired for this internship, but I had worked as hard as I could. Boy, was I grateful to my mentors Doug Mills and Steve Crowley, my editors, colleagues, parents, and God.

The day before I left town, Doug threw a little going away shindig for me at a local brewery across the street from the *New York Times'* Washington bureau. Scores of my friends from various wire services, newspapers, and magazines turned out to bid me farewell and shower me with gag gifts that referenced various inside jokes we shared from the past year. That evening I felt something that I had been chasing for a long time. I was one of the gang.

Despite my gratitude, a piece of my heart simply couldn't stomach the thought of going back to school. Much as President Obama had expressed to me on Air Force One, I did not understand why I needed to go sit in a classroom to prove that I could do the job I had already been doing for the past year. The whole point of higher education, in my mind at least, was to receive training to work effectively in the professional world. Working in Washington felt as though I had skipped ahead to the best part of the movie. I could not understand why my editors wanted to send me back to then classroom.

Just as I was starting to feel like I belonged, it was time to uproot and move back to Kentucky. I packed up my car on a late August morning in 2010 and started the ten-hour journey back to school. As I merged onto the westbound lanes of I-66, feelings of doubt and fear began gnawing at my insides. "What if I never make it back here again," I wondered. Upon arriving back at Western, I shouldered a full course load of photography and journalism courses. Any time I wasn't in class, I took on as many photo assignments as I possibly could for the school paper, the *College Heights Herald*. Although I did the best I could to distract myself, I deeply missed the camaraderie I experienced working in Washington.

I couldn't see it at the time, but campus was, in fact, where I belonged. I was young and still had a lot to learn. The excitement and sexiness of covering the White House had blinded me to the fact that there was much more to life outside the DC political bubble. There were experiences to be had that didn't involve velvet ropes, press conferences, and podiums. There were lessons I had learned in Washington that I needed to bring back to school and share with my friends, classmates. I had grown professionally in DC, but still had much room to grow personally. It would be a few years, however, until this perspective became my own.

Scan this code for photos from Chapter 1

2. THE WHITE HOUSE

Upon leaving Washington, I did my best to settle into life back in Kentucky. Over the course of the next year, I continued to mature as both a person and a photographer. I attended classes and chipped away at required course like intro to newswriting. I photographed as many assignments as possible for Western Kentucky University's school newspaper, the *College Heights Herald.* In fact, I enjoyed shooting for the school paper so much that I once skipped my weekly three-hour photo class in favor of shooting a sports assignment for the *Herald.* My professor was none too pleased and docked my grade significantly. It didn't matter. The feeling I got when I was on assignment for the paper reminded me of my internship with the *New York Times.* In my mind I was preparing for the day when I would be able to return to Washington and work as a photojournalist again. Why sit in a classroom when I could be out doing the real thing? I often daydreamt of being called back to work in the White House press pool once again. Not even the best that college had to offer could top that.

Then one day, it happened. I was walking across campus on a beautiful fall afternoon in 2011. My last class for the day had just adjourned and I was on my way to the dining hall for a late lunch. Sauntering down the sidewalk in my sandals, I felt my front pocket buzz. I fished my phone out and glanced down at the caller ID. As soon as I saw the number, I stopped dead in my tracks. The *New York Times* was calling. *Maybe an editor was reaching out with a freelance assignment?* A few had come my way since leaving Washington the year before. I cleared my throat and answered the phone.

"Hi, Luke," a pleasant and familiar voice said on the other end of the line. "It's Beth Flynn at the *New York Times.*"

Beth was a senior photo editor who hired me for my first year-long internship back in 2009. Throughout my year in DC, she was a warm, supportive advocate for me on the desk in New York. It was always a pleasure to hear from her.

"How would feel about coming back to DC on contract to help us cover the 2012 presidential campaign?" she asked.

I froze. I couldn't believe what I was hearing. This was THE very phone call I had spent the last year daydreaming about.

It was actually happening.

Without a moment's hesitation I accepted the offer. I couldn't wait to get back to DC. I couldn't wait to see my pals and start covering the White House again. Exchanging goodbyes with Beth, I pocketed my phone and took off at a run. My backpack flopped against my back as my legs propelled me down the hill. An enormous smile spread across face. I was going back to DC. Somehow, I managed to finish out the rest of my semester with good grades in my classes. I remember the weeks between that phone call and the end of the semester just dragging by. As much as I loved my time at Western, I simply could not wait to get back to the White House. Covering politics was my one true love, and it had been much too long since I had felt her embrace.

My first experience photographing politics came as a White House intern when I was 19 years old. On the heels of my freshman year at Western Kentucky University, I was accepted for an internship in the White House photo office during the summer of 2008.

The photo office is responsible for editing, distributing and archiving photographs taken by the Chief Official White House Photographer. Ever since Cecil Stoughton was first appointed to the role by President John F. Kennedy the photo office has existed to support the administration's official photographers.

During the Bush Administration Eric Draper held the position. Eric, a veteran photojournalist long before he came to the White House, worked as a staff photographer for newspapers in Seattle, California, and New Mexico before joining the Associated Press in the nineties. During his tenure at AP, he covered the Kosovo conflict in 1999, the 2000 Summer Olympic Games in Sydney, Australia, and eventually traveled with the press pool on George W. Bush's first presidential campaign. As soon as it became clear that Bush would be inaugurated as the 43rd president, Draper asked him personally if he could be his White House photographer. President-elect Bush was reportedly so impressed by both the quality of Draper's work and his gumption that he agreed. Draper would go on to spend the entire eight years of George W. Bush's Presidency at his side with a front row seat to history.

I spent the majority of the summer of 2008 in a suit and tie running errands around the Eisenhower Executive Office building. The EEOB is located inside the White House compound and houses the offices responsible for most of the executive branch's official business. All but the highest-ranking White House officials work out of the EEOB. My summer consisted of performing menial tasks in the basement of the EEOB. This included answering phones, delivering photo albums, and most importantly replenishing the office's ever-dwindling supply of Diet Coke. Another one of my official duties consisted of rotating White House photos that were displayed prominently on the walls of the West Wing. Every seven days our office's photo editors chose the best of the previous week's photos and made large 2-foot-by-3-foot prints nicknamed *jumbos*. Various offices in the EEOB competed fiercely for access to the newest crop of jumbos to hang on their own walls. Realizing that they possessed a hot commodity in the underground economy of the executive branch, the photo office shrewdly used this to our advantage and bartered for all sorts of favors on the EEOB black market. The most lucrative of these trades was the doubling of our weekly soda ration that we negotiated with the White House soft drink cartel. Thanks to the stellar work of the White House photographers, our cups runneth over with Diet Coke.

One week, my boss tasked me with changing out some jumbos on the ground floor of the West Wing. I carried a handful of photos across Executive Drive, past a Secret Service checkpoint and into the hallway where I had been instructed to proceed. As I swapped out a handful of photos from their thick black frames, I did my best to stay out of the way of foot traffic. Upon hanging the last of the pictures, I took a step backwards to admire my handiwork. In doing so I accidentally backed into someone walking down the hall.

"Oops, excuse me," a woman's voice said.

Startled, I turned around to see who I had bumped into. It turned out to be none other than the Secretary of State, Condoleezza Rice. I was mortified and terribly embarrassed. I began apologizing profusely. She was incredibly gracious and complimented the photos on the wall before continuing on her way.

To my delight I was occasionally invited to photograph official events across the street in the White House proper. The first of these was a Presidential statement in the White House Rose Garden. President Bush's chief photographer, Eric Draper, escorted me from the photo office to the briefing room and left me in the care of the White House press corps. A few minutes later we filed into the Rose Garden and prepared to cover the statement. I watched as photographers set up aluminum step ladders emblazoned with the logos of the specific outlets for whom they were shooting. I geeked out as I spied ladders belonging to the Associated Press, Reuters, AFP, Getty Images, the *New York Times*, and the *Washington Post*.

I followed a group of photographers to the northwest corner of the Rose Garden that afforded a view looking down the White House colonnade. The iconic shot of the President walking past rows of white columns is a classic photo in political photography. I was excited to try my own hand at the shot. I was even more excited to be rubbing shoulders with some of the best news photographers in the country.

Shortly before the start of the event, an announcement came over the speaker system,

"Two minutes. Two minutes."

A few of the photographers echoed the announcement in case anyone in the Rose Garden had failed to hear the crystal-clear warning from a moment before.

"Two minutes!"

President Bush emerged from the Oval Office in a grey suit and strode confidently down the colonnade toward a podium bearing the Presidential seal. A chorus of clicking camera shutters erupted as soon as Bush came into view. I did the same and fired away with my camera. The statement only lasted a few short minutes, so I did my best to capture as many different angles of the scene as I possibly could. Before I knew it, the event was over. President Bush concluded his statement as he normally did.

"Thank you. May God bless the United States of America." He walked back to the Oval Office to carry on with the morning's business.

Upon the conclusion of the statement, members of press corps began breaking down their television cameras and packing up their step ladders. I walked back to the photo office and reflected upon the thrill of the morning. What a rush it was. I wanted to do it again.

And again.

And again.

I decided then and there – this was exactly what I wanted to do for a living. I wanted to be a political photographer covering the White House.

Eric Draper was kind enough to invite me to photograph several more presidential events. These included other Rose Garden statements, East Room events, Marine One arrivals, and the annual 4th of July celebration and fireworks viewing on the White House South Lawn.

The summer was a blur. The feelings of self-importance that my proximity to power provided were intoxicating. Weekdays were spent at the White House running errands and occasionally photographing Presidential events. On the weekends I woke up early, threw every piece of photo gear I owned into my camera bag, and set out into the District looking for things to photograph. I rode the Metro for hours on end listening to music and taking photos along the way. It was an exhilarating three months.

As the summer drew to a close, the intern class gathered in the East Room of the White House for a group photo with the President and Vice President. We stood lined up on a set of bleachers and excitedly awaited the arrival of the VIPs. For some interns, it would be their first time laying eyes on the President in the flesh.

"Two minutes!" a White House aide announced.

The excited chatter that permeated the room a moment earlier died down in an instant. Hairdos were fixed and ties were straightened in the last moments before the President's arrival. Everyone wanted to look their best.

A short fifteen seconds after the two-minute warning, the President burst into the room. "Good morning, everyone!" President Bush practically shouted. His energy immediately filled the East Room. "How's everybody doing?"

The eight-year presidency had taken its toll on George W. Bush. The burden of leadership had aged him considerably, as the office tends to do to those who occupy it. No longer was he the energetic, youthful-looking Governor of Texas who took office in 2000. His face was now wrinkled considerably. His hair was completely grey. The president took his place at the front of the bleachers for a group photo.

As he did, Vice President Dick Cheney strode in to do that same. Cheney acknowledged us with a wave and a noticeably less-sunny greeting. "Hello," he said, as he walked to stand at the President's side for the photo.

I did my best to keep my eyes open and forgo blinking as an assistant White House photographer snapped a few group photos. "Thank you, Mr. President," he called out as he lowered his camera. The Vice President wasted no time leaving, but to our satisfaction, President Bush stuck around for a few minutes to take questions from the eager crowd. One intern raised her hand and was quickly called upon by the President.

"How does it feel to know that thousands of Americans are praying for your every day?"

The President answered that he needed the prayers and was grateful for them.

"How do you think the United States should deal with North Korea?" another intern asked.

President Bush responded immediately by stating that a seat at the negotiating table is a bargaining chip in and of itself. Unless North Korea's leaders started respecting the human rights of their people, our government had no interest in negotiating with them, he explained. Until they started treating their people right, the United States government would keep its hands around their neck. Bush was alluding to economic and political sanctions that had been enacted against the North Korean regime.

The last question of the Q&A concerned what it was like to live in the White House. "You know, the White House is like a big museum. And without my wife Laura by my side, well, it can get pretty dang cold in a museum."

Less than a year later, I would return to the White House again as an intern. This time, I wouldn't be working for the administration. Instead, I would be covering Washington for the *New York Times.*

To my surprise, my editors at the *Times* treated me more like a staffer than an intern. There was very little handholding. I was immediately thrown into the mix of day-to-day political coverage. Less than a month into my internship, I would find myself flying aboard Air Force One.

I joined a team comprised of two veteran political photojournalists, Doug Mills and Stephen Crowley. Both men took me under their respective wings when I showed up as a green, eager, college student. Whatever natural talent I possessed as a young photographer was cultivated by these two men. Without their mentorship, direction, critique, and friendship I doubt I ever would have become a successful news photographer. Between the two of them, they have been awarded an astonishing four Pulitzer Prizes. Simply put, I learned from the best.

Before coming to the *New York Times,* Doug was an experienced wire photographer with the Associate Press for decades. A wiry, short-haired man with a well-groomed mustache, Doug covered countless Olympic games and was in the White House travel pool with President Bush on September 11, 2001. He snapped the famous photo of the President receiving the news of the attack as he sat in an elementary school classroom in Florida. Later in the day, Doug would be the only photographer allowed to accompany the President aboard Air Force One as he flew to Barksdale Air Force Base and later to a secure bunker at Offutt Air Force Base outside Omaha, Nebraska. As soon as I showed up, Doug began working to cultivate a never-quit attitude in me. He stressed the importance of always being prepared and anticipating where the next photo might occur before anyone else.

Toward the end of my internship, I reached out to him during a particularly bad week. I was making garbage photos and felt demoralized by my subpar performance. "Doug, how do you get out of a slump?" I asked in an email. His reply landed in my inbox a mere five minutes later.

"WTF, when did you get in a slump?" His email began. "There is no such thing in photography. You make your own luck, and you continue to take chances. Be positive and always remember, never, never give up. You are far too talented to let one or two days of being one inch off get you down!!"

Meanwhile, Stephen Crowley instilled in me a deep conviction to be unrelentingly fair in my coverage as a journalist. The bespectacled man was always sharply dressed in a navy-blue blazer and vest. He wore his thick head of silver hair parted to one side. Steve knew the lay of the land on Capitol Hill like no other. He knew where Senator's secret offices were located and could often be found stalking the halls of Congress as he tracked down the major players of the day's news cycle. In Steve's view, no side of the political aisle nor personality in power was to be spared a ruthless examination by the press. Accountability was non-negotiable. Additionally, Steve viewed each photo he made as an opportunity to say something to the reader. His photos always had a witty, insightful, or humorous layer to them.

Crowley was a source of constant encouragement and inspiration. Revered across the board by photographers in Washington, I cherished the time I was able to spend with him. "Luke, my boy!" was his constant refrain any time I called him up on the phone. He never passed up an opportunity to look at my work and provide feedback.

His mentorship did not end with the conclusion of my internship. During my transition back to photo school at Western, he swung through town while traveling to an assignment in Tennessee. Over a dinner of cornbread and steak, I shared my how much I missed the fast-paced excitement of Washington. Hearing the notes of doubt and melancholy in my voice, Steve looked me in the eyes and told me that there were stories on campus that only I could tell. I was here for a purpose.

These were life-giving words for a 21-year-old who feared that his glory days in the news industry might be behind him.

As I settled into my internship, I would often fill in for Doug at the White House. Those were long but exciting days on the clock for the *New York Times*. In addition to doubling as the President's office and home, the White House grounds also serve as the backdrop for a dozen or more televised media events in a given week. Bill signings, cabinet room meetings, Rose Garden press conferences, meet-and-greets with foreign dignitaries in the Oval Office, and receptions in the State Dining room are just a handful of examples of events open to media coverage by the White House Press Corps. One of the most versatile venues on the grounds is the White House East Room. Located on the ground floor of the residence, the spacious rectangular room runs the width of the White House from North to South. The historic space, with its vibrant yellow curtains and tall windows, makes one feel like royalty upon entering. A handful of ornate crystal chandeliers hang gracefully from its tall plaster ceiling. A majestic life-size oil painting of President George Washington, the single U.S. President who left office before the White House's completion, is displayed prominently on the room's east wall. For obvious reasons, the East Room has been a favorite television backdrop of presidential administrations for decades.

While most of the events I covered in the East Room during my stint in Washington have blurred together, one stands out in my memory: an evening concert featuring Sir Paul McCartney. President Obama was slated to award him a Gershwin Prize for Popular Song in recognition of his contributions as a member of The Beatles. The Public Broadcasting Service would be recording the evening's events and airing the program at a later date. While most of the journalists cleared out of the briefing room around 5pm, I stuck around into the evening to cover the event.

In addition to the pressure that comes with representing the *New York Times* at the White House, one of my photo editors informed me that a decision had been made to hold the paper back from publication until they received my photo from the event. The East Room concert was set to take place at the same time the paper normally went to press. A small army of copy editors and page designers would be waiting at their desks in Manhattan for my photo. Postponing the Times' print-edition deadline is as rare as it is costly. The pressure was on.

With about an hour to spare until our gather time, I left the White House compound to grab some dinner. Settling on a sandwich shop nearby at the corner of Pennsylvania Avenue and Jackson, I picked up a footlong meatball sub and brought it back to the White House. Back at my desk I made quick work of the meal, polishing off all 12 inches of the sandwich and a bag of chips. A short time later my stomach began to feel funny. I brushed it off and started to prep my gear form the impending shoot.

An announcement came over the briefing room intercom giving us a five-minute warning. I joined the other handful of photographers who were staying late to cover the East Room event and found a spot in line. Five minutes passed without any wrangler showing up from the lower press office. My stomach was really starting to bother me. "What is going on down there," I thought to myself. I crouched down along the wall and pulled my knees close to my chest to get some relief from the growing pressure in my belly. Another 10 minutes passed. There was still no sign of our wrangler. My thoughts turned to the bathroom only a few steps away in the press break room. I really needed to use the restroom, but I didn't want to risk missing the event. Once the press was escorted over to the East Room there wouldn't be any way for me to catch up with them. Unsurprisingly the Secret Service won't let you wander around the White House grounds if you are a member of the press. Having a staff escort is non-negotiable. I noticed the discomfort shift from my stomach to points south. Just as I was about to make a run for the bathroom, our press wrangler emerged from behind the sliding door that separates lower press from the briefing room.

"Get ready, everyone" she announced. "We will be heading up to the East Room momentarily."

Despite the announcement from our wrangler that we would be leaving any minute, we continued to hold our position in the briefing room. As each minute passed, I thought about how I should have just run to the bathroom and done what I needed to do. My fear of missing the evening's only escort upstairs kept me in line. I looked longingly toward the restroom as the agonizing minutes ticked by. My brain was consumed with urgent signals from my gut.

"Hey boss, I know you can hear us down here. We really need you to get us to a toilet. Pronto." Finally, I gave in and decided to make a run for the restroom. Just as I set my cameras down on the briefing room carpet our wrangler re-emerged from lower press.

"Here we go everyone. Follow me," she said.

Well, isn't that just perfect timing? I picked my cameras back up fell in line with everyone else. We filed out the back of the briefing room, past the restroom that I had failed to patronize, and up a flight of steep concrete steps outside. With my cameras on my shoulder and aluminum step ladder in hand we walked under the towering North Portico and into the White House. The event was in progress as we filed into the East Room inconspicuously through a back entrance. A stage with professional lighting had been set up, effectively transforming the historic space into a concert venue. Sir Paul McCartney was onstage playing a guitar and signing a familiar Beatles tunc is his trademark British accent. I spied POTUS sitting in the front row with his wife Michelle and their two daughters, Malia and Sasha.

I set up my ladder at the back of the room and climbed up a few steps to gain a height advantage over the crowd. As I did so, I felt a drastic shift. Apparently aware that a bathroom visit was not in my immediate future, I began to feel sick to my stomach. Waves of intense nausea started rolling over me. I tried to power through the rebellion being waged against me by my own body. *Must. Make. Photos.* I urged myself on. Despite my best effort to resist the uprising in my stomach, my body finally won out. I vomited into my camera bag.

I looked up from the carnage in a daze. President Obama was standing onstage with the Presidential Medal of Freedom in hand, moments away from handing it to Sir Paul. This was the photo I needed. I raised a camera to my eye and fired off a half dozen frames. The audience rose to its feet in applause. At that moment our press wrangler pulled us out of the East Room. "Thank you, Press." She announced in passive-aggressive manner meant to communicate that we were no longer welcome at the event. I folded up my step ladder and moved gingerly toward the door, careful not to make a bigger mess than I already had. I felt awful as I shuffled outside. My strength had left me along with the meatball sub.

Under the hanging iron chandelier of the North Portico, I surveyed the damaged. While my camera bag had caught the majority, my blue button-down shirt became collateral damage of widespread splattering. I grasped the cast iron handrail of the staircase and struggled to descend the North Portico steps. I realized I couldn't go back into the briefing room in this condition, so I collapsed into a miserable heap on the asphalt at the base of the North Portico steps.

I cracked open my laptop and set it on the pavement in front of me. With New York holding the paper for my photo, I scrambled to send my best photo to the National desk. The Times' printing presses were on standby waiting for my photo. The morning edition on the East Coast couldn't be printed until I had done my job. I felt the pressure of the deadline weighing on me as I pulled the best frame from my memory card. After slapping a pre-written caption on the photo, I quickly tweaked its exposure and color balance in photoshop and sent the photo off to New York.

As I sat there frantically working, a Secret Service agent from the Uniformed Division interrupted my deadline scramble to inform me that I was not allowed to sit where I had camped out.

"You need to go back inside the briefing room, sir" he informed me coldly.

"Officer, can't you see I'm covered in my own vomit? Give me a break here," I replied exhausted and exasperated. Despite my plea for mercy, he would not budge.

I staggered inside thoroughly embarrassed. I cleaned up as best I could and packed up my gear for the long trek home. Even though I had stained the carpet in the East Room and soiled the clothes of one of my colleagues in front of me (sorry, Kevin), I still managed to make deadline. My thoughts turned to the humming printing presses in New Jersey duplicating my photo of Sir Paul on hundreds of thousands of newspapers.

Next time, I vowed, I would listen to my gut.

For as many events as I covered inside the White House fence, the area surrounding the executive compound never failed to draw its share of newsworthy happenings. Protests of all stripes and sizes were a common occurrence on Pennsylvania Avenue. Perhaps the most memorable thing I photographed outside the White House fence was the flyby of the. retired space shuttle, Discovery. In 2011 the end of the space shuttle program was announced by NASA, America's space agency. Barring a pair of fatal mishaps over the decades that claimed the lives of nearly a dozen astronauts, the space shuttle was generally regarded as a successful platform. It ferried personnel between cape Canaveral and various space stations orbiting the earth over the course of thirty years. The shuttles had served their purpose well for more than 130 missions.

It was announced that Space Shuttle Discovery would be transported to its permanent home at the Smithsonian's Air and Space Museum at Dulles International Airport. Plans called for NASA's 747 jumbo jet to perform a flyby over the District of Columbia with the shuttle mounted atop, piggy-back style, before landing at Dulles International Airport. On the morning of the flyby, I emerged from the orange line Metro stop at Farragut Square and hustled over to Pennsylvania Ave. The street was teeming with people hoping to catch a glimpse of the once-in-a-lifetime spectacle.

Positioning myself directly in front of the White House North fence, I took a few test photos and waited for the shuttle to appear. Camera in hand, I scanned the crowd of office workers and bureaucrats who had spilled out into the streets. Suddenly a woman's scream pierced the morning air. I reflexively turned to pinpoint the origin of the sound. In doing so I saw a man point to the sky.

"There it is!" exclaimed another person excitedly. I swung back around toward the White House to see for myself.

There it was. Space Shuttle Discovery was soaring through the air atop its 747 transport plane. I raised my camera and took a burst of photos as the two aircraft floated through the District's tightly controlled airspace. A pair of Secret Service counter-snipers stood on the roof of the White House peering through pairs of military grade binoculars at the majestic sight.

The crowd on Pennsylvania Ave. let out a collective gasp. A hush fell over the crowd. Not only had I never seen a jet aircraft flying so low over the District of Columbia, but the sheer sight of Space Shuttle Discovery perched on the back of the NASA 747 was magnificent. The shuttle made a single pass and then turned to begin lining up for its approach at Dulles. As the craft disappeared from our sight behind the DC skyline, the crowd began to disperse. The shared experience of witnessing such a remarkable sight far outweighed my satisfaction with the photographs I had produced. In the days leading up to the event it had been the talk of the town. The television airwaves were blitzed with coverage surrounding the event. Yet none of that prepared me for witnessing the scene. It was a truly unexpected, curious, and downright fantastic event. The whole thing was an awe-inspiring symbol of human accomplishment.

Another highlight of covering the Obama White House was the opportunity to tag along on Presidential motorcades around Washington, D.C. Being a member of the protective pool meant shadowing the President's every move. Whether he was driving to Capitol Hill to deliver his annual State of the Union address, or simply going out for dinner with First Lady Michelle on a date night, someone from the *New York Times* would provide protective coverage from inside the press pool. There was simply no telling when big news might break unexpectedly.

Riding in the motorcade quickly became my preferred mode of travel through the city. One such in-town movement stands out as especially memorable. On April 21, 2009, President Obama's White House schedule was uncharacteristically light. A large block in the morning was conspicuously absent of public events. I arrived at the White House and settled into the *New York Times'* small desk at the very back of the James S. Brady Briefing Room. Built atop the former White House swimming pool, the press area was where journalists spent their time waiting to cover any White House events, planned or otherwise, that might pop up.

Shortly after reaching my desk, the travel pool received a visit from an administration official. She informed us that in a few minutes we would be motorcading to the Central Intelligence Agency's headquarters in Langley, Virginia. On top of the general excitement of traveling with the President of the United States, this would be a motorcade movement to remember.

A few minutes later a Secret Service agent led us through the White House Rose Garden toward the motorcade. By the time we arrived, the convoy was already staged on the blacktop driveway that spans the South Lawn in a graceful arch. I walked past the pair of armored Presidential limousines that would lead the procession and noticed my khaki pants and blue button-down shirt reflected in the vehicle's shiny black finish. A Secret Service agent polished the hood of one of the limousines with a cloth as another affixed two small flags, one the stars and stripes, and another featuring the Presidential Seal, to the front bumper of the highly modified Cadillac.

Behind the limousines came several black Chevy Suburbans that would transport the President's Secret Service detail and members of the White House Military Office. The Counter Assault Team's vehicle, "the war wagon," brought up the rear of the Suburban convoy. Following the CAT team was a black extended-cab Ford Super Duty truck that resembled an ambulance. It was rumored that this vehicle could act as a safe haven for POTUS in the event of a nuclear, chemical, or biological attack on the motorcade. Behind the formidable looking truck, a handful of 12 passenger vans that would transport White House officials and members of the press followed along. The two press vans at the very back of the motorcade were nicknamed Wire 1 and Press 1. My colleagues from the Associated Press and Reuters newswires peeled off from the group and climbed into Wire 1 with their respective pool reporters. I proceeded a few more steps to Press 1 and loaded myself into the rearmost bench seat with a few other members of the in-town press pool. My favorite feature of the sleek black press vans was a small sunroof cut into the ceiling of each vehicle. Grabbing my cameras, I clambered up through the opening and emerged from the roof of the van at waist level. A chrome handrail surrounded the rectangular sunroof on all four sides. This position would afford me an excellent view of the entire motorcade as we made our way to Langley. A camera man from one of the national television networks did the same and emerged from the roof of Wire 1 just in front of me. Great minds think alike.

In the distance I watched as President Obama emerged from the Oval Office. He walked down the colonnade along the Rose Garden and proceeded toward one of the two limousines at the front of the motorcade. An agent held open the door of the Presidential vehicle nicknamed "The Beast" as President Obama climbed inside. A few seconds later the President's limousine started driving forward. Following the leader, the rest of the motorcade followed suit. I watched as the perfectly manicured grass of the South Lawn passed by on either side of me. We passed the Obama girls' wooden play set complete with swings and plastic slide outside the Oval Office. Looking over my shoulder, I watched as the tail vehicles of the motorcade, a White House communications Suburban and a local DC Fire Dept. ambulance passed through the fortified South Lawn gate.

A few turns later, we emerged onto Pennsylvania Ave. to begin the ten-mile trip to CIA headquarters. The U.S. Army driver behind the wheel of Press 1 gunned the engine to catch up with the rest of the motorcade that stretched down the road ahead of us. I gripped the chrome railing with one hand to steady myself as the van accelerated violently. DC Police motorcycle cops blocked off each intersection that we passed through. Bystanders lined the sidewalks along the motorcade route as we sped past in a blur. Continuing westward toward the Kennedy Center, we descended into a tunnel along the E Street Expressway. I raised my camera and took a photo as the flashing red and blue lights of the motorcade danced off the reflective tile ceiling of the tunnel. The wail of sirens filled the space as we zipped underneath the gridlocked surface streets above. We crossed the Potomac River on Route 50 and merged onto the northbound lanes of the George Washington Parkway. The tree-lined highway was devoid of all vehicular traffic as we followed the Potomac River upstream toward Langley. The vehicles at the head of the motorcade ignored the 45mph speed limit as they weaved in and out of the parkway's lane markers in a graceful ballet of tactical driving.

The frigid April air stung my cheeks as I continued to occupy my favored spot in the sunroof. As we approached Langley, the motorcade passed a large road sign that read "George Bush Center for Intelligence, CIA, Next Exit." The string of black vehicles exited the parkway and slowed considerably as they approached the North boundary of the CIA.

My colleague, Jason Reed, a crack photographer for Reuters whose skill behind the camera was rivaled only by his sharp wit and love of practical jokes, emerged from the roof of Wire 1 ahead of me.

"Hey Luke," he called out to me in his thick Aussie accent, "put your cameras down inside the van."

I followed his advice as we passed a slew of sternly worded signs posted on the shoulder of the road: "No Trespassing." "Authorized Personnel Only." "No Photography!"

The motorcade snaked between multiple reinforced guard shacks and vehicle barriers that comprised the CIA's back gate. A cacophony of security cameras pointed outward from the checkpoint in every conceivable direction. Numerous heavily armed security officers dressed in black fatigues watched intently as Press 1 passed them by. I returned the gaze of one of the officers with a polite nod. My subtle greeting went unacknowledged as we left the checkpoint behind.

As the CIA building came into view, the front two thirds of the motorcade split off ahead of us en-route to a back entrance. Our mini motorcade of press vans pulled around to the CIA's east entrance. For the first time since we had left the White House fifteen minutes prior I popped back down into the body of the van. Our press wrangler turned around in her seat and gave us some good news. Instead of holding inside the vans for the duration of the President's visit we would be allowed to visit the official CIA gift shop inside the building. There was only one catch: all cameras, laptops, and cell phones had to stay inside the van.

I left my electronic devices on my seat and stepped outside with my colleagues from Press 1. I jogged to catch up with my friends from Wire 1 and descended a concrete ramp into the belly of the Central Intelligence Agency.

While President Obama addressed a gathered audience of CIA members on the hot-button topic of enhanced interrogation techniques in the Global War on Terror, I was busy plundering the CIA gift shop. The small store took up about as much real estate as your average airport bookstore. The walls were jam-packed with intelligence memorabilia. Sweatshirts, T-shirts, coffee mugs, and shot glasses emblazoned with the CIA crest lined the shelves of the world's most exclusive souvenir stand.

My travel pool colleagues and I spread throughout the shop intent to do as much damage as possible. I perused store shelves looking for something that would meet the following criteria: small, affordable, and meaningful. I briefly considering purchasing a set of etched CIA crystal bourbon glasses, until I spotted the price tag.

In line with my meager intern salary, I left with only a few small items: a keychain lanyard with the words "The Agency" on it, a baseball cap with an Air America logo embroidered on the front of it, and a commemorative Soviet challenge coin. The memento featuring the face of Vladimir Lenin was too ironic to pass up. Capitalism and the West had won out in the end.

I handed my souvenirs to an employee standing behind the checkout counter. To the left of the cash register I noticed a small laminated the sign with a friendly reminder to agency employees: "If you are clandestine, do not use your credit card. It will blow your cover." In my imagination I could picture intelligence analysts from hostile nations pouring over the credit card statements of suspected American spies until they found the smoking gun: a charge labeled "CIA Gift Shop." As a photographer whose name regularly appeared in newspapers, albeit in microscopic font, blown cover was something I didn't have to worry about.

After paying for my purchases, I exited the gift shop and rejoined the rest of the travel pool waiting outside in the hallway. A steady stream of employees passed by in the corridor. One woman dressed in unremarkable business casual garb walked along carrying a Starbucks cup. Her hot caffeinated beverage reminded me that my cousin Chris had once spent the better part of a year working at the agency's in-house Starbucks. Unlike other Starbucks locations, baristas at the CIA store do not write their customer's names on their cups. The true identities of their clientele are often classified. With President Obama's visit nearing its conclusion we returned to the motorcade for an uneventful ride back to the White House.

Most official motorcade movements are accompanied by a phalanx of Washington, D.C. Metro Police motorcycle officers. On weekdays, that is. During my tenure at the White House, I noticed that on weekends the President's motorcade made its way through the District without a police escort. On one such occasion we were returning from Andrews Air Force Base. Any weather deemed prohibitive to the safe operation of Marine One triggers a weather call. This meant that POTUS must motorcade home from Air Force One, rather than flying by helicopter.

Instead of ignoring posted speed limits and stop signs as we usually did, the motorcade made its way back toward the White House at an agonizingly slow pace. Without a motorcycle escort, we obeyed the rules of the road just like any other vehicles must. It was a strange contrast compared to our usual weekday motorcade movements. Normally we blew through traffic lights without regard to their color. After all, was the leader of the free world expected to be kept waiting? I watched from my rooftop perch in Press 1 as we uncharacteristically slowed to a stop at a red light in DC's Anacostia neighborhood.

As we waited for the light to turn green, I noticed a man panhandling with a cardboard sign at the intersection ahead. He was dressed in tattered clothes and wore scruffy, untamed facial hair. The panhandler leapt to his feet and approached the President's limousine with an empty McDonald's cup in his outstretched hand. He came within nearly an arm's reach of "The Beast," the President's highly modified, armored, Cadillac. A moment later, a black assault rifle extend from the open window of a nearby Secret Service Suburban.

An authoritative voice belonging to a Secret Service Agent yelled from inside the SUV, "Get back!"

At the sight of the rifle, the man stopped in his tracks and threw his hands in the air. He hastily retreated from the motorcade as the agent continued yelling orders. Before the confrontation could play out any further, the traffic light turned green and the motorcade accelerated down the road. The panhandler sat back down against the light pole with his McDonald's cup woefully empty.

On days where weather wasn't a factor, the President usually took Marine One from Joint Base Andrews directly to the White House South Lawn. These helicopter arrival and departures quickly became one of my favorite White House events to photograph. During seasons of extensive Presidential travel, election years specifically, it was not uncommon for there to be a half dozen or more South Lawn arrivals or departures over the course of a week.

About thirty minutes before a scheduled arrival, White House Press office officials would make an announcement over the intercom in the briefing room. Any press wishing to cover the arrival should be gathered outside the Palm Room doors in five minutes. Grabbing my two cameras and an aluminum step ladder, I made my way through the break room and out the back door to where the line was forming. Every line of press photographers is subject to a pecking order. The Associated Press was always first in line. Given how many newspapers, websites, and magazines subscribed to the AP around the world, it only made sense that they would have first dibs when it came to claiming spots at White House events. Next came other international newswires: Reuters and Agence France-Presse. As a representative of the *New York Times,* I claimed my spot fourth in the line behind AFP.

Behind me stood my colleagues from Getty Images, the *Washington Post*, UPI, the *New York Daily News*, and other outlets. South Lawn arrivals were always open press, meaning no limit was placed on the number of journalists in attendance. Other White House events such as Oval Office bill signings, cabinet room meetings, and diplomatic room statements were restricted to the "tight pool" only due to a lack of physical space.

While covering the White House is often glamorous and exciting, there's plenty of sitting around as well. "Hurry up and wait," was a common phrase thrown around. Ten or fifteen minutes passed before a Secret Service Agent opened the Palm Room doors from the inside. He glanced at each of our White House press credentials as we passed through the doorway on our way to the South Lawn. We passed through another set of doors with large glass windows into the White House Rose Garden. A team of groundskeepers from the National Park Service worked to make sure the grass was cut, and flowers trimmed to perfection. I was always struck by the beauty and serenity of the space. The Rose Garden was a peaceful respite from the non-stop urban hustle and bustle that surrounded it in the nation's capital.

I picked a spot on the White House driveway and plopped down my aluminum step ladder onto the blacktop. A cursive script *New York Times* logo was proudly fastened to the handle with a strip of clear tape. With my spot claimed, I took a few moments to relax and take in the scenery. The sprawling green grass of the White House South Lawn spread out for acres. Perfectly manicured trees, hedges, and shrubbery surrounded the wide-open space. First Lady Michelle Obama's vegetable garden stood toward the southern-most fence. The White House South Portico towered above me. A collection of massive white columns supported a pair of balconies, one on top of the other. It was always humbling to find myself in this space. So few Americans could say they had stood in this spot. Why exactly was I allowed to be one of them? I couldn't tell you. All I could do was resolve to make the most of every opportunity I was given to be present on such storied, historic soil.

The minutes ticked by as we awaited the arrival of President Obama's helicopter. To pass the time I scanned the sky to the south for any sign of Marine One. Nothing yet. I raised the camera to my eye and spied on the tourists who were congregating at the base of the Washington Monument. My bored voyeurism was interrupted by the announcement of a TV camera man.

"Here we go folks," he called out.

I looked up from my camera to see three identical Sikorsky VH-3D helicopters flying in formation low over the National Mall. The trio passed behind the Washington Monument and banked to the North on approach to the White House. The distant sound of their engines reached my ears. In no time they had closed the distance between the monument and Constitution Avenue. The sound of Marine One and the two decoy choppers grew steadily louder.

The aircraft approached three abreast until they were directly over the ellipse. With room for only one chopper to land on the South Lawn, I wondered which of the three carried President Obama. At the last possible second two of the helicopters peeled off to the left and to the right, revealing the middle bird to be Marine One. The overpowering engine noise from the two decoy choppers echoed off the stone facade of the Eisenhower Executive Office Building for a moment before fading away almost instantly.

"Expose for the fireball," quipped one of my colleagues wryly.

What sounded on the surface like a friendly bit of photography advice relating to camera settings and exposure, was actually gallows humor. These Marine One arrivals were so common and generally so uneventful that such coverage opportunities were morbidly referred to as "death watch." It was an unspoken fact that the pictures we were about to shoot would likely only be of significant historical value if a tragic accident occurred during takeoff or landing. As commonplace as covering the White House can become to those who have done it for years, there was no telling when the defining event of a presidency could unfold right in front one's camera. It was good practice to expect the unexpected.

With the two decoy choppers out of the picture, Marine One approached the press pool head on. Through my telephoto lens I could see the pilot and co-pilot through the Sikorsky's sloped windshield. Headsets sat atop their high and tight haircuts. Boom mics extended down to the base of their chiseled jaw lines. Ribbons and medals adorned their crisply pressed khaki dress shirts. Flying Marine One was a coveted assignment for any Marine aviator.

The bird approached ever closer. Some thirty yards from the apex of the driveway it slowed to a hover directly above the grassy South Lawn. Marine One's rotor blades beat mercilessly at the air, forcing it down toward the ground in an effort to defy the laws of gravity and create lift. I felt the deafening sound waves reverberate through my chest. The hair on the back of my neck stood on end. It seemed as if the chopper was right on top of us. With the sharp blades of the aircraft spinning in such close proximity to my colleagues and me, I marveled at the skill of the crew piloting Marine One. The grass on the South Lawn bent outward in concentric circles from the middle of Marine One.

The Marine pilot began a steady ninety degree turn until the helicopter's nose was pointing in the direction of the U.S. Capitol building. As he turned, I extended my left foot and shifted my weight forward like a football linebacker defending his team's goal line. A gust of wind from the helicopter's tail rotor, sudden as it was fierce, slammed into my torso, nearly shoving me back from my spot on the driveway. The front two feet of my stepladder went airborne as the wind caught hold of the lightweight aluminum rungs. I grabbed for the ladder with one arm and leaned forward once more into the relentless gale. Out of the corner of my eye I saw a female reporter's long, shoulder-length hair being tossed around in the tempest. The press pass hanging around her neck fluttered about chaotically as she tried in vain to regain control of her hair.

The violent blast of rotor wash abated as soon as Marine One's landing gear touched down on the South Lawn. I joined the rest of my colleagues in a quick reconstitution, corralling my windswept hair and straightening my necktie. I untangled my twisted *New York Times* lanyard from the death grip it had taken around my neck.

As the Sikorsky's engines powered down to an idle, a set of steps unfolded from the front entrance of the Helicopter. An enlisted Marine in distinctive dress blues, white cap, and matching belt descended the stairs. Cursive script adorned the grey carpeted risers: "Welcome Aboard Marine One." The Marine made an about face with his back to the helicopter, snapped to attention, and saluted. A Secret Service Agent quickly exited the door and took up a position a few yards to the left of the aircraft's nose.

With the agent in position, President Obama emerged from Marine One, returning the enlisted Marine's salute as he descended the steps in a dark suit and tie. I fired away with camera as he walked across the South Lawn toward the covered awning of the White House residence. The president gave a friendly wave before heading inside to the oval shaped diplomatic reception room on the ground floor. With POTUS inside and photos in hand, I packed up my step ladder and retraced my steps back through the Rose Garden and into the briefing room. I sat down at my desk to send my best photos to New York with the noise of Marine One still ringing in my ears.

Perhaps my favorite part of covering the White House was the opportunity to accompany President Obama as he traveled around the United States campaigning, fundraising, and conducting official business as the nation's chief executive. This travel usually originated from the Washington, D.C., area onboard Air Force One. Whenever POTUS needed to traverse a distance too short to justify a flight aboard Air Force One, but too far away to motorcade, he would fly via helicopter.

A squadron of specially modified Marine Corps helicopters are used to transport the President. The fleet's widely recognizable green and white paint job, which Marine One wears so well, sets it apart from all other helicopters in the aviation world. If the President is traveling by helicopter usually that means his entire entourage is as well. White House staff, military support personnel, Secret Service Agents, and the travel pool usually follow along behind Marine One in support helicopters. The sophisticated planning and execution of these helicopter flights left a lasting impression on me. Any day traveling with the Marines was a good day.

One such memorable helicopter lift took place above the cornfields of central Iowa. I was accompanying President Obama on a campaign swing out west as he campaigned for re-election in 2012. After touching down at Des Moines International Airport my colleagues and I photographed President Obama as he disembarked Air Force One and boarded Marine One.

As soon as POTUS made it safely onboard, my colleagues and I turned to run and catch our own helicopter, Nighthawk 4. On that particular lift in Iowa, the Marines were using a variant of the CH-53 Sea Stallion helicopter painted the same shade of green as Marine One. First flown in 1974 during the Vietnam war, the massive single-rotor helicopter has been a workhorse for the U.S. Navy and U.S. Marine Corps for decades. Two of these behemoths would be joining Marine One and another decoy chopper in formation as we flew to our first campaign stop of the day.

With my laptop on my back and two cameras hanging from my shoulders, I sprinted toward the pair of Sea Stallions idling across the tarmac from where Air Force One had come to rest. Standing in a wide stance outside the helicopter was a Marine dressed in a dark green flight suit and white helmet. A black-tinted sun visor, like the type utilized by fighter pilots in the movie *Top Gun,* covered the top half of his face. The Marine held a clip-board sized placard with a large number four printed on it. This signified our helicopter's callsign: Nighthawk 4.

I slowed my run to a jog as I approached the rear ramp of the helicopter. The pair of General Electric turboshaft engines that were mounted on either side of the fuselage emitted a deafening roar even at an idle. Each engine could produce 4,380 horsepower to keep us airborne on our journey. I ducked my head and stepped inside the fuselage of the hulking metal beast. Two long benches ran the length of the carpeted interior. Having passed the rest of the press pool during my sprint across the tarmac, I had my pick of seats on the bird.

I walked all the way to the front of the helicopter and took the first available seat on the starboard side. In doing so, I positioned myself right next to an open window that Nighthawk 4's Marine crew chief would use to monitor our takeoff and landings. Laying in my seat was a pair of foam earplugs. I quickly ripped them from their packaging and crammed them into my ears. The painful whine of the helicopter's engines receded to a more bearable level as the foam earplugs expanded in my ear canal. I buckled into my seat as the rest of the press pool filed inside.

Shortly thereafter, the Marine whom I had passed outside climbed aboard and sat down in a rear-facing canvas crew seat near the entrance to the cockpit. I gave him a nod and watched as he went about accomplishing his list of designated tasks required for takeoff. The pilot and first officer up front in the cockpit began flipping switches on the CH-53's control panel. The helicopter's engines powered up and we started taxiing forward down the tarmac. The Super Stallion's massive rotor blades began to spin up for takeoff. With the tinted helmet visor still covering his face, the crew chief leaned halfway out his square window. He glanced up at the rotor, down at the pavement, and then side to side as he scanned the surroundings for any obstructions to our flight path. I noticed a funny sensation develop in my stomach as the horizon began to fall from view. We were airborne.

The helicopter's all-encompassing vibration rattled up through the floor and into my legs. As soon as we gained sufficient altitude, the crew chief took his seat back inside the fuselage. I raised my camera and took a few photos of the clear blue Iowa sky reflecting in his helmet visor. To pass the time on our lift I pulled out my laptop and began to work on the photos I had taken at the Airport in Des Moines.

As I sat with my laptop on my knees, I began to feel the sensation of something dripping on my left shoulder. I turned to investigate and noticed a few dark spots had appeared on my light blue button-down shirt. Intrigued, I started to look around the interior of the fuselage to pinpoint the source of the leak. The interior of the helicopter was lined with a hopelessly complex jumble of electrical wiring, cables, and riveted aluminum panels. Try as I might, I couldn't figure out the drops were emanating from.

I turned to the Marine crew chief next to me and tapping him on his knee.

"Hey, I think we're leaking something" I yelled over the noise of the helicopter. I pointed at my stained shirt and then up toward the ceiling of the Sea Stallion's fuselage.

A smile broke across his face as he leaned in toward my ear.

"That's hydraulic fluid," he yelled back.

My eyes widened in disbelief.

"Aren't you worried that we're leaking fluid?" I questioned.

"Actually, it's a good sign. It means we still have hydraulic fluid. I would only be worried if we *weren't* leaking hydraulic fluid," he replied with a grin.

With the helicopter at capacity, there were no spare seats to which I could move. I watched with resignation as the drips of hydraulic fluid continued to splatter and stain my Oxford shirt for the duration of the flight.

A few minutes before we reached our destination, I fished a small notepad out of my backpack. Turning to a blank page I scribbled down a message: "Write down your email address and I will send you photos." I handed the notebook and pen to the Marine crew chief and pointed to the message.

He gave me a thumbs up and scrawled his contact information across the paper.

As he handed back my notepad, I returned his thumbs up and turned my attention back to the window to watch as our Super Stallion came in for a landing at a small regional airport. The short asphalt runway was extensively cracked, though thankfully this did not pose much of a problem for our helicopter. The crew chief rose to his feet and again leaned out the starboard window to perform his duties. I slipped my laptop back into my backpack and began gathering my equipment to disembark the helicopter. We touched down gently on the landing strip. The bench seats quickly emptied as my colleagues in travel pool stepped off the aircraft and onto the cracked runway.

At the bottom of the ramp, another crew member standing beneath the Sea Stallion's tail section. I framed up a quick portrait of the black Marine. A warm beam of sunlight partially illuminated his face as he stood there wearing an expression of confidence and pride.

As I stepped off the ramp to run toward the motorcade, I felt a firm hand grasp my non-soiled shoulder. I turned and made eye contact with the crew chief who had given me his email address a few minutes earlier. Questions darted through my mind. *Did leave something behind on the helicopter? Was he mad that I had stopped to take a photo of his teammate?*

Without a word the crew chief answered my question. In one smooth motion he ripped his HMX-1 squadron patch from his flight suit and handed it to me.

I looked down at the worn HMX-1 unit insignia that he had placed in my hand. Four yellow helicopter blades in the shape of an X filled the circular logo. Each quadrant formed by the rotor blades featured a different icon relating to the unit. In one quadrant was the United States Marine Corps globe and anchor emblem. Another housed the storied unit's coat of Arms. A third featured a bold number one denoting their place in military history as the first Marine helicopter squadron in existence. The fourth and final quadrant featured a drawing of the U.S. Capitol Rotunda. Some 75 years earlier, HMX-1 was incorporated at Marine Corps Base Quantico, in Virginia.

I looked up and met the gaze the Marine crew chief with a smile of my own. To serve in this unit was an honor bestowed on very few Marines. Although I was not a Marine myself, I understood the message behind the simple gesture. It felt almost like he was making me an honorary member of the unit.ta

"I will send you some photos!" I yelled as best I could over the deafening engine noise. I clicked an imaginary shutter button with my index finger to help get my point across. He flashed another thumbs up as I turned to run and catch up with the rest of the travel pool. I barely made it into my assigned press van before the motorcade started rolling. As I rode toward the next campaign event, I proudly affixed the worn Velcro squadron patch to my laptop backpack.

Throughout my tenure covering the White House, few experiences topped flying with the Marines. On one fundraising trip to the West Coast, we boarded helicopters near the Golden Gate Bridge in San Francisco. Later during that same trip, we choppered from Los Angeles International to Burbank Airport en route to actor George Clooney's house for a closed fundraiser. As President Obama rubbed shoulders with Hollywood A-listers, I sat in Clooney's garage with the rest of the travel pool. I watched as one of my star-struck colleagues, a middle-aged female reporter, giddily tried on one Clooney's leather motorcycle jackets that hung in the otherwise empty space. On another trip, our helicopter landed at historic Fort McHenry in Baltimore Harbor where Francis Scott Key composed the words to the *Star-Spangled Banner*. In 2010 we utilized a massive Chevron heliport situated on the Gulf of Mexico during the Deepwater Horizon oil spill. Whenever the President traveled to New York City we choppered from JFK International Airport into Manhattan. Our route took us down the East River and directly over top of the Brooklyn Bridge. The scenery from Nighthawk 4 on those lifts was unmatched. On practically every helicopter trip I day-dreamed about dropping out of school, joining the USMC, and flying with HMX-1 as an enlisted Marine. Something inside me craved the challenge, the sense of purpose, and the brotherhood that I imagined I might find in the military. At the same time, a competing path beckoned to me. I had barely scratched the surface of what photojournalism could offer. For as long as I had the opportunity to cover the White House for the *New York Times*, I should probably capitalize on it. Boot camp could wait.

A short helicopter flight to the West of Washington, D.C. lies the Presidential Retreat: Camp David. When measured against the opulence of the White House, the rural compound's cabins, guest houses, and meeting spaces are comparatively rustic. Nestled on Catoctin Mountain, Maryland, the grounds of the retreat boast a swimming pool, tennis court, chapel, skeet shooting range, and other amenities. President Franklin Delano Roosevelt was the first U.S. President to utilize the site back in the 1940's. Ever since, Camp David has offered Presidents the opportunity to escape the grind of the White House and unwind in the midst of its secluded pine forest. In addition to acting as a weekend getaway, Camp David has served as a host facility for peace accords and international diplomatic summits. In May of 2012, a Group of 8 summit was hosted on the grounds of the

Presidential Retreat. World leaders from Canada, France, Germany, Italy, Japan, Russia, the UK, and the European Union joined President Obama for what Reuters called "A rustic sleepover" at the mountain getaway. Rarer still, select members of the press were allowed inside the notoriously camera-shy compound to photograph the G8 summit. My editors at the *New York Times* asked if I would be interested in covering the rare event. *Would I ever!*

Plans called for President Obama and other world leaders to be ferried to Camp David by HMX-1. My colleagues and I took the bus. We gathered in nearby Hagerstown, Maryland and set out on the 30-minute drive to Camp David. Our charter bus took its time climbing the winding roads toward the wooded summit of Catoctin Mountain. A wooden sign that looked like it was fashioned from felled trees stood outside the front gate of the Presidential Retreat. It was not unlike something you might encounter at a Boy Scout camp or your local state park.

Being a U.S. Naval installation, Camp David is heavily defended by a detachment of U.S. Marines who take their jobs very, very seriously. Whenever POTUS was present at Camp David, all attention turned to guarding the perimeter of the thickly wooded compound. Judging from our exceedingly cold reception by the guards at the front gate, one could be forgiven for assuming that our arrival had not been communicated to the necessary authorities. A pair of Marines dressed in camouflage and carrying assault rifles emerged from a fortified guard shack whose mirrored windows looked to be thick enough to withstand gunfire. The guards forcefully demanded that our civilian bus driver stop the vehicle and kill the engine. More guards emerged and began to perform a thorough search of our charter bus with the help of bomb-sniffing dogs and other explosive detection countermeasures. With the suspicions of Camp David's Marine Guards apparently diminished, our bus driver was instructed to restart his engine and proceed slowly through the front gate and onto the installation.

I peered out my window as the thick metal gate in front of us slowly inched open on its own accord. On either side of the guard shack was a small clearing through the woods. A pair of tall security fences extended the length of the clearing around Camp David's perimeter. As our bus crossed the fence line, I reflected upon the fact that I was now on the inside of perhaps the most impenetrable and well-defended 140 acres in America, second only to the United States Bullion Depository at Fort Knox.

The summit events we were allowed to cover were not all that different from the G8 summit I had covered in similarly rural Muskoka, Canada two years prior. There was a cheesy "family photo" where all the Group of Eight leadership gathered on a stage and waved to photographers in unison. In addition to the canned photo ops that always seemed to accompany these diplomatic summits, we were also granted a few seconds access inside working lunches between the eight world leaders in attendance. Recognizable personalities like German Chancellor Angela Merkel, Prime Minister Dmitry Medvedev of Russia, and UK Prime Minister David Cameron sat across from President Obama at a large wooden table scattered with documents and water glasses.

Later that day, several foreign reporters and photographers from other delegations joined the White House pool. About fifteen minutes before the next photo op was scheduled to being we were escorted down a shaded trail to Laurel Lodge. Plans called for President Obama to participate in a meet-and-greet outside the handsome log cabin. Each of the attending world leaders would shake hands with POTUS and pose for a photograph before entering the lodge. Although this type of photo-op was all too familiar to anyone who had photographed a G8 or G20 summit, the environment in which it was taking place was quite foreign. Rather than mild-mannered State Department officials directing our coverage of each photo-op, U.S. Marine Corps non-commissioned officers assumed these roles.

As the expanded press pool arrived at our predetermined spot outside the lodge, we were treated to a rather unique meet-and-greet of our own. In front of us stood a U.S. Marine dressed in a form-fitting polo shirt and pressed khaki trousers.

"Attention!" the Marine demanded.

His commanding demeanor caused a hushed silence to permeate the otherwise chatty group of journalists. With a booming voice he quickly explained what we would and would not be allowed to photograph during the photo op.

"This is your left-most lateral limit" the Marine informed us with a wave of his muscular am. "This is your right-most lateral limit," he repeated as he extended his arm on the alternate side our group. "If anyone points their camera beyond these lateral limits, their equipment will be confiscated," he half-yelled at us.

While this level of restriction and micro-management would never fly on the grounds of the White House, we weren't at "the people's house," as President Obama sometimes referred to 1600 Pennsylvania Avenue. We were at Camp David, and this house clearly belonged to the United States Marine Corps.

At the same time our instructions were being shouted to us, I began to suspect that one member of the press pool was not giving his undivided attention to the briefing. In fact, it sounded like someone was carrying on a separate conversation altogether. I turned and saw one of the foreign press reporters speaking French rather loudly on his cellphone. My eyes widened. I had a feeling that our drill instructor would be none too pleased. I was right.

"Sir!" the Marine interjected incredulously.

The Frenchman was oblivious to the verbal butt-kicking that would soon be visited upon him and continued to speak loudly into his smartphone.

"SIR!" barked the Marine in an even more authoritative tone.

By this time the entirety of the press pool had turned to stare at the unsuspecting French reporter. Still, he exhibited no awareness to the situation unfolding around him. Deciding that decisive action was needed, the Marine quickly closed the distance between himself and the reporter. With his previous entreaties having gone unheard, the Marine unleashed a torrent of verbal commands at point blank range.

"Discontinue use of voice comms, IMMEDIATELY!" the Marine bellowed at the top of his lungs.

At this, the poor reporter jumped three feet into the air and managed to hurriedly shove his phone into his pocket before his feet hit the ground. Having no desire to participate in a similar confrontation, I discreetly reached for my own phone and triple checked that it was on silent mode.

Certainly no one would be able to accuse our Marine guide of being overly colloquial. And while he did not choose to employ familiar turns of phrase, his intensity of delivery left no question as to whether the rules would be strictly enforced. Having set the tone for the afternoon, the meet-and-greet went off without a hitch. No lateral limits were violated. For the rest of the weekend, I looked for opportunities to rib my fellow photographer colleagues about their own use of "voice comms."

In between photo ops the press pool was positioned inside Camp David's Evergreen Chapel. We filed into the modest sanctuary and spread out amongst the pews. Sunlight filtered in through a dozen panes of stained glass on either side of the chapel. Wooden beams supported the lofty, vaulted ceiling. My colleagues and I wandered around the front of the chapel to stretch our legs and pass the time. Near the chapel's piano stood a small wooden bookshelf complete with hymnals, Bibles, and a handful of theological texts. As we stood looking at the shelf, a pair of enlisted Marines approached us from behind. Without so much as a word, the men walked up to the bookshelf, lifted it off the ground, and carried it clear out of the chapel.

Camp David was the Marines' world. We were just living in it.

As G8 summit ended, my colleagues were anxious to get back home to Washington. It had been a long weekend. In the media filing center, I overheard a Reuters photo editor trying to find a volunteer from his staff to stay behind and fulfill their role as the protective photo pooler. The White House Correspondents Association had lobbied that a photographer always be present any time the President lifted off in Marine One, including at Camp David. The AP, Reuters, and AFP all shared this duty. This time it was Reuters' turn in the rotation.

Even though I was a *New York Times* intern, I spoke up and volunteered to be the protective pooler. The Reuters staffers had spent the entire weekend working and were ready to go home. I, on the other hand, had nowhere to be. It seemed like a once-in-a-lifetime opportunity to spend a few extra hours hanging out at Camp David.

The Reuters editor took me up on the offer on the condition that I enter into a handshake agreement should the unthinkable happen to Marine One during takeoff.

"If anything happens, those are Reuters' photos. Is that understood?" the Reuters editor said.

"Of course," I replied, worried that he might rescind the offer at the last minute.

The rest of the press cleared out as the afternoon progressed. Roughly an hour before the President's scheduled departure I grabbed my two cameras and met my escort back at the front gate. He was a young Corporal with bulging biceps and high-and-tight haircut typical of the Marines stationed at Camp David. When the time came, we walked down a wooded path toward Camp David's helicopter landing zone. The pine trees surround the path gave way and opened into a small clearing. There, backlit and gleaming in the late-afternoon sun, sat Marine One.

My muscular escort instructed me to place my cameras on the ground facing away from the landing zone. I was not to touch my cameras except in the unlikely event of an emergency. I complied and made small talk with the corporal to pass the time.

"How long have you been in the Corps?" I asked. "Where are you from? Have you deployed anywhere? How was boot camp?"

He was a man of few words. Despite his tight-lipped demeanor I did learn that whenever the President was not on the premises pretty much all the Marines did was "eat, sleep, shoot guns, and lift weights."

"That sounds like a pretty good time," I remarked.

Our conversation was interrupted by the whine of Marine One's engines as they powered up. It was a telltale sign that POTUS would be arriving soon. The landing zone was buzzing with activity. Marines and Secret Service agents spread about the clearing in anticipation of the President's arrival. Without the ability to take photos, I watched helplessly as the fascinating scene played out in front of me. My hands felt noticeably empty with my cameras sitting on a bed of pine needles a couple feet behind me. A few seconds later a golf cart sped out into the clearing.

President Obama was in the driver's seat. He hopped out and walked swiftly toward the waiting Helicopter. Returning the salute of the enlisted Marine standing outside the aircraft, the President trotted up the carpeted stairs into Marine One.

It occurred to me in the moment that this was the first time I had ever laid eyes on President Obama absent the phalanx of press and television cameras that normally follows the man around. It's human nature to behave differently when you know you're being watched and recorded. In the few seconds it took for President Obama to hop out of his golf cart and board the chopper I felt as if I was stealing a private, unfiltered look at the most-photographed man in the world. Despite being a hundred yards away at the edge of the clearing, the moment felt strangely intimate. I was also unaccustomed to simply watching the President with my own two eyes. Usually, I had a camera pressed against my face and was consumed with the task of making compelling photographs.

Marine One powered up and lifted off from Camp David with ease. Thankfully there were no catastrophic engine failures, bird strikes, or anti-missile countermeasures deployed. Thus, my two cameras remained on the ground for the duration of the departure. My escort and I walked the path back to the front gate as the sound of Marine One's rotor blades faded into the distance.

My second year in the nation's capital came to an end on January 21st, the day after President Obama's second inauguration. It had been a fantastic run, but again, school was calling. I was one semester away from graduation. Just a few more classes stood between me and my undergraduate degree. If I could just check that box, I thought, I would be able to get back to Washington, D.C. and continue what I *really* wanted to be doing.

As my *New York Times* paycheck faded in the rearview mirror for a second time in as many years, I again questioned the decision of my editors to send me back to school. Another talented *New York Times* intern would soon be taking my place in the Times' D.C. bureau. I wondered if there would there be a place for me in Washington after I graduated that Spring.

Would I be remembered by my colleagues, or promptly forgotten like so many other interns who rotate in and out of Washington with the changing of the seasons? Would the inroads I had made in the industry remain, or slowly fade away? I had felt such a sense of belonging and purpose working in D.C. This was where I belonged. I could feel it in my bones. Was this the curtain call on my dream of covering the White House as professional photojournalist? Would I ever find that sense of calling again? Was it all downhill from here?

Scan this code for photos from Chapter 2

3. SEAL BOATS

The camouflaged boat slipped quietly through the dark waters of the Pearl River. Illuminated only by the faint green glow of their night vision goggles, a half dozen shadowy figures scanned the night for signs of the enemy. The subdued hum of the boat's diesel engine echoed gently across the surface of the star-lit river. Bullfrogs and cicadas signaled rhythmically to one another as the U.S. Naval craft churned slowly downstream. Suddenly, a rapid succession of gunshots rang out from the riverbank, shattering the peaceful calm of the evening. *Thump, thump, thump.* A voice called out from amongst the boat's crew.

"Contact right!"

In an instant, the aluminum craft exploded with a hail of return fire. The sailor closest to me swiveled his 7.62mm M240-Bravo machine gun toward our attackers and let loose. *Pow, pow, pow, pow.* His weapon retorted with a blistering pace. A moment before, the boat had been bathed only in the faintest beams of moonlight. Now, muzzle flashes enveloped the craft, illuminating it like the mid-day sun.

At the stern of the boat another sailor swung his Browning .50 caliber machine gun toward the enemy position and opened up with the long-barreled weapon. It's slow, deliberate cadence was instantly recognizable over the cacophony of machine gun fire streaming from our boat toward the shore. The coxswain revved the engines of our SOC-R boat and took evasive action to escape the ambush. Two other patrol boats identical to our own followed our lead, their guns blazing all the while. The machine gun nest on the river's bank abruptly went quiet. Our boat put some distance between ourselves and the original ambush site before throttling back down to an idle. In the ensuing silence each gunner called out how much ammunition remained for his weapon. Smoke hung low over the surface of the water as the smell of gunpowder permeated the stagnant air of the swamp. I noticed my hands shaking with adrenaline as I knelt behind the port gunwale of the riverine craft to which I had been assigned. Tightening my hand's grip on my camera, I did my best to regain my senses. I could feel sweat beginning to soak through the t-shirt I wore beneath my bullet proof vest. No sooner had serenity returned to the river than another bust of gunfire came from the opposite bank.

"Contact Left," our coxswain called out once more.

Another eruption of gunfire exploded from our craft in response. The muzzle flashes of the dueling automatic weapons illuminated the river with a vibrant orange glow. The sailor nearest me spun to his left and trained the craft's sole M134 minigun in the direction of the enemy. A modern adaptation of John Gatling's original rotary design, the weapon could provide a staggering rate of fire of up to 10 rounds per second. The sheer power of the gun would hopelessly overwhelm anyone unlucky enough to be on its receiving end. The telltale whirring sound of the gun's electric motor spooling up reached my ears. Half a second later, fire poured from its six spinning barrels. I squinted through the viewfinder of my camera toward the blinding muzzle flash of the minigun and mashed down the shutter button with my index finger. The gun's overpowering noise consumed my ear drums and seemed to fill every square inch inside my skull with sound and vibration. The gun's intense shockwave brought on a curious physical sensation that I decided could only be my internal organs ricocheting off one another with reckless abandon. With my one free hand I reached up to stabilize the Kevlar helmet that was bouncing around on my head due to the intense vibration of the gunfire. I moved to a different position on the starboard side of the SOC-R as the volleys of gunfire continued. Hundreds of shell casings littered the deck of the boat. The piping hot brass rolled in every direction as we pitched and turned sharply in the middle of the river. The slippery bullet casings made it practically impossible to keep my balance and maneuver at the same time.

Again, we broke contact and zig-zagged over the surface of the Pearl River in response to our attackers along the bank. A pattern began to emerge from the chaos evening's operation: patrol, ambush, return fire, break contact, reload, repeat. After spending a few hours engaging in this cycle, our boat's supply of ammunition began to run low. The order was given to break contact one last time and take off downstream at high speed. I lost track of time as we rocketed through the moonlit swamp at a breakneck pace. I couldn't help but marvel at the skill of the men piloting the three boats in our riverine patrol. We continued to zig and zag around sharp turns and fallen trees as we progressed deeper into the swamp. I used what little moonlight there was to take some slow-shutter photographs of one of the operators on our boat. He sat with his back to the riverbank and stared stoically downstream through a pair of night vision goggles that hung from his helmet. Small beams of faint green light illuminated each of his eyes behind the pair of night vision tubes. The vegetation behind him blurred together like an impressionist painting as we navigated the constant bends and turns of the river. Even though we had been firing blank rounds, my heart pounded out of my chest. This may have only been a training exercise, but it sure felt like the real thing.

It was the Spring of 2013 and I had been granted access inside Special Boat Team 22, the U.S. Navy's premier special operations riverine unit. SBT-22 is headquartered at NASA's John C. Stennis Space Center on the western edge of Mississippi's Gulf Coast. The unit trains extensively in the region's vast swamps and bayous in support of their primary tasking: combat insertion and extraction of U.S. Navy SEALs and other special operations units in hostile maritime environments. Their boat of choice is the Special Operations Craft Riverine, or SOC-R. A sturdy flat-bottomed swift boat with a shallow draft, a fully equipped SOC-R bristles with up to five machine guns and an impressive array of communications and navigation equipment. In the aftermath of Hurricane Katrina in 2005, SBT-22 deployed to neighboring New Orleans in order to aid search and rescue teams. These Navy men spent days fishing survivors out of the floodwaters that had inundated the city's Lower Ninth Ward.

Back on the Pearl River, our trio of SOC-Rs raced up the tributary at a blistering pace. "Brace, Brace, Brace!" the coxswain yelled. Mimicking the stances of the crewman around me, I found a handhold and crouched down to lower my center of gravity. The boat slammed violently to a halt as if we had just impacted an invisible brick wall. I crouched down as low as I could and gripped the boat's metal railing for dear life. A gigantic wall of water shot up some fifteen feet in the air in front of us as the SOC-R ground to an immediate stop. My body smashed into the boat with a violent crash. Hoping to shield my cameras from certain destruction, I instinctively turned my back toward the tidal wave of water that our bow had thrown aloft into the night sky. My pair of white knuckles gripping the aluminum boat was the only thing that prevented me and my cameras from flying overboard headfirst into the Pearl River. A second later, the wall of water cascaded down on me on the rest of the crew, soaking my helmet, body armor, and camouflage pants.

We came to an abrupt stop near the edge of the waterway. The SBT-22 officer in charge of the training operation ordered the sailors off their boats and onto the riverbank. For the men of Riverine Troop 4, the evening would conclude with a miles long march back to base through the midnight abyss of the swamp. I watched from one of the newly vacated boats as the men fanned out to patrol through the darkness.

While their march through the moonlit swamp would likely yield few useable photos for my project, I still wanted to go with them. Something inside me had awakened while we were out on the water. My inner warrior was stirring. This spirit inside me desires to be trained, disciplined, tough, and lethal. This inner warrior had been with me for as long as I can remember.

As a boy I was fascinated with World War II. Long before I picked up my first camera my childhood was filled with green plastic army men and G.I. Joe cartoons. Like so many little boys, past and present, I was captivated by Jeeps, tanks, aircraft carriers, and submarines. Something inside me couldn't help but be excited by the stories of America's fighting men who helped free a continent from the tyranny of national socialism and all its genocidal evils.

Growing up in North Texas, I spent most of my Saturdays at the Fort Worth public library consuming every book, magazine, and movie about World War II that I could get my hands on. My favorite film in the VHS cassette section was undoubtedly the 1949 black and white movie "Battleground." Starring Hollywood heartthrobs Van Johnson and Ricardo Montalban, the film chronicled the exploits of the famed 101st Airborne Division as they held the line against Germany's 12th SS panzer Division during the snowy Battle of the Bulge. I dreamt of fighting alongside the "battered bastards of Bastogne" with a 101st screaming eagle patch sewn on my shoulder. Alas, I was born 63 years too late.

If I wasn't hidden away in the library stacks with a pile of World War II history books, I was out marauding through the streets of my neighborhood battling imaginary Nazis. Armed with bazookas fashioned from cardboard shipping tubes and tennis ball hand grenades, I spent hours upon hours leading patrols through my backyard. Time and again the imaginary soldiers under my command would be ambushed by enemy forces unseen and rely on my leadership to outflank and outgun the bad guys. Nothing excited me more than stumbling upon a shallow ditch or small mound of mulch during my make-believe military adventures. The power of imagination transformed these otherwise commonplace terrain features into impenetrable battlefield foxholes and bunkers. To my delight other boys from the neighborhood would often join in for epic campaigns that would stretch all day until the streetlights flickered on at sunset.

Every penny of my allowance, birthday, and Christmas money was spent at Omaha's, a local military surplus store. For a 10-year-old boy, the place was better than Disneyland. To this day I can recall trembling with excitement as I rode to Omaha's in the backseat of the family minivan, my wallet stuffed full of one-dollar bills. As we drew closer to the store a pair of World War II-era training bombs mounted to a telephone pole in the shape of a "V" would become visible on the horizon. The curious sight was a welcomed signal for many a young boy on pilgrimage to the hallowed surplus store on Fort Worth's North side. The skeleton of a tank turret complete with gun barrel and crew seats sat outside the front entrance, beckoning all who passed to climb inside. Beyond the turret, a maze of government surplus shipping crates and ammunition canisters stood between customers and the store's entrance.

Stepping inside the store was like stepping into the past. The old warehouse was overflowing with row after row of camouflage uniforms. Helmets, belts, pouches, and canteens filled the expansive space. Oversized classroom replicas of machine guns hung from the ceiling with belts of ammunition draped over them, Rambo-style. In one corner sat a collection of massive wooden artillery shells used to train sailors aboard Navy ships. A cardboard container full of long-expired U.S. Government issue rubber gas masks sat in another. The air inside the store smelt of mothballs, rusty fuel cans, and cosmoline. Omaha's owner, a matter-of-fact gentleman with graying hair and a kind demeanor, was a constant presence behind the counter. He never failed to answer the myriad of questions that I pestered him with during my many visits to his place of business. With the man's help, I managed to cobble together a collection of surplus equipment that served me well for years of backyard battles.

It was a privilege to have spent my evening in the company of this elite group of SWCC operators. It was also a challenge. These were hard men. Tough men. They were seasoned sailors well-acquainted with the stifling summer heat, ornery water moccasins, and maddening swarms of mosquitoes that infested the swamps of southern Mississippi. I couldn't help but wonder how I measured up to them. Was I man enough, brave enough, or tough enough to hang with these guys? Could I make it through SWCC selection like they had? I didn't know the answers to these questions. I did know, however, the depths of admiration that I possessed for these men who volunteered to join the ranks of U.S. Naval Special Warfare. I was grateful that there were still units where men could be unabashedly masculine. I was grateful to be among this group of dedicated men where courage, competence, aggression, and lethality were rewarded.

The world is a dangerous place. We need men like this.

Shortly after returning from Washington, D.C. to Western Kentucky University, I began work on the capstone project for my photojournalism degree. I set out to produce a photo essay chronicling the U.S. Navy's Special Warfare Combatant-craft Crewmen (SWCC) My plan was to follow a Navy recruit through enlistment, basic training, and SWCC selection in order to tell the story of our country's Naval Special Warfare personnel as they trained and operated in the shadows. To do this would require approval from multiple chains of command in the Navy.

During my time working for the *New York Times* in Washington, I made friends with a military veteran named Haraz Ghanbari. For years

Haraz had worked in Washington, D.C. as a photographer for the Associated Press. Easily identifiable by his perpetual high and tight haircut, Haraz's intense energy, magnetic personality earned him a well-known reputation Department of Defense. Having served in both the Army and the Navy, his influenced reached across service branches. Haraz possessed an uncanny ability to network within circles far exceeding his comparatively junior rank. The first time I met him in person I was caught off guard by his thick Northern Ohio accent. Born and raised in the Buckeye state, Haraz's father emigrated from Iran to the United States in the 1970's and worked as a photographer covering news and sports across Ohio. His son Haraz followed in his footsteps in more ways than one, simultaneously adopting the vocations of both photojournalist and service member in the U.S. Naval Reserves.

Haraz quickly became someone whom I admired as both a military veteran and a photographer. We shared a deep love for our country and the many symbols of its freedom and liberty. Haraz would often cruise around Northern Virginia and the District of Columbia keeping a sharp eye out for any American flags that might have been displayed in a manner incongruent with the U.S. flag code. He frequently passed out replacement flags if an offending emblem was deemed, in his judgement, to be too faded or torn for continued display. Rumor has it that he once went so far as to enlist the help of a local fire department's hook and ladder company to replace a torn and tattered star-spangled banner; a task which the flag's owner apparently couldn't be bothered to perform.

When news broke that a deadly structure fire had claimed the life of a homeless veteran in Toledo, Ohio, Haraz went to work on behalf of the man. In the days following the fatal fire, details surrounding Raymond Vivier's tragic death emerged. The Marine Corps veteran lost his life while rescuing three others from a decrepit boarding house that had been set ablaze by arsonists. Haraz found Ray's service record and successfully secured a funeral with military honors at Arlington National Cemetery for the late veteran. Haraz embraced the concept of "leave no man behind" as seriously as anyone I had ever met.

Thanks to Haraz's generosity, I landed a sit-down meeting with a Captain in the U.S. Navy's Office of Public Affairs. In the weeks leading up to my meeting I compiled a collection of the best military photos I could muster from my portfolio. When the day of my appointment finally arrived, I caught a blue line Metro train from the White House to the Pentagon. I emerged from the underground subway station and walked to the Pentagon's main entrance to pick up my visitor's badge. This was my first visit inside the impressive five-sided structure.

Constructed in 1943, the Pentagon is home to some 23,000 Department of Defense employees. Legend has it that during the Cold War,

Soviet officers regularly analyzed satellite imagery of the structure in hopes of gaining insight to America's military operations. The Russians noticed that every day as the clock struck noon, dozens of personnel would convene and enter a structure in the inner courtyard of the five-sided building. The Soviets' brightest minds surmised that this gathering must be a highly classified mid-day briefing in a hidden underground command bunker. Not until the fall of the Berlin Wall and the collapse of the Soviet Union would the truth be revealed to the curious Russian intelligence analysts. The daily noontime gathering was nothing more than a pilgrimage to the Pentagon's popular snack bar. For decades, Soviet intercontinental ballistic missiles had been aimed to inflict maximum damage upon a hot dog stand.

Inside the Pentagon I made my way through a dizzying maze of corridors until I arrived at the office of Navy Public Affairs. Captain Greg Hicks, a career Navy officer with an outgoing personality, welcomed me into his office with a firm handshake. He looked over a selection of my photographs that I had brought with me and reviewed the contents of my proposal to shadow the members of the Navy's Special Boat Teams.

"Mr. Sharrett, the Navy would be happy to support your project. Let me know how I can help."

We shook hands and I left with a big smile on my face. Upon returning to Kentucky to finish my last semester at Western, I contacted the subject who would open my project. The young man was a teenager named Jeremiah who had plans to join Naval Special Warfare and become a SWCC operator after graduating high school. I traveled to New Carlisle, Ohio to spend a few days with him as he got ready to ship out for boot camp.

We met up at his local YMCA where a retired Navy SEAL mentor was coaching a group of young Naval Special Warfare hopefuls. I took photos as the group of young men swam countless laps back and forth in the aquatic center pool. Those in the water hoped to become SWCCs, SEALs, Aviation Rescue Swimmers, or Navy Divers. Young men who sought membership in these elite military units would have to endure months of rigorous training. Brutally high attrition rates awaited the men who were brave enough to enter the Naval Special Warfare training pipeline. Only a small percentage of the young men who were swimming in the YMCA's pool would come close to achieve their goals. For some reason I had a gut feeling that my subject Jeremiah would be one of them.

With pool training complete, we drove to Jeremiah's high school football stadium for another workout. As soon as we arrived at the school, he began sprinting up and down the steep bleachers with a heavy metal chain draped across his shoulders. With his favorite metal band, Five Finger Death Punch, blasting through his headphones, he attacked those stair sprints like a wild animal. A look of pure determination remained on his face as he sprinted up and down those stadium steps again and again. Finally, he had nothing left to give. Thick drops of sweat poured from his brow as he hunched over to catch his breath. After his grueling workout, we dropped by his grandparents' house a short drive from the high school. There he scarfed down a snack of scrambled eggs and peanut butter toast while sitting at his grandparents' kitchen table. He spoke with his grandfather LeRoy about his own Naval service in the 1960s.

"We're a Navy family," remarked the silver-haired man.

A U.S. Navy keychain lanyard hung from his grandson's neck as they chatted away at the kitchen table. I studied LeRoy's face. The pride that he felt for his grandson was evident. There is a certain type of respect that can only be found between men. I could see it clearly between the two of them as they sat together in the kitchen. I took a few photos of them together then bid Jeremiah farewell. I wished him luck with the intense training regimen that lay ahead of him at Naval Amphibious Base Coronado in San Diego, California.

The next stop in my journey took me to Navy boot camp at Great Lakes, Illinois. Located approximately 37 miles north of Chicago on the western shore of Lake Michigan, Great Lakes was home to the U.S. Navy's Recruit Training Command. The base saw some 40,000 recruits pass through the installation annually. At Great Lakes, recruits would learn basic military discipline and acquire the fundamental skills required to become U.S. Navy sailors.

I arrived at the training base on a weekday evening just in time to witness a busload of new recruits arrive for in-processing. A co-ed group of 100 or so young men and women dressed in civilian clothes filed off the charter bus that had picked them up from Chicago's O'Hare International Airport. A cadre of drill instructors was waiting for them with specific instructions.

"Stand at attention. Line up shoulder to shoulder. Drop your personal belongings. Shut your mouth and pay attention to your drill instructor," one instructor said brashly.

As I photographed the first few minutes of boot camp, I noticed a range of emotions become apparent on each recruit's faces. Fear. Confusion. Bewilderment. Confidence. I suspected that the new recruits who looked right at home would be the ones I should focus on. My suspicions were confirmed when a Chief Petty Officer pointed out to me the candidates who had enlisted with contracts to go SWCC. I began to shadow this small group of recruits as they progressed through in-processing. They took a drug test, donned uniforms composed of yellow Navy T-shirts and black gym shorts. Once outfitted with their uniforms, they proceeded to the barber shop where the last vestiges of their individuality would be sheared off. Over the coming weeks they would learn the Navy way to walk, dress, eat, sleep, and brush their teeth. The bathroom was "the head." A bed was a "rack." The kitchen was the "galley."

Drill instructors further divided the recruits into individual class-sized units. In each recruiting class the special warfare candidates were grouped together in a special unit called an 800 division. All recruits in this division would be subject to extra training after graduation at a school called Naval Special Warfare Preparatory Training, or NSW Prep. The whole point of NSW Prep was to whip candidates back into shape. The classroom portions of Navy basic training were so time-consuming that 800 division recruits were falling hopelessly out of shape over their eight weeks boot camp. To the dismay of NSW leadership, the young men who had arrived at boot camp in top physical condition were falling far beneath the required NSW physical fitness standards. From a time-standpoint, it was practically impossible for a recruit to stay in the tip-top shape that their NSW training demanded of them. At boot camp there are only so many hours in the day, and much of that time is dedicated to learning the ins-and-outs of U.S. Naval history, discipline, and skills training. Many special warfare candidates over the years have made it a habit to sneak out of their racks after lights-out in order to practice calisthenics in their barracks. As the rest of their class slept soundly in their beds, NSW candidates were quietly doing hundreds of combined push-ups, pull-ups, and sit-ups in the bathroom of their new home at boot camp.

During my second day on base, I attended a graduation ceremony where an earlier class of recruits was recognized for completing basic training. Family members packed into a gymnasium to watch their loved ones receive the title of U.S. Navy Sailor. Following much fanfare, recruits were allowed to reunite with their families after eight weeks away from home. I watched as smiles stretched across the faces of the 800 division recruits. A few wiped away tears of joy. All seemed to beam with pride for having accomplished a major milestone. While most of their fellow sailors would receive orders to report to the fleet, the special warfare candidates would remain at Great Lakes to attend NSW Prep.

Located on the northern edge of the base, NSW Prep employs the use of two Olympic-sized swimming pools for much their training. Inside the humid pool enclosure, I watched as NSW recruits swam laps back and forth ad nauseam. Freestyle, breaststroke, and combat sidestroke were the main tools employed by recruits looking to move efficiently through the water. The normally calm surface of the pool looked like it was boiling as arms and legs thrashed about every which way. NSW Prep instructors, all active-duty members of Naval Special Warfare units themselves, blew their whistles at specific intervals to signal a break. A calisthenics break, that is.

Hearing the whistle, recruits exited the pool, paired off, and performed dozens of sit-ups a piece. NSW regulations require sailors to be able to bang out at least fifty sit-ups in under two minutes. A few of the slower sailors received extra "encouragement" from the cadre. There's a well-known saying in NSW: It pays to be a winner. In training the inverse is true as well. Finish near the rear of the pack and you will quickly find yourself with an instructor breathing down your neck who is all too eager to "smoke" you with extra calisthenics.

I turned my gaze away from the sit-up session for a moment and noticed a line of olive drab canteens lined up neatly against one of the pool's mustard yellow walls. The last name of each special warfare candidate was stenciled onto a piece of masking tape and affixed to their respective canteens. Dempsey. Marlow. Miller. I wondered how many of these guys would make it through their training. I prayed silently that any of these men who might go down range would return to their loved ones in one piece.

Having satisfied the instructors with their sit-ups, the recruits hustled next-door with their abdominal muscles aflame. I followed the group through a garage door-sized opening to find myself in another equally humid pool enclosure.

"Pull-ups!" an instructor barked.

The recruits quickly formed single file lines in front of six sets of pull-up bars and began banging them out rapid fire. Mounted above the pull-up station on the wall was a wooden trident, the coveted symbol of the U.S. Navy's SEAL teams. Expressions of pain and determination flashed across the faces of the newly minted sailors.

"Push-ups!" Another instructor ordered.

The men dropped to the pool deck to work their already exhausted arm muscles.

Packed shoulder to shoulder and bathed in yellow-green, fluorescent light, the sailors began counting their reps out loud. *One, two, three, four.* Each man wore a pair of UDT shorts; high-cropped khaki swim trunks adopted in World War II by the Navy's Underwater Demotion Teams. The experience of standing in the midst of the push-up formation as a sea of muscular men convulsed up and down was nearly vertigo-inducing. Heaven knows how many push-ups later, the instructors decided that the men had paid their anaerobic debt for the moment and ordered them back to the pool deck from which they had come.

As the pack of sailors disappeared from view, I set my cameras down and leapt up to take hold of the pull-up bar directly beneath where the SEAL trident hung from the wall. I banged out a measly four pull-ups, well short of the minimum requirement of 15. I dropped back to the ground with arms that felt like Jell-O. Perhaps I should re-think being a

Navy SEAL as my backup career, I thought to myself. That, or keep practicing my pull-ups.

With my time at Great Lakes coming to an end, I hit the road back to Kentucky. Back in the Bluegrass I began to sort through the hundreds of photos I had taken in Illinois. I also started planning my next visit in the SWCC training pipeline. Upon graduating NSW prep, SWCC candidates receive orders to Coronado, California for their next training evolution: Basic Crew Training. Not unlike SEAL training, BCT was as a kick in the pants that served to weed out the mentally weak from the ranks of prospective SWCC operators. The sailors would soon settle into a brutal training routine. Every day they would run for miles on soft sand, perform seemingly endless calisthenic drills on the beach, and be pounded by the crashing waves of the frigid Pacific Ocean. Despite having the Pentagon's approval for the project, I still needed the green light from each of the local commanders aboard any installation where I planned to photograph. Even though I had made multiple appeals to Navy brass, I was unable to secure an invite out to Naval Base Coronado. Apparently, the commanding officer wanted his men to be able to train without the intrusive gaze of a civilian photographer in their midst. My disappointment at the news quickly faded once I received an invite to the SWCC base on the opposite coast: Joint Expeditionary Base–Little Creek in Virginia Beach, Va.

Little Creek is a small Naval installation hidden in the shadow of the massive Norfolk Naval Station located directly to its west. The base is home to Special Boat Team 12, the SWCC unit tasked with operating in open ocean environments. The east coast even-numbered conventional SEAL teams had their team compounds only a stone's throw from SBT-12's dock in Little Creek cove. The Special Boat Team would often conduct Visit, Board, Search, and Seizure (VBSS) training on the high seas with their SEAL comrades onboard. VBSS missions were a staple for the SEAL teams and one of the missions for which SBT-12 trained constantly.

Upon arriving at Little Creek, the unit's public affairs officer picked me up at the front gate and toured me around the SWCC compound. When called upon, SWCCs have the capability to parachute into the sea with their boats from high altitude and conduct operations as needed. I photographed sailors packing their own parachutes, working out in their extensive fitness training facility, and performing maintenance on their boats. The main vessel utilized by SBT-12 is called the Rigid Hull Inflatable Boat, or RHIB. The open-air boats are painted dark gray and feature a collapsible superstructure mid-deck that houses advanced communications and navigation equipment. The RHIB is 36 feet long and can operate in close proximity to comparably massive vessels such as oil tankers, cruise ships, and naval destroyers.

Down by the water, a half-dozen or so RHIBs sat docked in SBT-12's marina. I stood on the dock with my escort watching a group of SWCC sailors gearing up for an evening of training out on the Atlantic Ocean. I wanted more than anything to go with them. I wanted to gear up and be out in the thick of it. I imagined what it would feed like to pull up beside a massive U.S. Navy destroyer underway in the Atlantic. I imagined the boat bobbing in the choppy seas as Navy SEALs practiced climbing rope ladders with the use of their night vision goggles. Alas, my escort had not planned on spending his night out on the high seas. Nor was he going to be convinced. Instead, he had scheduled a date with his girlfriend that evening. As a civilian, I would not be allowed on the training mission without him. My fate was sealed. I watched longingly as the SWCC operators huddled together for their mission briefing. The semi-circle of young men standing before me brought back thoughts of the many adventures I had playing army as a little boy.

The only thing better than a trip to Omaha's, my favorite military surplus store, was a rendezvous with my best friend Joe Stackpole. He was a good friend who always had my back on the battlefield. One Friday in the spring of 1999, Joe and I attended a half-day at school and then relocated to my house for the afternoon. We didn't have cable; thus, soap operas and daytime talk shows comprised the only programming my family's television had to offer. Instead of vegging on the couch, Joe and I dressed head to toe in camouflage and set out to play at a local park in my neighborhood. Working in tandem, we maneuvered down my street using parked cars for cover and concealment. I imagined myself as a British commando sneaking through the rubble of Arnhem, Holland during Operation Market Garden in World War II.

After covering a couple blocks, we arrived at our destination: a huge playground complete with slides, rope bridges, towers, and monkey bars. Joe and I had a blast using our imaginations and fighting a make-believe battle on the playground. Unbeknownst to us, the nation was still in a state of shock as they mourned the deadliest mass school shooting in modern memory at the time. The Columbine High School shooting had taken place just a few weeks earlier.

As we played at the park, we happened to catch the attention of a playground monitor at an adjacent elementary school. Located next-door to the park, Oakmont Elementary was a grade school that served the growing population on Fort Worth's south side. Joe and I took a break from playing to watch as some of the school's students played outside at recess. Suddenly we a heard a panicked voice come over the school's loudspeaker.

"Code red. Code red. Everyone inside the building immediately," a female voice implored over the intercom.

All at once the children on the playground let out a collective scream and bolted for the nearest entrance. It took only a few moments for the school playground to empty out completely.

Joe and I locked eyes and seemed to read each other's minds. We had better get home, and quick. Gathering up our gear, we ran in a panic back in the direction of my house. My heart pounded as the home-made cardboard shipping tube bazooka I had slung over my shoulder bounced every which way. The wail of distant sirens grew steadily closer as the Fort Worth Police Department closed in on two suspected school shooters. Judging by the sound I thought there must have been at least a half dozen police cars careening down the street toward us in hot pursuit. I shot a panicked glance over my shoulder and saw a squad car come into view just down the block from where we had come. A short time later we reached my front door and disappeared inside the two-story red brick house.

Once inside we bolted upstairs to my room and closed the door. Without a word between us Joe and I took off our camouflage jackets and hid our canteen belts under my bed. We sat cross-legged on my floor in a sea of LEGO bricks, terrified and out-of-breath. I hoped desperately that the police hadn't seen us duck into my house. Less than a minute later the front doorbell rang. Immediately I felt sick to my stomach. I listened from upstairs as my mom answered the door and called me down to the foyer.

I emerged from my room and descended the staircase to find an intimidating-looking police officer standing in the front doorway of my house.

"Son, were you playing at the park a few minutes ago?" he queried.

"Yes sir," I responded sheepishly with my head hung low.

The officer asked me to retrieve the toy gun I had been playing with. I retreated to my room and returned with a miniature replica of a wild west rifle that I had purchased from The Alamo the summer before. "Old Betsy: Davy Crockett's Rifle" proclaimed a shiny gold sticker on the wooden stock of the souvenir cap gun. I only succeeded at keeping my emotions in check for a short time. Before I knew it a flood of tears was streaming down my face. The emotion brought on by the afternoon's events was too much to keep inside. The police officer continued his line of questioning. He asked for my name and birthday and scribbled the answers into a small notebook that he retrieved from his belt. A full-sized black handgun filled the holster on his duty belt. Two embroidered Fort Worth Police Dept. patches were stitched onto each shoulder of his pressed blue duty uniform. I absorbed the authoritative energy radiating out from the officer as he occupied the threshold of my home.

Upon finishing the police report he scolded me to be more careful in the future. Tears continued to roll down my cheeks as I internalized his harsh tone. There was no mistaking the disappointment in his voice.

"You should know better," he said before turning to leave.

As the front door clicked shut, I choked back the last of my tears and slowly climbed the staircase to the second floor. Back in my room, I fumbled around with my LEGOs and did my best to put the afternoon's events behind me. A little while later Joe's mom stopped by to pick him up, leaving me alone for the remainder of the day.

I sat back down on the floor of my now-vacant room. The camouflage fatigues that I had so hastily hidden were just barely visible beneath my bedspread. I sat and stared at them as I soaked in a puddle of negative emotion. Fear, confusion, and painful embarrassment swirled around my heart. In the coming days, a sense of deep shame would descend upon me. With my parents trying to raise three kids and make ends meet, I didn't have anyone to help me make sense of what I was feeling. At ten years of age, I had few tools, if any, for processing the events of that afternoon. I imagined the teachers and students gathered in the elementary school's auditorium, learning the identity of the boys who scared them all half to death. I waited for another knock at the door, this time from the chief of police who might handcuff and take me downtown for more questioning. I feared that television news crews might set up their cameras outside my front door and wait to catch a glimpse of me. While none of these fears came to fruition, the shame stuck around. In the weeks following the incident, any time my family drove past the school I would slink down in my seat for fear that a mob of angry carpool moms might spot me and surround our car in justifiable maternal rage.

For months I just couldn't shake the feeling that there was something really wrong with me. On a cognitive level I had a good understanding of the situation for a 10-year-old. Of course, the teachers at the elementary school were on edge after the Columbine shooting. Of course, two kids dressed in camouflage with weapons would seem alarming in the middle of the school day. Everything made sense to me rationally. My heart, however, was a different matter.

Why did I feel so much shame? I was just trying to play at the park with my best friend. I was only doing what came naturally to me. I was just being a boy. Yet in the naive zeal of my youth, I sent an elementary school into lockdown and had been chased home by the Fort Worth Police Department. I began to question if boys like myself belonged in my neighborhood. While these questions swirled in my mind, one thing had become painfully clear: I needed to find a better place to re-enact the battles of World War II. Where could I go to mimic my heroes, those brave Allied soldiers who fought to save the world from the Axis? Where could I go to embody courage, proclaim the truth, and bring order to chaos? Fourteen years later, those questions again demanded an answer as I stood on the dock watching the SWCC operators prepare for their training mission.

I returned to Little Creek the next day to take more photographs of SBT-12. While I couldn't tag along on the overnight training mission, I was given the opportunity photograph a pair of SWCC boats operating closer to shore.

With permission from the unit commander, I boarded a slightly smaller, less exciting Navy patrol boat called a SAFE boat. We followed a pair of RHIBs out into the Chesapeake Bay in order to photograph one of their training evolutions. One of the unit's RHIBs was back in the water for the first time following extensive engine maintenance. I photographed the vessel as it tore across the Bay and crashed through the Chesapeake's choppy waves. Large sheets of water sprayed up in front of my lens as the SAFE boat collided with waves of its own. A little while later one of the SBT-12 RHIBs pulled alongside our SAFE boat. The boat's tall, fit coxswain called out to me. "Hey, hand your cameras over here and come aboard with us." I resolved not to let my cameras sink like bricks to the sandy bottom of the Chesapeake Bay and leapt from the pitching deck of the SAFE boat onto the RHIB. Behind the boat's controls stood the stout coxswain. A pair of Oakley sunglasses wrapped around his face. Shaggy blonde hair protruded from beneath his fitted SBT-12 platoon baseball cap.

"Welcome aboard," he said as he offered me a handshake.

I met his grip and readied my cameras to take more photos as he put the RHIB through its paces. A few minutes later the coxswain reduced our speed and yelled over the roar of our motor.

"Do you want to drive?"

"Yeah, alright." I responded, trying to hide my excitement and play it cool.

He gave me a crash course in the boat's controls and off we went. I've never been behind the wheel of a Formula1 race car, but I imagine this boat was its waterborne equivalent. Time became a blur as we zoomed across the surface of the Chesapeake Bay with yours truly at the helm. The coxswain gave me instructions as we sped across the surface of the water.

"Turn Left on my command," he ordered. "Ready? Turn."

I yanked the boat's steering wheel sharply to our port side and nearly careened over the bow thanks to Sir Isaac Newton's First Law of Motion. With a little more practice and some on-the-job training from the coxswain I helped push the RHIB to its limits for the duration of our allotted training time. With fuel running low we motored back to the serene Little Creek lagoon. An American flag flew from the superstructure of our boat, its edges worn and tattered by months of salty Atlantic gales. As we pulled back into the SBT-12 dock I thanked the SWCC coxswain with a hearty handshake and set off for the front entrance of the base. The thrill of being given command of such an impressive watercraft left me practically buzzing for the next hour.

At the end of the semester, I turned in my project to my photo professors. A group of faculty members, fellow classmates, and a panel of visiting industry professionals gathered in an auditorium on Western's campus for the presentation. Having poured my heart and soul into the project I was deeply satisfied to finish my college career with high marks, good feedback, and a project that I still consider to be some of my best work more than a decade later.

For a time between my junior and senior year at Western, I flirted with the idea of trying out for Naval Special Warfare myself. I shed thirty pounds and whipped myself into shape for the first time in my adult life. I was motivated by the opportunity to serve my country. Nearly every day I ran long distances in a Kevlar vest, stopping each mile to do pushups, sit-ups, squats, and burpees along my running route. I even went so far as to get Lasik eye surgery in order to qualify for an NSW boot camp training slot.

To my chagrin, the fire in my belly got the best of me. Halfway through an early morning training run I tore the meniscus in my right knee. Instead of taking things slow, I had pushed my body too far, too quickly. Due to this injury, I watched my dream slip away before I even had a chance to realize it. Running eight miles every morning before sunrise on the concrete sidewalks of Bowling Green, Kentucky did me in. Day after day, mile after mile, I pulverized my knees on that unforgiving cement. With sharp pains shooting up my right leg, I limped back to my house carrying the crushing weight of a dream deferred. Back at home I strapped an ice pack to my swollen knee and began to face reality. I would never wear a trident in a SEAL Team. I would never man a machine-gun on a SWCC boat. I would never jump from a helicopter into the ocean as a U.S. Naval Rescue Swimmer. It was a bitter pill to swallow.

When I reflect on my time spent with the men of the Navy's Special Boat Teams, I am struck by their professionalism and mastery. Their skill in navigation, boating, and shooting sets them apart from most any other maritime unit worldwide. Only the toughest of the tough make it through the rigorous SWCC selection process. It takes years of discipline and determination to land a spot in an SBT unit.

Spending time near men of such dedication prompted me to do some soul-searching over the course of my project. Even with a healthy knee, did I have what it takes to succeed? Could I have made it through such break-neck training? These were dedicated men. In what areas of my life did I need to be more dedicated? During my final semester at Western the men of the Navy's Special Boat Teams became both an ideal and a judge against whom I measured myself. How could I work to embody the masculine traits exhibited by these sailors? How could I increase in courage, commitment, strength, bravery, mastery, and dependability? It didn't take long for me to realize that there was significant room for growth in all these areas of my life.

I was not aware of it at the time, but my photo project allowed me to follow roughly the same path that I would have taken had I ended up enlisting in the Navy. Not until the completion of my senior year did this realization fully dawn on me. As it did, I felt a sense of peace begin to take root in my heart. I didn't belong in the pool or on the pull-up bars at Great Lakes. I didn't belong in the sand of Coronado Beach or on a SWCC boat in the Atlantic Ocean. I belonged behind the camera using my gift as a photojournalist.

Shadowing these men helped me arrive at a new realization. While it may not have been my calling to serve in the ranks of Naval Special Warfare, I still had a mission to accomplish. There was a heroic journey of my own that I needed to embark upon. This journey would require discipline, courage, and commitment. My mission would be to become the type of man that my family, friends, and coworkers could depend on. I would strive to be masculine in a world in desperate need of men.

Scan this code for photos from Chapter 3

4. SECTION 60

A shiver ran up my spine as I sat on the deserted railway platform not far from the Baltimore airport. My thin jacket did little to prevent the frigid January temperatures from chilling me to the bone. I checked my watch. My train to Washington, D.C. was running late. The hustle and bustle of airports, baggage carousels, and shuttle busses had insulated me temporarily from the emotional weight of the trip. With every exhale, my breath condensed into a small cloud of moisture. For a fleeting moment it hung suspended in the air in front of me. Then, as suddenly as it had appeared, it dissipated into the night. In the cold silence of the dimly lit station, another wave of grief began to roll over me. I was on my way to Arlington National Cemetery to bury my cousin.

Eleven days before I boarded my flight to Baltimore, my Uncle Dave and Aunt Vickie received the dreaded knock at the front door of their townhouse in Northern Virginia. A U.S. Army casualty assistance officer and a chaplain stood on their front porch with the worst imaginable news. Their son, private first class David H. Sharrett, was dead. He had been killed in a firefight a few hours earlier in Iraq. It was January 16, 2008. Word spread quickly through our close-knit family. I was home from college on Christmas break when my cell phone rang. It was my dad calling with the terrible news. My heart sank. *Lord, have mercy.*

My dad is the youngest of three brothers. Since before I was born, the three Sharrett brothers and their families have gathered for beach week every summer on the Outer Banks of North Carolina. In the 1980s, our family staked their claim in a small neighborhood a few miles south of the historic Corolla lighthouse. Referred to as "Section A" by the local vacation realty firms, the humble enclave is comprised of a trio of cul-de-sacs lined with stilted beach cottages. Not only is Section A a foundational part of

Sharrett family folklore, it also happens to be the setting for all my fondest memories of my cousin, Dave.

I grew up seeing Dave at the beach every summer. He was nine years older than me, and the ringleader of the Sharrett first-borns mafia. My older brother Mike, my cousin Allan, and Dave composed a boogie-boarding, troublemaking threesome whose antics have cemented themselves in the annals of Sharrett family mythology. The fathers of every teenage girl would break into a cold sweat any time these three showed up to a beach bonfire or fourth of July picnic in Section A. Their cocky attitudes, handsome good looks, and sheer mastery that comes naturally to every Sharrett made them a triple threat. I looked up to Dave both literally and figuratively. When I think of him, I can hear his infectious laugh. I can see his muscular, tattooed frame running across the beach playing two-hand-touch football against my dad and my two uncles. I remember his wide grin as he emerged from the Atlantic Ocean exhausted from hours and hours of surfing. I recall watching with rapt attention as Dave schooled my big brother in a plastic army men battle that stretched the entire length of our rental cottage's screened in porch.

In the evenings, my cousins and I would break out our arsenal of toy guns and follow Dave into battle against legions of imaginary enemies. Dressed head to toe in surplus army gear, we marauded through the sand dunes defending the shores of our beloved Section A from wave after wave of make-believe foes. Sometimes it was Russian invaders. Other times it was a fearsome cabal of bad guys who proclaimed loyalty to the firstborn female Sharrett cousin: Lizzie's Troops. We chucked firecrackers and smoke bombs at each other with reckless abandon. We explored the crumbling ruins of an old coastal defense bunker leftover from the Battle of the Atlantic in World War II. Dave was our leader and we had lost him.

My train of thought was broken by a nearly unintelligible announcement over the train station's loudspeaker. After a long delay, the train was approaching the station. The rickety Amtrak coach gave me a reprieve from the bitter cold outside. I put on my headphones and found a reprieve from the dull ache in my heart. The empty train that I caught to Union Station mirrored how I felt inside: hollow, alone, numb, sad.

The next morning, I woke up in the basement of my Uncle Dave's townhouse and got dressed for the funeral. He asked me to photograph the day like a photojournalist would. Despite having completed only a single semester of photo school, my uncle believed in me. I would take on this role for our family, and for Cousin Dave. I accompanied my grieving family to Dave's memorial service at a family friend's church in Arlington. A standing-room only crowd packed into the small chapel. Dave's flag-draped coffin sat at the front of the sanctuary as family members and friends delivered eulogies in his memory.

My dad, a Presbyterian pastor and gifted public speaker took the pulpit and delivered a short benediction.

"I want to say what we're all thinking," he started. "This STINKS. Dave's death is horrible. This is not the way it's supposed to be," he forcefully exclaimed.

My dad read the shortest verse in the Bible, John 11:35. It's only two words long: Jesus wept. When Christ stood outside his friend Lazarus' tomb he was moved in spirit and snorted with anger. Then he burst into tears. Jesus had lost a friend. He was angered at death itself. He trembled at the thought of the tomb that he would soon experience before his own resurrection.

I do not know how a good God can allow so much pain and suffering in the world. But I do know that we do not suffer alone. Jesus knew what it was like to carry deep pain in his heart. The fact that our hearts ache in the face of tragedy and loss are evidence that we were not created for a world where death has a home. Yet, in the face of this agony, we have this hope: for those who follow Jesus, death is not the end of the story.

After my cousin's closest family and friends had spoken, my uncle took the stage to deliver the final eulogy. A criminally underrated high school Shakespeare teacher by trade, he shared how he had raised his son Dave as a single father. Known affectionately by the nickname "Bean," Cousin Dave would crawl around the floor of my uncle's high school classroom as his dad taught English literature at the front of the room. Over the years he grew up to be revered district-wide on the high school football field. Those of us who had squeezed into the church laughed, cried, and laughed again at the heartwarming stories my uncle shared of his late firstborn son.

My uncle shared a story from when Dave was seven or eight years of age. One summer at the beach, cousin Dave was standing on the sand watching my uncle bodysurf out on a sand bar in the Atlantic. Spying his little boy on the shore watching him, my uncle waved an arm in the air to say hello. Suddenly cousin Dave ripped off his T-shirt and ran into the surf. He swam wildly through the breakers toward the sand bar. Fearing that his little boy might not be able to make it all the way through the choppy waters, my uncle swam to meet him halfway. Upon reaching his boy, my uncle grabbed him and startled treading water. Red hot tears were streaming down my cousin Dave's flushed cheeks.

"What's the matter? What's wrong?" My uncle asked.

Cousin Dave replied that when he saw him waving from the sandbar, he thought he was drowning and calling for help. Little Dave was swimming out to sea to rescue his father.

The service ended with my uncle playing a rendition of Amazing Grace on his Martin acoustic guitar. A harmonica hung around his neck, its soulful notes filling the space between the verses of the well-known hymn. A collection of Dave's closest high school friends and his younger brother Chris carried the casket down the aisle and outside to a waiting hearse. Soldiers who attended the memorial snapped to attention and saluted as Dave's body passed by. A crowd of mourners who had been unable to fit inside the church stood reverently outside as the scene unfolded. A group of motorcyclists known as the Patriot Guard Riders stood at attention along the sidewalk in front of the church. Although they had never met my cousin, they spent their morning holding U.S. flags in memory of Dave's service and life.

The funeral procession left the church and drove the short distance down Route 50 toward Arlington National Cemetery. Motorcycle officers from the Arlington Police Department escorted the procession along the way, blocking off intersections from cross traffic. The first tears of the day came to my eyes when I spotted an officer snap to attention and salute as Dave's body passed by. As the funeral procession entered Arlington Cemetery, I did my best to re-focus on the task at hand: documenting this day with my camera for my family. I shoved my emotions down and picked up my camera instead.

There's something about a camera that can serve as an insulating layer between myself and the emotional reality of whatever I'm photographing. Not only does the act of bringing a camera to my eye obscure me physically from the situation at hand, it can also serve as an emotional barrier. Peering through a lens necessarily communicates that I'm not here to be present or engaged. I'm here to document and record. I've got a job to do.

We made our way slowly through acre after acre of uniform marble headstones. Dave's body was about join the resting place of tens of thousands of his fellow brothers in arms. All had dedicated their lives to serving their country. I stared out the window as the funeral procession snaked through the cemetery. Try as I might, I was unable to tear my gaze away from the hallowed gardens of stone that lined both sides of the road. We were not the first family to make this journey through Arlington Cemetery to bury a loved one, nor would we be the last.

A short time later, the procession arrived at the gravesite. Dave was to be buried in Section 60, the cemetery plot reserved primarily for America's war dead from recent conflicts in Iraq and Afghanistan. We parked our cars in a line and emerged to watch an eight-man casket team remove my cousin's body from the back of the hearse. The soldiers wore the U.S. Army's first class dress uniform. A curved blue patch with the words "Honor Guard" stitched into it adorned each of their left shoulders.

Light blue braided shoulder cords encircled their right arms. These men were soldiers from the 3rd U.S. Infantry Regiment "The Old Guard." Based at Fort Myer, they would be responsible for performing Dave's funeral with full military honors.

A hushed silence fell over the already somber scene. Every eye was glued to Dave's flag-draped casket as it came into view. I watched the body of one of America's fallen sons emerge from the hearse. Grief hung heavy in the air. The soldiers removed Dave's casket with steady intentionality. The coordinated movements between the honor guard's arms and legs were executed with robotic precision. In unison, the soldiers turned 90 degrees toward the field of graves where Dave would be interred. The way they wore their dress uniform caps, with polished black visors pulled down low over their eyes, gave one the impression that the funeral party could have completed the task with their eyes closed.

My Uncle, his wife, and his two surviving sons followed in the wake of the casket. A sea of mourners dressed in black trailed along behind the funeral party at a slight distance. They walked at an un-naturally slow pace, mimicking the speed of the Old Guard soldiers carrying their brother in arms to his final resting place. Maybe if I walked a bit slower, I could delay the inevitable painful goodbye that await me. Maybe I could turn back the clock.

Concluding their solemn march, the burial party set the casket down on a rectangle of green AstroTurf that surrounded Dave's six-foot-deep grave. A rectangular hole had been carefully excavated from the Northern Virginia soil by the cemetery's groundskeepers. Dave's family members and friends filled in around the gravesite in a horseshoe pattern. A few rows of white folding chairs sat facing the casket. My uncle settled into the most hellacious front row seat that a father could imagine.

Beneath a gloomy overcast sky, the honor guard lifted the draped American flag to reveal Dave's bare silver casket. Each soldier held a piece of the flag in their white-gloved hands. They methodically folded it into the shape of a perfect triangle. The Purple Heart and the Bronze Star were presented to my family. The cherished medals symbolized Dave's courage in battle and sacrifice for his country. A group of high-ranking military officers and local congressmen offered their condolences to each person seated in the front row.

A seven-soldier firing party stood at attention nearby with M-14 rifles at their sides. In the distance, a bugler lifted a polished brass horn to his lips and played *Taps*. The mournful notes echoed off the sea of white marble headstones in Section 60.

"Ready, fire." the firing party commander ordered in monotone.

Three volleys of gunshots were fired into the sky in quick succession. The sharp report of their riles rang out across the cemetery. The distinct smell of gunpowder reached my nostrils as the last notes of taps faded from the bugler's horn. Having accomplished their mission, the honor guard turned to march away. The funeral was over.

With my job complete, all the of the pent-up emotion of the day came rushing out. I put my camera down on the grass and bawled. The dam had broken. My mom embraced me as I sobbed with grief. I buried my face into her shoulder to muffle my crying. The flood of tears falling from my eyes left a damp patch on her jacket.

With tears still in my eyes, I reached out and touched Dave's cold silver casket. I tried hard to savor the last few moments that my cousin's body would be above ground. That was where he belonged. He belonged in his Army uniform with a 101st Airborne patch on his shoulder. He belonged on the deck of a beach cottage smoking a cigar and sipping Knob Creek bourbon during our annual Thanksgiving family reunion at Section A. He belonged at the gun range where he taught his little brothers how to shoot his AK-47. He belonged above ground, not surrounded by cold, dark earth. I pressed my camera's shutter button and took one last photo: my hand on his casket. *Goodbye, Dave.*

That evening I caught a flight back to Kentucky to resume the second semester of my freshman year at Western. Having never grieved the loss of a loved one before, I was surprised to experience lingering feelings of sadness come and go for some time. I remember sitting in the dining hall on campus trying to drown my sadness with food. A plate piled high with pepperoni pizza sat in front of me as I stared out the huge plate glass window next to my table. I focused my gaze on an American flag flying at half-staff in front of Western's basketball arena. Flags statewide had been lowered in honor of three Fort Campbell soldiers who had been killed in Iraq. Dave was one of them. A deep sense of sadness, with which I had become familiar over the past week, again overcame me. This time, however, I noticed the presence of a new emotion coupled to the sadness. It was pride. I was so proud of my cousin. He was a warrior to his core. There was no other way he would have wanted to go out, than fighting alongside his squad mates.

The rest of the Spring semester flew by. As final exams loomed, I learned that I had been selected to serve as a White House intern during George W. Bush's last summer in office. As mentioned in a previous chapter, I would be spending the summer in Washington, D.C. lending a hand in the White House Photo Office. Long-time family friends Brian and Diane Webster offered me a place to stay in their home for the summer. The handsome two-story house where they lived sat tucked away in wooded neighborhood in Arlington, Virginia. It was only a stone's throw from Fort Myer and Arlington National Cemetery. The house was so close, in fact, that if you stood outside in the backyard, you could hear *Taps* play each night at 5pm as the American flag was lowered on base. In a strange twist of fate, every Christmas a handful of holiday greeting cards addressed to none other than General David Petraeus arrived in the Webster's mailbox on Jackson St. At some point the distinguished four-star Army general had lived in the same house. A few people in his rolodex apparently didn't make the cut when he sent out his change of address notice.

Over the course of the summer, I returned a handful of times to Arlington Cemetery and visited Dave's grave. Such was a privilege of living close to Fort Myer. My first trip back to Section 60 was an emotionally heavy experience, to my naive surprise. I ventured into the cemetery and was immediately disoriented. America's losses in the War on Terror had continued to mount over the last five months. When we buried Dave on January 29, his grave stood two thirds of the way down on the front row of Section 60. Since then, another row of headstones had appeared and buffered Dave's grave from the rest of empty cemetery plot. Over the coming months and years this space would fill in, slowly but surely, with the bodies of fallen soldiers, sailors, airmen, and marines from our wars in Iraq and Afghanistan. I struggled to find a reference point for Dave's burial site. Eventually I was able to pick his headstone out of the row of graves. Chiseled into the white granite stone was a black cross along with his name, rank, service branch, birthday, and the date of his death. "Bronze Star," "Purple Heart," and "Operation Iraqi Freedom" filled in the lower third of the headstone.

Tears began to well up as I stood there reliving the funeral. After a handful of seconds, a single tear finally escaped the corner of my eyes and rolled lazily down my cheek. I let it linger along my jawline for a moment before wiping it away. A strange sense of relief came over me. It felt good to let that bit of grief escape from inside me. *Why was that?* Immediately, I knew the answer. I was terrified that I might visit my cousin's grave and feel nothing. Yes, the sorrow surrounding Dave's death was still present in my heart. Following the funeral, I had shoved those emotions aside in order to focus on my academic, social, and professional goals back on campus in Kentucky. I had not dealt with the grief of Dave's passing.

The day of his funeral was the last time I had really cried. It had been nearly six months since then. Simply stepping foot on the hallowed ground of Section 60 was enough trigger the wellspring of pain and sorrow that still lingered in my heart. Amidst the gardens of stone, it was again bubbling up inside. It was escaping the clenched fist of my soul. The fist that spent its time trying to regulate my negative emotion. I was still sad. This realization reassured me of my own humanity. My body remembered. This plot of grass along the Potomac River was a place for sadness. Here, of all places, it was OK to mourn. My grief was a sign of membership in a terrible club; a club where deep sorrow and deep pride coexisted at once.

One morning near the end of my White House internship, I was sitting at my desk scrolling through the White House photo archive. One of the perks of working in the photo office was the ability to access the trove of digital photos taken throughout President Bush's eight years in office. Sadly, many compelling pictures of the 43rd President were never released to the public. Some were determined to contain classified information. A whole host of photos from the September 11th terrorist attacks fell into this category. In the middle of the attack, White House photographer David Bohrer followed Vice President Cheney as he was whisked away to the bunker beneath the White House. Bohrer took photos the entire way and throughout the morning inside the Presidential Emergency Operations Center, or PEOC. Due to the shroud of secrecy surrounding the White House bunker, most were never approved for public consumption.

Other photos in the archive were deemed too politically sensitive to see the light of day. One such example included a photo of President Bush shouldering a gold-plated MP5 submachine gun in the Oval Office. The gaudy firearm had been gifted to him by a visiting prince from the oil-rich nation of Saudi Arabia. Someone in the West Wing had decided that publishing a photo of the President brandishing a fully-automatic, German-designed 9mm firearm fielded by tactical units around the world could backfire politically. Then there was a collection of serene landscape photos taken on a ranch in Southern Texas. Hunting dogs were pictured walking through a tall, grassy field as men wearing blaze orange clothes cradled double-barreled shotguns in their arms. I came to learn that the photos were taken in the moments leading up to Vice President Cheney's infamous 2006 quail-hunting accident that left Texas attorney Harry Whittington in an intensive care unit.

As I sat scrolling through the archives of forbidden photos, my boss Jody called my name.

"Hey Luke," she said. "You're wanted across the street."

I spun around in my swivel chair with a puzzled look on my face.

"What do you mean?" I asked.

All she would tell me is that someone would be over to escort me to the West Wing soon. I walked nervously to the restroom to spiff up my hair and make sure my necktie was tied properly. A short time later my friend Jonathan came to get me from the photo office and escort me across Executive Drive and into the White House. Jon was the executive assistant to White House Photographer Eric Draper and had urged my parents to have me apply for the internship. His folks attended the same church as my parents in Lynchburg, Virginia where I had finished high school. That summer, Jonathan and his wife often gave me a ride home from the White House, so I didn't have to cram into the packed Metro trains that ran during the afternoon rush hour.

On the way over to the West Wing, Jon informed me that President Bush would be signing a bill renaming a U.S. Post Office in memory of my cousin Dave. To rename a post office requires an act of Congress as well as a Presidential signature. Someone in the West Wing had found out that I was serving as an intern and requested that I be present at the bill signing.

My heart started to pound as we entered the West Wing. We ascended a staircase that was lined with official White House photos taken the previous week. Jon led me through a narrow hallway to a couch that sat just outside the Oval Office. He wished me good luck and retraced his steps back downstairs to Eric Draper's office. I sat tensely on the plush couch, unsure of what to do with my hands. A Secret Service agent from the Presidential Protection Division stood with his back to the curved Oval Office wall. He looked the part perfectly with his dark suit and clear earpiece. I passed the time examining historic photos and valuable oil paintings that hung on the walls of the West Wing. I sniffed my cheap intern suit and wrinkled my nose. I probably should have had it dry-cleaned more often that summer. It was too late now.

Suddenly, the door to the Oval Office opened. White House Chief of Staff Joshua Bolten appeared in the doorway.

"We're ready for you, Luke."

I stood up from where the couch and stepped into the Oval Office. President Bush stood up from his desk and welcomed me with a warm, boisterous greeting. He wore a charcoal gray suit and strode out to meet me with his hand extended. I had heard rumors in the past about the man's exceedingly firm handshake, and I must say, it did not disappoint.

"Luke, where are you in school?" The President asked as he made eye contact with me.

Before I could respond, he attempted to answer his own question.

"Virginia Tech?"

"No sir, Mr. President. Western Kentucky University."

"Hilltoppers!" He interjected with a half-shout.

"Yes sir," I replied with a nod.

The President invited me around behind his desk to witness the bill signing. I looked around at the rest of the Oval Office as I followed his lead. Aside from the President's photographer, Eric, President Bush and myself were the only ones in the room. I thought to myself how astounding it was to be receiving this type of personal attention from the leader of the free world.

I stood behind the Resolute Desk at the president's right hand as he added his signature to the bottom of the leather-bound bill. The text of the document read "An act to designate the facility of the United States Postal Service located at 10449 White Granite Drive in Oakton, Virginia, as the 'Private First Class David H. Sharrett II Post Office Building'. Be it enacted by the Senate and House of Representatives of the United States of America in Congress assembled." He closed the bill and extended his hand to me for another handshake.

"Tell me about your cousin," the President said.

"He was an incredible man," I replied. "He loved his family and he loved America. There was no other way he would have wanted to go out than fighting for his country."

The President nodded and rose to his feet.

President Bush pressed a heavy metal coin into my hand. It was about the size of a silver dollar. One the front of the challenge coin was a Presidential seal. On the rear was a bronze rendition of the With House South portico with the words "George W. Bush, Commander in Chief" on it. I felt the weight of the coin in my hand and clenched my fist around it.

"Luke, I want you to have this coat" the President said.

"Thank you, Mr. President," I replied, somewhat confused. *Did he mean to say coin?*

"This note," the President corrected himself, tongue tied.

"Thank you, Mr. President," I again replied.

President Bush paused for a second and corrected himself.

"Wait, that's not a note, that's a coin."

The President and I chuckled together for a moment.

"Yes sir, Mr. President. That's correct," I responded with a smile.

The day before our meeting, President Bush had returned from the Beijing Olympics aboard Air Force One. Instead of sleeping in, he had elected to get an early start, as he usually did. Due to this decision, he was suffering from a serious case of jet lag. The President gave me one more handshake.

"Thank you for serving as intern," President Bush said.

"Thank *you*, Mr. President," I replied as I turned to leave. "It's my pleasure."

A few weeks after Dave's death, the President met privately with my Uncle Dave, Aunt Vickie, and my two surviving cousins, Chris and Brooks. I was grateful for the lengths he went to honor the sacrifice that the Sharrett family had made for the United States. I could tell that the casualties that resulted from the Iraq war weighed heavily upon him. In the years following the conclusion of President Bush's second term, he began painting portraits of some of the servicemen and women who had been wounded in the War on Terror. It's not hard to imagine the haunting sense of guilt that must plague a commander in chief who sent troops to their death in battle. Nor is it hard to pick up on this theme in President Bush's paintings.

Over the next three years, new information regarding my cousin's death would come to light. Evidence began to emerge that my cousin was not in fact killed by insurgents, but instead was mistakenly shot in the back by his own commanding officer. Dave's death was a tragic case of friendly fire. As questions surrounding my cousin's killing began to mount, a family friend opened his own investigation into the matter. That friend was veteran investigative journalist James Meek. Back in the day, James had been of my uncle's students at Langley High School. The two kept in touch over the years as James spent the ensuing decades reporting on national security topics for publications like the *New York Daily News* and ABC.

According to one of his sources in Iraq, an un-manned Predator drone circling high above the battlefield captured the circumstances surrounding Dave's death on video. Shortly thereafter, the existence of a second infrared video recorded by a nearby AH-64 Apache helicopter gunship was also confirmed. A much clearer picture of what really happened was beginning to emerge.

In the pre-dawn hours of January 16, 2008, Dave's squad was inserted via Blackhawk helicopter to a small village north of Baghdad called Bichigan. Upon dismounting their helicopter, Dave and his fellow squad mates patrolled on foot through a grove of orange trees. Intelligence reports suggested that armed insurgents were hiding in a thicket not far from their position. Gripping his rifle, my cousin peered through his night vision goggles as he walked methodically through the citrus grove. With each step, the 101st Airborne soldiers drew nearer to a hidden enemy position. Suddenly, the stillness of the night was shattered. Insurgents opened fire at close range with AK-47s and hand grenades.

The bright flashes of the enemy gunfire immediately rendered useless the American soldiers' night vision goggles. Two of Dave's squad mates, Cpl. John Sigsbee and Pfc. Danny Kimme, were shot and killed immediately as they attempted to move out of the line of fire. The video feed of the friendly Predator orbiting overhead showed Dave hit the deck and seek cover from the onslaught. Gunshots erupted all around him as the insurgents fired over his head only a few feet away. A few long minutes after the ambush started, Dave leapt to his feet in a desperate attempt to fall back and rejoin the rest of his squad. While making his escape, he turned to open fire in the direction of the enemy. Spent cartridges ejected from his rifle as he fought to turn the tide of the ambush. At that moment the Predator circling overhead lost sight of Dave. A large tree momentarily obscured my cousin from the drone's line of sight. As soon as he came back into view, my cousin was down on the ground, writhing in pain. Dave was hit. Chaos reigned supreme on the battlefield.

Upon receiving the report of American casualties, a medevac chopper landed nearby to retrieve two other soldiers who had suffered non-fatal wounds in the attack. Dave's commanding officer, 1st Lieutenant Timothy Hanson, boarded the UH-60 Blackhawk and left the battlefield without accounting for the whereabouts of my cousin or the two other Americans who lay dead near the thicket. Some forty-five minutes after the ambush had commended, another force of American soldiers arrived and coordinated an air assault against remaining enemy. Apache gunships attacked the thicket from the air and silenced the ambush, once and for all. Darkness fell as they searched frantically for my cousin. One member of the search party launched a flare into the air. A bulb of burning phosphorous suspended beneath of small silk parachute painted the desert in an otherworldly glow. A few moments after launching the flare, they discovered Dave under a nearby bush. His pulse was faint. Dave was a fighter, and he was still clinging to life.

His comrades picked him up and carried toward another medevac chopper that had landed outside the orange grove. They placed him onboard the helicopter and in the care of the flight crew. A huge cloud of dust enveloped Dave's surviving squad mates as the UH-60 helicopter became airborne. Time was of the essence. If the medics onboard could stabilize Dave and make it to a field hospital in time, they might be able to save his life. Tragically, Dave didn't make it. He passed away on a Blackhawk helicopter somewhere between Bichigan and an air base in Balad, Iraq.

An autopsy performed at Dover Air Force Base a few days after his passing would reveal that the single round that struck, and eventually killed, my cousin was fired from an American weapon. The bullet came from a rifle belonging to none other than Dave's commanding officer, 1st Lieutenant Hanson. In the heat of the moment, Hanson had mistaken Dave for an enemy fighter and opened fire on one of his own men. This missing piece of the story would remain hidden by the U.S. Army for far too long.

With more and more new information coming to light, the grieving process for my uncle and his family was interrupted again and again. Over the course of three years, the Army lied continually to my family and to those advocating on our behalf like James Meek. We knew nothing would bring Dave back to life. But at the very least, we wanted to hear the truth about what really happened from the Army. Amazingly, no one in Dave's chain of command received disciplinary action for the multiple failures and regulations that had been broken in the incident. The Army even attempted to promote the LT Hanson after knowing full well that he had shot and left one of his own men behind on the battlefield to die. Dave had answered the call and done his duty for his country. Now it was our turn to make sure that the U.S. Army learned the painful lessons it needed to learn from his death. With the help of Virginia's United States Senators and other members of the Senate Armed Services Committee, LT Hanson's promotion was eventually reversed. Although we could never get Dave back, it was a small consolation to know that an officer who had inexcusably abandoned his own men in battle would never again lead American soldiers into harm's way. It was a fitting end to a long, painful saga. Or so I thought.

On Veterans Day 2011, I was covering the White House for the *New York Times.* That morning, I accompanied President Obama to Arlington National Cemetery where he laid a wreath at the Tomb of The Unknown Soldier. On our way back to the White House, the motorcade made an un-announced stop at Section 60. With a light drizzle falling, President Obama walked through the neat rows of headstones with a somber expression on his face. His demeanor mirrored the mood of the cold, wet, dreary day. It reminded me the day Dave was buried nearly four years earlier.

I grabbed my cameras and scrambled down a row of graves toward the middle of the cemetery to document the scene. A handful of mourners had braved the rain to visit their loved ones in the cemetery that morning, unaware that they would be running into the commander in chief. President Obama stopped to speak with a couple of the mourners. One such man towered over the rest at six feet, seven inches tall. He wore a blue raincoat and stood in front one of the many white, marble headstones that spread out through the cemetery in uniform rows. I raised my camera and fired off a few frames of the man as he spoke to President Obama. The two men stood with their backs turned to me, facing the headstone of the grave nearest them.

A moment later our White House press wrangler for the day corralled the travel pool back to the motorcade as President Obama continued to speak to the man in blue. Back in the van, I opened my laptop and started sending photos of the impromptu stop to my editors in New York. While waiting for my memory card to download, I looked out the window back in the direction of Section 60. I thought of my cousin and wished that I had been able to share his story of courage and sacrifice with yet another sitting U.S. President.

Later that afternoon I received an email from the man in the blue rain jacket. It was none other than James Meek, the reporter who helped my family blow the lid off the U.S. Army's coverup surrounding Dave's death. James had been visiting Dave's grave when the motorcade arrived and was subsequently able to share my cousin's story with President Obama. Although Dave was gone from this life, those he left behind made sure that he would never be forgotten.

Losing Dave shattered my long-held romanticized notions of combat. This was not a movie. This was real life. I would never see my cousin again. My uncle would never hug his firstborn son again. My cousins would never be able to smoke another cigar with their big brother. I saw the effects of pain and grief rip through my family. Even though I was only experiencing the horrors of war second-hand, I realized how naive my attitude toward war had been as a child and a teenager. War is hell.

Scan this code for photos from Chapter 4

5. HOUSTON FLOODS

I sat upright in bed with a start. A moment before, I was sound asleep in my North Houston hotel room. My groggy eyes darted around the room as I tried to get my bearings. *Where am I? What am I doing here? What time is it?* I squinted toward the alarm clock sitting on the nightstand to my left. The neon green light of the clock's digital display seemed outrageously bright to my groggy eyes. It was quarter to four in the morning. I struggled again to figure out where exactly I was.

Suddenly, an urgent thought struck my sleep-deprived brain: the floodwaters were rising, and I had left my laptop on the hotel floor. It wouldn't be long until the carpet was under a foot of murky water. My laptop would be ruined. Without a working computer I would be completely ineffective as a journalist. I still couldn't figure out where I was, but I knew time was of the essence. I needed to act quickly.

Swinging my weary legs onto the carpet, I stumbled like Frankenstein's monster toward the power outlet where I left my MacBook plugged in the night before. I hastily unplugged it and placed it on top of the hotel room dresser. My cameras weren't safe either. I scooped up my two Canon digital SLRs and placed them in the same spot beside my laptop.

Satisfied that my quick thinking had purchased me a few more hours of precious sleep, I collapsed back onto the king-sized mattress. If the water made it up to my bed, my hope was that I would wake up in time to escape before I drowned in my hotel room. Content with my plan, I passed out and fell back asleep immediately. A few hours later I woke again in the same bed. I noticed my room subtly illuminated by the soft pre-dawn light filtering in through the half-drawn window curtains. It must be morning, I reasoned. Rolling onto my side, I peered down at the carpet.

It was bone dry.

There was no sign of floodwater anywhere in my room.

Sheets and pillows went flying as I burst out of bed and flung open curtains. My eyes registered the parking lot three stories below me. Also bone dry.

Thus began my third day covering the aftermath of Hurricane Harvey.

Harvey was a Category 4 hurricane that devastated Houston, Texas, in late August 2017. The monster storm gained strength for days in the Gulf of Mexico before essentially grinding to a halt over Texas's Gulf Coast communities. According to estimates by The National Oceanic and Atmospheric Administration, Harvey dumped upwards of sixty inches, or five feet, of rain on the Houston metro area over the course of just a few days. Low-lying areas in the city saw catastrophic flooding.

I was some 900 miles away in Kentucky sitting in my living room when the first of Houston's roadways started to flood. An image of a completely submerged interstate began going viral on social media. I looked up from my computer and glanced around the enclosed sun porch where I sat. A woven basket of vintage Fisher-Price toys belonging to my two young sons sat in one corner of the room. A television that played Disney's beloved 1973 animated classic, *Robin Hood,* practically on repeat sat in another. Sunlight flooded in through the large windows that lined my favorite room in the 1920's era two-story home where I lived outside of Louisville. I felt an all too familiar feeling take hold. Whenever national news breaks, something inside me longs to be there. On the ground. In the mix. I felt a tug calling me to leave the comfort and safety of home and go do what I was made to do. My train of thought was interrupted by a chime signifying that a new email had just landed in my inbox. The message was from one of my editors at Bloomberg News.

"How soon can you get yourself to Texas?" it read.

Not soon enough, I thought to myself. I replied to my editor that I would start packing my bags ASAP. I closed my laptop and immediately started getting spun up for the trip. Both airports in Houston were shut down due to flooding, so I elected to fly into Dallas and drive the 250 miles that separated Texas' two most populous cities. If all went well, I could be on the ground in Houston by midnight.

Working in hurricanes and similar austere environments is no walk in the park. My six years of experience covering natural disasters up to that point had taught me that preparing for an extreme weather event could be just as challenging as enduring one. On my way to the airport, I stopped by my local Walmart and purchased eight, six-gallon plastic gas cans to bring with me to Texas. If you've never lived or worked along the Gulf Coast, you might not know that in the days leading up to a storm's landfall, the first thing to disappear from store shelves are gas cans. At this point in time, finding one on the shelf of a local Walmart in Houston would be an absolute pipe dream.

In similar fashion, rain jackets, ponchos, batteries, duct tape, and bottled water all tended to disappear from the shelves of retail stores in the run-up to major storms. Whenever I was sent to cover a hurricane, I opted to bring as many of these necessities with me from out-of-state as possible.

To be an effective news-gathering unit on the ground during a natural disaster requires complete self-sufficiency. I needed to be able to survive on my own for up to a week without relying on anyone else for food, water, fuel, electricity, or a place to sleep. I booked the largest rental SUV I could find and purchased as much supplementary insurance coverage that money could buy. In order to cover as much ground as possible upon reaching Houston, I needed to maximize my ability to navigate flooded roads. An SUV would allow me to do just that. I ended up with a Yukon XL, a vehicle not all that different from a Chevrolet Suburban. The copious amount of trunk space that the Yukon afforded me would easily hold a week's worth of supplies and gear. It could also double as a place to sleep in a pinch.

In advance of big storms, agencies like the Federal Emergency Management Agency (FEMA) will often snatch up any available SUVs to supplement their existing vehicle fleets. It's not uncommon for local rental car lots to be completely cleaned out of their SUV rentals. Scoring a Yukon at this stage in the game was a big win. It felt good to scratch such an important item off my to-do list.

As soon as my flight touched down in Dallas, I loaded into my rental car and headed again for a nearby Walmart. As I pulled into the parking lot my heart sank: the shopping center was buzzing with activity. Nearly every space was filled. People were pushing empty shopping carts toward the front entrance of the store in a hurry. Some of the more dire news reports coming out of Houston had predicted widespread power outages throughout Texas as a result of Harvey. Judging by this level of activity on a Sunday evening, panic-buying had already reached the Dallas metro area.

I made a beeline for the front entrance, weaving hurriedly through a maddening traffic jam of cars and shopping carts in the parking lot. I envisioned the worst-case scenario inside: bare shelves, no bottled water, no beef jerky. Lines to checkout might stretch throughout the store, like on Black Friday. But while the scenes inside Walmart were as busy as I had imagined, the contents of peoples' shopping carts surprised me. Instead of being piled high with canned food and peanut butter, almost every cart was filled with boxes of crayons, backpacks, notebooks, rulers, and safety scissors.

It was August in Texas. I hadn't stumbled upon hurricane-inspired panic buying; this was just last-minute, back-to-school shopping—a tradition as old as public education itself. I felt a mixture of relief and embarrassment that my expectation had failed to materialize. Houston may have been under water, but it was still life as usual in Dallas.

My own cart was quickly filled with essential supplies: three cases of bottled water, a dozen packages of beef jerky, an armful of canned salmon, trail mix, and a couple boxes of peanut butter granola bars for dessert. I also picked up a pair of rubber muck boots, a stack of bath towels and 10 pairs of socks before heading to the checkout. I remembered what my photo mentors in Washington had taught me. I should be prepared to endure days without electricity or running water.

Having completed my hurricane shopping list, I hit the drive-thru of a local In-N-Out Burger for what could very well be my last hot meal for a few days. The last bit of color in the sky from the late-summer sunset had finally given way to night. I merged onto I-45 south, set my cruise control a hair over the speed limit, and settled in for the three-and-a-half-hour drive. During the drive, I tried to anticipate what the situation in Houston would look like. I imagined scenes from Hollywood disaster movies playing out in front of me. Assuming law enforcement and first responders would be stretched thin, what would the vibe be like on the streets? Would I be able to stay safe? Would there be cellular service for me to send photos back to my editors in New York? How long would the electrical grid hold up?

As I drew closer to the city, I began thinking about my fuel stockpile and the still-empty gas cans sitting in the back of the Yukon. When natural disasters wear on, few things become more precious than unleaded gasoline. A lack of fuel will severely hinder your mobility and thus your ability to report what's happening on the ground. So, with that weighing on me, I exited the interstate and pulled into a Buc-ee's.

Easily recognized by their cartoon mascot—a smiling beaver in a red ballcap—Buc-ee's is an institution, known throughout the state for their colossal fuel pumps, even bigger convenience stores, and the "cleanest restrooms in America." In keeping with the state tradition of everything being bigger in Texas, there are more than 100 gasoline pumps available for motorists. The attached convenience stores are the size of a Walmart. Inside, every snack, candy bar, and beverage known to man is available for purchase along with a mind-numbing assortment of souvenirs featuring Buc-ee the Beaver himself.

One would never have guessed it was 1:00 in the morning judging by the crowd of vehicles outside at the gas pumps. I found an open spot and felt like a gas hog as I began filling my eight spare gasoline canisters. You could feel the tension in the air. People were on edge and tempers were short. No one wanted to be without fuel for their pickup trucks and generators. With my gas cans filled to the brim, I topped off the Yukon's tank and jumped back on the highway toward Houston. A few miles north of the city, I found an open hotel along the interstate and caught about four hours of restless sleep. If memories from reporting on previous storms served me right, a spike of adrenaline the next morning make up for the short night.

My first experience covering natural disasters came during my sophomore year at Western Kentucky University, when I was sent to cover the most severe aftermath from the largest tornado events in history: the 2011 Super Outbreak. The disaster occurred across four consecutive days. During that time, tornadoes were recorded in a whopping 21 states. Alabama was the hardest hit. On April 27, 2011, a powerful line of severe weather passed through south central Alabama. The weather system spawned over 200 tornadoes that day, including a monstrous EF4 tornado that tore through Tuscaloosa and Birmingham. The twister was, at times, a full mile and a half wide and stayed on the ground for over 80 miles. By the end of the night, a staggering 238 people were dead.

The news of the devastation broke as I was sitting in one of my photo classes at Western. I reached out to my good friend Daniel Houghton and asked if he wanted to drive down to Alabama together to cover the aftermath of the storms. Daniel was a year ahead of me in the photo program and a frequent companion on photo safaris. While many of our classmates enjoyed staying out late on the weekends, he and I forewent the booze and instead focused our energy on building our portfolios. I admired Daniel's work ethic and identified with his desire to constantly improve at his craft. Because of his hard work, he would eventually become CEO of the internationally-known travel company Lonely Planet.

After class we met up and skipped town. With our photo gear and sleeping bags packed in the trunk of his Honda Element, we drove down I-65 South until we crossed the Alabama state line. Despite growing up in Tornado Alley, I had never witnessed tornado damage first-hand. Daniel and I pulled off the highway at the first sign of damage, just west of Huntsville. We were awe-struck. Brick homes were reduced to rubble. Steel-framed billboards along the road had been bent and twisted like pretzels. Entire forests of trees were stripped of their leaves, snapped at the base, and scattered like matchsticks. In one neighborhood, a pickup truck had been flipped upside down into the deep end of a half-empty community swimming pool, its chlorinated contents having been vacuumed up by a passing tornado. We later learned that the tornado that affected this town was just one of the many that touched down in Alabama the previous night.

As darkness fell, we dined on beef jerky and spent the night in Daniel's SUV surrounded by our spare gasoline canisters. The next morning, we awoke with a pair of painfully raw throats. Throughout the night we had been inhaling gasoline fumes as we slept. We were novices in the storm-chasing game and didn't know never to sleep in a poorly-ventilated space, especially with gasoline present. Following a breakfast of granola bars and Pop Tarts, we headed South toward Birmingham. Many neighborhoods located to the west of downtown had taken direct hits from the storms. The remnants of trailer homes were spread far and wide across one subdivision that we visited. In another we saw vehicles that had been picked up and tossed in every direction like toy cars.

Daniel and I spent the next few days driving around Alabama reporting for our respective newspapers: him for the *Lexington Herald-Leader* and myself for the *New York Times*. It was rewarding to see our work displayed online, despite being inexperienced college students. There was something intoxicating about knowing that millions of eyeballs were seeing my photos and reading my byline. Two years had passed since I completed my first year-long internship in Washington for the *Times*. All those feelings of status, importance, and accomplishment came rushing back as I traversed the state with my friend. While I did feel empathy for the people I met, at that stage in my career I was more concerned with making a name for myself than anything else. A desire to be seen as dependable in the eyes of my editors and successful in the eyes of my classmates helped me overcome the awkwardness of sticking a camera in someone's face during their time of need. However important newsgathering may be, personal motivation matters more. As a 19-year-old I still had some maturing to do. I wasn't thinking about helping. I was thinking about getting on the front page of the paper, above the fold.

A steady rain began falling in Houston as I fired up the Yukon. At this relatively early stage in the disaster, the first order of business was to try and find where water rescues were taking place. I was unsure where exactly I should head to find the action. A quick scroll through Houston's local news websites revealed widespread flooding and water rescues in progress across the metro area. I programmed my GPS to take me downtown. It seemed like the logical place to start given the photos I had seen of flooded underpasses in the city center.

Interstate 45 took me in the right direction. Only a few minutes had passed before my progress was stymied.

"There is a road closure in 3 miles," my phone announced in an annoying cheerful tone.

A cursory glance at the map revealed that an extended section of the interstate had been shut down due to flooding. I would have to take back roads if I wanted to get anywhere near downtown Houston.

While I contemplated my next move, a convoy overtook me on the highway. A half dozen pickup trucks pulling fishing boats of various shapes and sizes zipped past me in the left lane. *Those guys look like they know where they're going.* I stepped on the gas pedal and accelerated until I caught up with the line of trucks. I was tagging along behind the Cajun Navy.

During Hurricane Katrina in 2005, the American public was introduced to this group of volunteer heroes. As New Orleans flooded with water from Lake Pontchartrain, boaters from across the Gulf Coast came to the rescue with their own personal watercraft in tow. Small boats normally reserved for duck hunting, bass fishing, and water skiing were pressed into service in the flooded streets of the Big Easy. In the days following the catastrophic breach of New Orleans' levees, Cajun Navy volunteers saved an estimated 10,000 lives according to then-Louisiana Gov. Kathleen Blanco.

I did my best to assimilate myself into the column of boats ahead of me. Mimicking the other vehicles, I turned on my hazard lights and brought up the rear of the Cajun Navy convoy. One of my good friends from Washington, Mark Wilson, taught me this tactic during Superstorm Sandy in 2012. Mark was well known for slipping through police checkpoints using this method. On one occasion, a sheriff's deputy figured out that the Getty Images news photographer had merged into the midst of a convoy of National Guard vehicles without permission. Mark rolled down his window as he slowed to a stop behind the wheel of his rental Suburban.

"Who are you with?" the suspicious deputy demanded.

"I'm with the federal media," Mark responded with faux indignation.

Of course, there's no such thing as the federal media. Yet somehow Mark's confident response got him waved on through the checkpoint.

I followed the convoy as far as I could on I-45 until the highway itself disappeared into flood water like a four-lane boat ramp. A Texas State Trooper was guarding the exit ramp in a police cruiser with blue lights flashing. I watched from my SUV as the lead pickup truck of the convoy pulled over to speak with the officer. The two exchanged words for a moment before the State Trooper motioned for us to proceed on our way through the roadblock. I hung my press credentials from the rearview mirror and placed a laminated piece of paper on my dashboard. The 8x10 placard read PRESS in bold red letters. The home-made sign, another storm coverage trick passed to me by Mark, lent my vehicle instant credence. I lifted two-fingers nonchalantly from my steering wheel as the officer waved me through with the rest of the group.

We proceeded from the highway into Spring, Texas, a suburb located north of Houston. A few minutes later the convoy came to a halt outside a subdivision just to the West of Spring's Hardy Toll Road. Just like the Southbound lanes on I-45, the road in front of me disappeared suddenly into a lake of floodwater that appeared overnight.

I split from the convoy and parked near the waters' edge. A hundred yards away across a submerged field stood the beginning of Spring's Highland Glen subdivision. A handful of Cajun Navy boats already on the scene were making their way toward me with passengers onboard. I took photos as displaced residents clambered down from one of them, a sleek bass boat. A few carried their shoes in hand and walked barefoot through the floodwaters toward less-soggy ground. One man sloshed to shore carrying a car-seat with an oblivious newborn baby strapped securely inside. Slung across his shoulders were backpacks stuffed full of dry clothes and blankets for himself and his family. The column of soaked hurricane refugees made their way toward a warehouse that stood a few dozen yards back from the waterline. The small business was acting as a temporary shelter for its neighbors who had been forced out of their homes. I followed along, taking photos to illustrate the human toll of the disaster. Another boat arrived from the neighborhood with three people and two dogs onboard. One of the passengers, a man in his forties, struggled to carry a large English bulldog away from the craft. The dog looked annoyed, apparently ambivalent that it had been rescued from such a perilous situation.

As soon as each boat unloaded its passengers, the Cajun Navy members would turn back into the subdivision for another rescue mission. After making a few more pictures of survivors coming in, I began asking boat owners if I could jump aboard and join them on their next trip.

The first boat owner I asked shot me a dirty look and motored away without a word. I propositioned the next boat in a similar manner.

"Can I jump in with you guys and take some photos for the news?" The boat's owner looked me over for a moment, no doubt noticing that I was, as of yet, unsoaked by the steady rain that had picked back up after a brief hiatus. My press credentials hung from my neck and a faded baseball cap that I had picked up a few years earlier at the CIA gift shop sat atop my head. This captain was far less surly, but still turned me down.

"Sorry man," he apologized with a Southern drawl. "I need all the space I can get for rescuing people. There are still a ton of people who need help."

It was hard to argue with his reasoning. I thanked him anyway and wished him luck.

Discouraged, yet undeterred, I noticed a larger bow-fishing boat heading in my direction. The sturdy green aluminum craft had a large flat deck with plenty of room for riders. Two younger men remained onboard after the last of their passengers had disembarked. Again, I approached and made my pitch. The man whom I took to be the owner of the boat squinted at me in silence for a few moments. He was skinny and absolutely soaked to the bone. A baseball cap sat backwards on his head. A rain-soaked pair of blue jeans and brown t-shirt clung to his skin. He wore an expression of deep fatigue across his stubbled face.

"What do you want to do?" He asked as he rubbed his eyes.

"I want to come along on your next trip back to the neighborhood with you. I'm a news photographer," I explained again. He paused and considered my proposition. I offered to email him a couple photos to sweeten the deal.

"Ok," he finally replied. "Hop on."

I waded into the water and climbed aboard. It was time to get to work. Wasting no time, we motored back toward the subdivision. The torrential rainfall had swollen a neighboring gully by orders of magnitude. The normally dry drainage ditch overflowed its banks by nearly half a mile. And the rain was still coming down. We found an access road and turned into the neighborhood. I estimated that the subdivision was under about six feet of water. The tops of backyard fences were barely visible above the water line and the wake left behind by our boat's motor lapped against the brick sides of the homes as we motored by them. We pulled onto a wide residential street lined with a mixture of single and two-story houses on each side. The boat's driver slowed our speed to a crawl as we began searching for anyone who needed to be rescued. I looked around in amazement. The floodwaters stretched as far as the eye could see, sparing nothing. The single-story homes were almost totally flooded out.

"Watch out for submerged cars," the boat's owner called out. The water level was high enough above the road that even pickup trucks were completely submerged beneath the muddy flood. I scanned the road in front of us for dark shapes beneath the waterline.

As we floated through the front yard of a handsome two-story brick house, I noticed a woman standing in a second story window.

"Do you need help?" the boat owner called out to her.

"I don't know" The grey-haired woman looked to be in her mid-fifties. She wore a strangely calm expression given the circumstances.

"If you need a ride out of here, grab your things and come on downstairs," the other rescuer said.

"I'm not sure if I want to stay or not," she replied. The two Cajun Navy members continued to try and coax her out. Unable to make up her mind, the woman finally called out to us. "Can you all come back in a few minutes? I want take a shower first."

A shower? I locked eyes with one of the rescuers on the boat. We each raised an eyebrow at the woman's seeming lack of concern for the situation that was unfolding in her front yard.

"The water's rising, and we've got more people we need to help," the boat owner retorted. "It's now or never."

To my amazement, the woman in the window elected to stay. I worried that she might regret that decision as the day wore on.

The rain continued to fall mercilessly as we pulled away looking for more survivors. The floodwater was rising. Time was of the essence, especially for those trapped inside one-story houses. We turned back onto the street and headed in the direction of the swollen gully responsible for the flooded neighborhood. A few houses down the street we spotted another person on the second floor of his home.

"Are you alright?" the boat driver called out.

The man gave us a thumbs up.

"Do you need a ride?"

The man shook his head no. He would be another holdout.

We continued on our way and encountered a stop sign with its metal pole completely submerged. Only the red octagonal sign was visible above the waterline. I held down the shutter button on my camera and captured a sequence of photos as we floated by. The following February, one of those photos would appear in a Verizon Wireless Super Bowl advertisement. But at that moment, the Super Bowl was quite possibly the farthest thing from my mind. Shortly after passing the stop sign, the boat shuddered unexpectedly. I grabbed for a handhold to steady myself as a muffled crunch emanated from beneath the water.

"Dammit! We hit a car." The boat driver yelled in an annoyed tone.

Thankfully the craft's thick aluminum hull emerged intact. We turned to look in unison as the stern of the boat passed over the submerged car. Just barely visible through the murky water was the roof of a blue SUV.

"Next time it floods, please park in your driveway," the other rescuer joked aloud.

As our boat progressed deeper into the subdivision, we still hadn't found anyone to rescue. Turning a corner, we encountered a red inflatable Zodiac motoring toward us. Inside the rescue craft were two men dressed in reflective raincoats. Judging by the differing shades of each man's fluorescent jacket, I guessed that one was likely a firefighter, and the other was a cop. A young girl in a purple life preserver and another adult sat huddled together in the center of the inflatable boat. The first responders stood tall, exposing themselves to the elements as they piloted the craft through the floodwaters. Our boats passed each other in the same manner that two neighbors out for a walk around the neighborhood might have on any normal day. Our boat's owner called out to the two public servants and asked if they knew of anyone else who needed rescuing. I raised my camera and took a photo of the two first responders pointing down the road toward the gully. There were more people in need just down the street.

Based on the advice of the first responders, we decided to penetrate as far into the neighborhood as possible before working our way back up the street. The plan made sense given that the residents who lived closest to the gully were likely in the greatest danger.

While passing the Zodiac, it occurred to me that the two public servants onboard were the first official first responders that I had laid eyes on since exiting the interstate with the Cajun Navy convoy. There simply were not enough public safety officials to go around given the sheer volume of flooding. There were even fewer boats available for water rescues. Local emergency services were stretched hopelessly thin. Thankfully, normal citizens had stepped forward to fill the void.

A block or two down the street, the first of many residents who needed rescuing came into view. A woman sat on the roof of her house calling out to us.

"Help! Over here!" She yelled and waved her arms frantically through the air.

"Hang tight, we will be back," our boat's captain yelled back.

Despite knowing full well that more Cajun Navy boats were on the way, it was gut-wrenching to leave her there.

A few houses later we passed by another survivor on the opposite side of the street. The man stood stoically in the front doorway of his house wearing a Dallas Cowboys football jersey. Raindrops impacted the floodwaters that came up to his chest. Behind him, I could see that the water had inundated the front living room of his house. I imagined how it would feel to be in his shoes. I pictured myself standing in front of my own house, a stout two-story block house with a long, sloping backyard, back in Shelbyville, Kentucky. What it would be like to see water seep through the windowsills and pool on the rustic hardwood floors that I vacuumed every Tuesday morning? How would I feel watching the green plastic army men I had played with as a kid (and since gifted to my two sons) float across the living room? I pondered what my reaction would be to having the sanctity and security of my own home, my sanctuary and my place of rest, upended so violently.

The man in the Cowboys jersey looked at me.

I cupped my hands around my mouth and yelled "We will come back for you!"

He gave a silent nod as we motored by his front yard.

The end of the street came into view. Our boat beelined towards a family of four, who were awaiting rescue with their dog. They stood in the bed of a red pickup truck that was parked in their driveway. Even with the added height of the vehicle working to their advantage, the floodwater came up to their knees. There was simply nowhere else for them to run. We pulled alongside the partially submerged pickup and the family climbed eagerly into our boat. With everyone safely aboard, we set course for the makeshift beach where I had first talked my way aboard. The boat's owner did his best to avoid submerged vehicles as we retraced our path back through the flooded streets. As expected, other Cajun Navy boats had shown up to rescue both the man in the Cowboys jersey and the other residents who we had passed up a few minutes earlier. Upon our arrival back at dry land, we offloaded our passengers and watched as they made their way to shelter.

At that point, the two Cajun Navy men who had given me a ride decided to throw in the towel and pull their boat out of the water. The pair had been up all night, rescuing people from their homes in a downpour. I could see on their faces that the two men were in serious need of sleep. They spoke briefly about how many more days each could afford to take off from work, and whether they would have enough fuel to continue doing water rescues the next day. These two blue collar guys had made the journey all the way from West Texas. They footed the bill themselves with no expectation of reimbursement, simply because they wanted to come help out.

We shook hands before parting ways.

"Thank you for the ride, gentlemen," I said. "Well done."

The next boat owner who I asked for a ride looked to be in his sixties. Rain dripped from the silver whiskers of his goatee as I gave him my pitch.

"Absolutely," he responded. "Jump on in."

He had just finished dropping off a married couple and was getting ready to go back into Highland Glen. I climbed aboard his Tracker bass boat and sat cross-legged on the carpeted deck. Although this boat was smaller than my first ride, we still had plenty of space for passengers.

My new captain revved his engine and we sped back into the heart of the flooded subdivision. Our craft snaked through the maze of neighborhood streets past row after row of inundated homes. I struggled to grasp the scale of the devastation. This was only a single neighborhood in a metro area of more than 2 million. By the time the floodwaters receded, more than 150,000 families would be forced out of their homes. Some estimates would place the damage to Houston at a staggering 125 billion dollars.

Most of the driveways in the neighborhood were occupied with one or more vehicles parked flush against their garage doors. Despite best efforts to position their car's engines at the apex of their sloping driveways, none managed to escape the reach of the flood.

As we passed one house, I noticed a dog that had taken refuge on the roof of one such flooded car. From what I could see, he didn't have a collar on. It was impossible to know if he was someone's pet, or simply a stray. Slowly but surely, the water continued to rise and began to threaten the dog's perch atop the water-logged sedan where he had sought refuge. Clearly agitated, he began barking angrily as we floated past him. Another Cajun Navy boat pulled in close to the car to see if they could rescue the stranded pooch. Our boat circled back around to try and lend a hand. Each time the captain of the other boat got close, the dog would let loose a vicious growl and snap angrily in his rescuer's direction. The poor canine was too stressed out to let anyone help him. Scared out of his mind and completely soaked, he viewed everyone and everything as a threat. After a few more unsuccessful attempts we reluctantly gave up and continued on our way.

"Good luck, boy," the captain of my boat called to the terrified dog.

We continued through the neighborhood in search of survivors. I pried my eyes away from the apocalyptic scene around me and checked on my equipment. Keeping the water away from my camera was a constant battle. Even the best rain gear available could only do so much against the steady, driving rain that had been falling since I left my SUV a couple hours earlier. My phone and car keys were safe for the time being inside a Ziplock bag in my rain jacket pocket. My camera was another story. While I usually shoot with two cameras, I had elected to leave my second camera body behind in the car, in case I fell overboard. If I had to lose photo equipment to the floodwaters, losing one camera would be far preferable to losing both.

Shortly thereafter, we happened upon another law enforcement officer who had hitched a ride in a civilian boat. The Harris County Sheriff's Deputy wore a cowboy hat and full-length fluorescent rain jacket. He gave us directions to a house that he suspected might still have people inside a few blocks away. After thanking him for the tip, both my boat and the other craft who attempted the ill-fated canine rescue sped off in that direction. We pulled onto the street where the officer directed us and began to search for any residents who might still be there. Single-story homes lined the cul-de-sac. In the center of the row stood a house with the porch light still illuminated.

Perhaps it was a signal.

The captain began honking his boat's horn repeatedly to communicate our presence to any residents who might be inside. The report of the horn bounced around the horseshoe of brick-walled homes. The echoing sound waves combined to create a concerto as melancholy as it was eerie.

The captain stopped honking the horn and listened for a response. Aside from the pitter-patter of the falling rain and the low gurgle of the boat's outboard motor, I could hear nothing. He honked the horn once more in a syncopated rhythm. Again, it's mournful sound filled the makeshift amphitheater in which we floated. Again, we listened intently in the silence.

Nothing.

Not wanting to leave prematurely, we decided to take a closer look. Our boat pulled beside a tree in the house's front yard and tied up to the thick trunk.

Despite the best efforts of my North Face rain jacket, I was soaked to the core. It was either the rain or my own sweat. Having spent hours outside in the muggy monsoon, it was impossible to know which of the two was the culprit. There was not a dry spot left on any of my clothes so, I reasoned, there was nothing to lose by going for a little swim. I held my camera above my head, swung my feet over the side of the boat, and lowered myself down into the flood. The water came up to my chest before my boots were able to find their footing on the house's submerged driveway.

A volunteer from the other boat in our flotilla waded through the water with me. We reached the front door and peered inside the otherwise dark home, scanning for any signs of life.

The volunteer pounded on the door.

"Anybody home?" he called.

We waited for a few moments, half-expecting someone to wade through the foyer and receive us on the front porch. No movement was visible through the windows. We had done our due diligence. Satisfied that no one was home, we waded back to our respective boats.

Once I was back aboard, the captain untied and cast off again into the middle of the cul-de-sac. Our boat turned to retrace our original path back through the subdivision. Before he throttled up, the captain let loose on the horn one more time for good measure. We sat and listened. Still nothing.

It may sound funny, but not finding anyone was bittersweet. On the one hand, I was glad that the homeowners and their neighbors had already evacuated. On the other hand, we had wasted precious time on what amounted to a wild goose chase.

That's all right. At least we didn't leave anyone behind.

As the boat started to accelerate out of the cul-de-sac, I glanced over my shoulder one last time . . . and noticed a figure peeking around the edge of one of the homes. My heart leapt into my throat.

"Hold on!" I shouted to the captain over the sound of the outboard motor. "There's someone back there!"

I turned again toward the house and saw an elderly woman with stringy white hair staring back at me. Deep lines on her wrinkled face communicated at once fear, dismay, and confusion. The falling rain had quickly started to darken the plain blue t-shirt and baggy black athletic shorts that she wore. She looked like someone who had endured a long, sleepless night.

The captain of the boat pulled a sharp U-turn and quickly closed the gap between us and the woman.

"Are you Ok?" the captain called out. "Do you need help?"

The woman paused for a moment. She seemed stunned at the sight of our two boats floating through her front yard. A flash of maternal worry and concern lingered in her eyes.

"Yes. Please." Her voice faltered. "My two grandchildren and our pets are inside. Please help."

I jumped from the boat back into the water and waded through her yard toward the front door. While the front yard was totally submerged, only two or three feet of water invaded the inside of her house. I followed the woman through the front door and into the home.

Inside her living room, a pair of sofas bobbed lazily up and down in the same muddy water that inundated the rest of the neighborhood. Somehow, the home still had electricity. A tungsten bulb screwed into the lone ceiling light bathed the watery room in soft, yellow light. The kitchen counters were piled high with pillows, books, and other items that had been moved to higher ground as the water rose. The woman's two elementary-aged grandchildren, a girl and her younger brother, stood nearby in the hallway, dutifully holding the collars of their three well-fed family mutts. The dogs were clearly stressed by the situation. They whined and looked down at the water that had begun to lap at their undersides. The children, on the other hand, exhibited a remarkable sense of calm considering that their house was actively flooding. At their grandmother's direction, each of them grabbed a bulging backpack stuffed with clothes. They followed her outside with their dogs close behind.

With everyone out of the house, the grandmother locked the front door out of habit and made her way toward our boat. The captain handed her grandkids two youth-sized life jackets and began helping the portly dogs aboard. I took a seat near the stern and turned my attention back to photography. I frantically searched myself for a dry patch of T-shirt to wipe away the moisture that had accumulated on the front of my camera lens. Thick raindrops fell from the tree branches overhead, frustrating my efforts. My wet shirt did little more than smear the water around on my lens. I gave up and lifted the camera to capture the moment unfolding in front of me. Each grandchild held on tightly to their respective dog as our boat pushed back from the woman's front yard. I clicked the shutter as the little boy wrapped his arms around his four-legged friend and pressed his face into the canine's fur.

What if the grandmother hadn't ventured outside when she did? What if we had left the cul-de-sac one minute earlier? What if we hadn't noticed her? Where would they have gone? What would they have done? I shuddered as I thought about those poor kids having to spend a second dreadful night in that flooded home. I felt a knot in my stomach again imagining a situation where floodwaters might slowly encroach upon my own neighborhood back on Walnut Street in Kentucky. I envisioned the water threatening the blacktop road, then my driveway, then my front yard full of Kentucky bluegrass and finally my front door. *Heaven help us.*

Back at shore, I disembarked the boat and helped our passengers down from the boat. The two kids shouldered their backpacks and stuck close to their grandmother's side as they waded to the waters' edge. Following close behind, the three dogs paused to shake the water from their soaked fur. Their tails wagged profusely upon reaching dry land.

With our passengers safe and sound, I pulled my phone from its Ziplock bag and quickly glanced at my email inbox. One of my editors in New York was asking how soon I could file my first batch of photos. My stress level spiked. No more boat rides through the subdivision for me. Taking photos was only half my mission. Now I had to get them to the photo desk. I thanked the captain for the ride with a soggy handshake and trudged hurriedly back to my rental car. Prior to getting in, I unzipped my rain jacket and began shedding layers of soaked clothing. I peeled off my T-shirt and dumped out the water that had accumulated inside my rubber muck boots. With my SUV's air conditioning up at full blast, I pulled out my laptop and began pouring over my photos. I could feel the mounting pressure of my editors' expectations. Tension built in neck and my heartrate increased as I worked to send two dozen of my best frames to the Bloomberg desk in New York City.

Being in the thick of things was exhilarating. It always is. There was nowhere else I would rather be than in the middle of a breaking news event. It's one big adventure. My line of work as a photojournalist aligns perfectly with this aspect of my personality. Heck, I was even being paid to do this, something I often forget. Still, somewhere inside me I felt a gnawing sense of discontent. I wondered if part of me wouldn't rather have traveled to Houston as a Cajun Navy volunteer, than as a journalist. The city was crawling with media. Would my absence really be felt if I was behind the wheel of a boat instead of behind my camera? I had long felt that working as a journalist was a high calling. But what if there was a higher calling than that?

By the time I finished transmitting photos, the water rescues were beginning to wind down at Highland Glen. Thankfully, everyone who had wanted to evacuate was able to find a ride. I began searching online for my next destination. According to news reports, a nearby apartment complex was currently being inundated with floodwater. It was not all that far from me as the crow flies, but flooding and subsequent road closures made getting there no easy task. About 45 minutes later, I happened upon a group of Cajun Navy volunteers launching rescue missions at the base of a flooded bridge. Another gully had filled with rainwater and swelled far beyond its banks. I noticed a husband and wife launching their aluminum bow fishing boat and ran to catch them before they set off downriver. The couple had driven three hours from their home in Tyler, Texas simply to contribute to the rescue effort. Before I could even finish introducing myself, the couple welcomed me aboard their boat. We took off down the swollen gully in the direction of the flooded apartment complex at a high rate of speed. I sat with my back to the bow of the boat and photographed the husband and wife as they scanned the water ahead for obstructions. A few minutes into our journey a massive water snake crossed our path. With nowhere to swerve, we ran over the monstrous serpent at full speed. The poor reptile could not have picked a worse moment to cross the river.

Not long after taking out the snake, the husband piloted his boat onto a flooded residential street that ran parallel to the river. We slowed our speed and began to keep an eye out for survivors. The houses in this particular neighborhood were mansions compared to the homes in Highland Glen. We floated by one whose three-car garage was totally flooded out. Peering through the open garage doors, I noticed a brand-new Mercedes Benz SUV and a massive ford F-series pickup truck parked inside. I guessed that both vehicles would be declared a total loss due to flood damage, judging by the water level inside. *I sure hope they have good insurance.*

Our boat passed a few more flooded mansions before we arrived at a large two-story apartment complex tucked away in the woods. The force of the water had scattered residents' vehicles throughout the complex, depositing them in curious locations. From the courtyard at the center of the complex, to the woods surrounding the parking lot, there was no telling where that amount of water could relocate a motor vehicle. Curiously, many of these cars and SUVs sat fully submerged with only their open trunks sticking up above the water line. I guessed that they might have been popped ajar by the sheer force of the floodwater.

Our boat circled the perimeter parking lot as we continued our search for survivors. A fluorescent orange rescue whistle hung from the wife's mouth as she scanned the second-floor balconies. Every ten seconds she blew a few short blasts in quick succession. We turned a corner along the outer edge of the complex and suddenly found ourselves nearly eye-to-eye with a middle-aged woman standing on her balcony. She leaned nonchalantly against the cast iron railing with a lit cigarette between her lips.

"Do you want to leave?" The wife called out to her.

"No, I'm staying put," the woman responded between drags. "My power's still on," she explained. "Why should I go anywhere?"

Sure enough, I could see the glow of her big screen TV from the parking lot. We wished the woman good luck and continued our route around the exterior of the complex. While our boat circled the property, we passed several other residents who seemed content to ride out the flood from their second story apartments. One man stared at us with a look of deep confusion, as if we were the strange ones in this scenario. Finding no takers at the complex, we returned empty-handed to the flooded bridge where we had originally put in. Although the trip yielded a few interesting pictures of flooded property, I knew I needed more photos of the human toll of the disaster. Homes can be rebuilt. Cars replaced. What really mattered was how people were being affected.

Back at my car, I studied a map of the area. Red-dashed lines denoting road closures branched across the map like a spiderweb. The closures acted as helpful landmarks toward which I would navigate. Leaving the flooded bridge behind, I drove a few miles and pulled into one of Spring's upscale neighborhoods. Down the block I noticed a dozen or more pickup trucks with empty boat trailers parked along the side of the road. Bingo. I was in the right place. I found a parking spot and donned my rain gear.

The water's edge was a flurry of activity. Cajun Navy members were busy launching boats and transferring people to shore. I asked one boat owner where the rescues were taking place. He informed me that a call had gone out a few minutes earlier for all available boats to assist with a nursing home evacuation. Volunteers from the surrounding neighborhoods gathered on the sidewalk with wheelchairs to help transfer patients from the rescue boats to vehicles waiting nearby. Where exactly these elderly residents were being taken, I wasn't sure. But almost anywhere would be better than here.

Wasting no time, I began trying to hitch a ride to the nursing home. The priority of all involved was to rescue as many of the elderly as quickly as possible. My presence in one of the boats would take up valuable space. Still, I knew that it was important to tell this story. The country needed to know what was going on here in the Lone Star state. It took me a few tries before I found a boat captain who was willing to take me aboard. I jumped in his bass boat and we set off into the deluge. As the craft sped down the flooded parkway, I noticed another volunteer launching his boat. He was dressed head to toe in duck hunting camouflage that matched the camo pattern of his boat. His rural motif stood in sharp contrast to the stately brick walls and neatly manicured grass median that ran the length the of the affluent suburban neighborhood.

Emerging from the boulevard, we crossed another flooded waterway. I raised my camera and took a photo of a small green sign denoting the name of the channel. Surrounded by water, the reflective letters on the roadside marker read "Dry Gully." As we motored down the flooded streets, we encountered a steady parade of other boats returning from the nursing home. Every few minutes or so a boat loaded with silver-haired passengers would pass us going in the opposite direction. We took a left off the main road and cut through a strip mall parking lot. Anchoring the shopping center was a Kroger grocery store. Plywood covered its windows. Bunkers of sandbags and plastic sheeting lined the entrance. Despite their best efforts, store management was unable to keep the water at bay. They never had a chance. My thoughts turned to what the scene inside must look like. I imagined boxes of Cocoa Puffs floating lazily down the cereal aisle, bananas bobbing around the produce section, and packs of Tic Tacs escaping the gauntlet of impulse-buy shelves flanking every checkout line. If only there was some way I could get inside that store. If only. I made a conscious decision to stop daydreaming about photos I had no hope of taking and instead re-focus on the mission at hand.

Shortly after passing the grocery store, we arrived in the parking lot of the upscale multi-floor nursing home. A flotilla of fishing boats bobbed in the water under the front entrance's portico like a nautical carpool line of sorts. Outdoorsmen wearing chest-high waders stood next to their watercraft in the choppy water. Rain dripped from their beards as they waited for the next batch of patients to emerge from the building. I disembarked into the middle of the parking lot and my captain took his place in line. Wading through the waist-deep water, I made my way toward the front entrance. A group of Cajun Navy members, nursing home employees, and a single local firefighter were helping the handicapped and infirm climb into boats. I estimated around a foot of water had already overtaken the ground floor of the nursing home. The stench of raw sewage hit my nostrils as I entered the lobby. My stomach turned. The nauseating smell of the facility's overflowing toilets stood in contrast to the calming floral decor of the lobby. Vases of light pink flowers sat on display as muddy water flowed through the common areas where residents normally passed their time playing bingo and watching television.

Unlike the flooded apartment complex, the nursing home lost electricity, thereby rendering their elevator obsolete. Volunteers formed a human chain and helped the elderly descend a long, carpeted staircase from the second-floor mezzanine down to the flooded lobby. The steady flow of senior citizens waiting for assistance down the stairs slowed momentarily. I seized the opportunity and climbed the steps against the flow of traffic. Once upstairs, I poked my head into one of the interior residential hallways. Except for a couple red emergency exit signs there was little ambient light to speak of. The dark corridor seemed to extend forever into the abyss. I couldn't imagine the home's medically fragile residents trying to survive in these conditions. Returning to the staircase, I continued to document the evacuation efforts.

At some point I caught the attention of the lone public safety official coordinating the rescue effort.

"Hey, you. Photographer," he called out in my direction. He was dressed in shorts with a red firefighter's helmet on his head. A fire department radio hung from the matching red life jacket that was strapped tightly around his torso.

"What can I do for you?" I replied.

"You can put your camera down and help get these folks out of here," he retorted with a hint of disgust. "This is no time to be taking photos."

I bristled at his assertion that the task I had been performing all morning was unimportant, or trivial. At this point in the day, I was approaching exhaustion. My fuse was short, and I did not have the emotional capacity to respond in a gracious manner. Instead of protesting or launching into a diatribe about the importance of a free press, I opted for the path of least resistance. For the time being I would take a break from shooting and comply with his suggestion. Usually, my goal as a photojournalist is to be as unobtrusive as possible. When shooting on assignment my mission is to *document* the news, not become an active participant in it. This case, however, seemed like a worthy exception to that policy. I didn't like the way the firefighter had barked at me, but I did like helping out.

I hung my camera from my shoulder and looked for a way to pitch in with the rescue operation. Back at the top of the grand staircase stood an elderly gentleman who needed to be helped downstairs to the lobby. My saggy nylon rain pants made a high-pitched swishing sound as I shuffled up to the mezzanine and extended my right arm to him. He clenched it firmly and began slowly descending the staircase one step at a time. We took a short breather halfway down the steps, then continued toward the ground floor. I felt the wrinkled man's arm grasping my forearm and thought about my grandfather who lived outside Philadelphia. We made it to the ground floor and joined the line of residents waiting for evacuation. A man only a few years older than myself stood along the wall near the front entrance. Locks of his wet hair hung down over his forehead as he a consulted a clipboard in his hands. As my elderly friend and I drew closer to the front of the line, the man with the clipboard checked his name against a manifest of nursing home residents. I gave him a nod. I appreciated his diligence in the face of the unfolding chaos. This certainly was neither the time nor the place to leave anyone behind.

Finally, we reached the head of the line. It was time for my friend to leave. The old man steadied himself on my arm as he lifted a leg into the flat-bottomed aluminum fishing boat before him. He took a seat on one of the boat's benches and began donning a life jacket for the voyage to the staging area back at the brick-walled boulevard. I was content with having lent a helping hand, however brief it may have been. But it was time for me to transition back into my role as a photojournalist.

The next evacuee was a frail elderly woman with wispy white hair. She wore a hospital gown and medical emergency alert button on her right wrist. The lone firefighter stood nearby to lend a helping hand as two others lowered the woman gently into the boat. I was struck by the look of fear that the woman wore on her gaunt face. I felt a stab of anger inside me.

How could the people in charge of this facility have let things get this bad? Why didn't they make the call to evacuate sooner? Did they wait until they noticed the floodwaters rushing through the automatic doors at the front entrance? This whole scene is outrageous.

I stopped photographing and took a moment to re-center myself. Choosing to sit and stew in these emotions would not be the best use of my time. I needed to keep a level head and focus on the task at hand. In fairness to the management of the nursing home, I did not have all the facts. It's doubtful that anyone could have anticipated how quickly the waters would rise. Many of the areas underwater in the Houston metroplex were not considered to be flood prone. Most importantly, there was no way to change the past. There was no use in throwing an emotional fit at a time that demanded cool, calm, decisive action by rational players.

I spent a few more minutes behind the camera as more of the nursing home's elderly residents were evacuated. As much as I would have liked to stay until the end of the rescue operation, I needed to get back to my car. It was almost evening, and my deadline was rapidly approaching. I needed to transmit this last batch of photos to New York.

Once again, I faced the challenge of securing for myself a coveted spot onboard a Cajun Navy boat. The flow of elderly residents, however, showed no sign of abating. I continued to take photos as I waited for my ride out. Finally, a long metal fishing boat with three bench seats bobbed up to the nursing home. Jackpot. Two older ladies joined me as we settled into the boat. They sat across from me with clear plastic hoods protecting their permed hairdos. The two were in good spirits and bantered back and forth with each other as we set sail from the nursing home.

"I can't wait to tell my grandchildren about this. This is such an adventure!" One of the women remarked.

"I don't remember a cruise being on our daily activity schedule," the other joked.

The captain of the boat navigated back in the direction of the Kroger parking lot. As he did, a heavy rain started to fall, and the wind began to pick up. The aluminum craft bobbed up and down in the chop. While the evacuees *were* wearing life jackets, it would not be pretty if we capsized here. We were still a long way from dry ground. I kept a close eye on the water level near the gunwales as we motored through the increasingly choppy floodwaters. We passed the grocery store and its neighboring tenants in the strip mall: A Goodwill thrift store, an income tax preparation business, and a physical therapy practice. All were breached by the floodwaters. Across the street stood a similarly inundated Shell gasoline station. Crossing Dry Gully signified that we were in the home stretch. It looked like we would make back in one piece. Volunteers waited on dry ground to receive our elderly passengers and shuttle them to temporary housing. The scene at the water's edge hit me in a different way than it had before. Neighbors were caring for their neighbors.

Back at the SUV, I filed my best photos from the nursing home and started shifting gears into logistics mode. My editors had asked me travel to Texas City, Texas the next day. A large oil refinery on the coast had suffered damage at the hands of Harvey and was experiencing flooding. Being primarily a business news outlet, Bloomberg was interested in the economic angle of the story. I found an open hotel on Houston's North side and snagged one of the last rooms available. During natural disasters, many hotels close their doors temporarily. With tourism and business travel being nonexistent, it makes more financial sense to shut down for a time than pay to staff an empty hotel. Due to the law of supply and demand, the few hotels that do choose to remain open fill quickly with national media and the first waves of displaced local residents.

To my surprise I also scored a hot meal for dinner. While rushing from one water rescue to the next, I ended up skipping both breakfast and lunch. On my way to my hotel, I found an open restaurant and picked up a massive pastrami Reuben with a slice of carrot cake for dessert. Having spent almost 12 continuous hours soaking wet, I checked into my hotel and dried off completely for the first time since that morning. I turned out the lights and collapsed into bed. I felt gratitude and guilt at the prospect of having a comfortable bed, hot shower and working air conditioning for the night. A great many families around the Houston metro area that evening were not afforded similar luxuries.

The next day I headed south to the Marathon Oil refinery in Texas City. With rain continuing to fall through the night, much of the flooding around the city had worsened. Many low-lying portions of the region's interstate system were underwater. Underpasses and exit ramps in flooded neighborhoods were practicality impassable. Thanks to my GPS, I managed to map out a circuitous route through the city. The interstates were completely deserted. Offices, businesses, retail stores, and restaurants were closed. There was no reason for anyone to travel anywhere. Not to mention, the logistics of doing so made it nearly impossible. Along the way, I pulled over at various spots and photographed flooding that was visible from the shoulder of the interstate. I photographed one man wading through floodwater toward the grassy highway embankment where I stood. He was carrying a full-grown pit-bull with both arms and his smartphone between clenched teeth.

Further down the road, I pulled over and photographed the town of Dickinson, Texas from an overpass along I-45. Utilizing my telephoto lens, I positioned myself above Route 517, a major six lane thoroughfare lined with fast food signs for McDonald's, Wendy's, and Taco Bell. At this stage of the disaster, it looked more like a canal than a main drag. The floodwaters extended to the horizon, easily a mile or more. Roofs belonging to flooded vehicles peeked above the waterline in no discernible pattern. Each sat where its owner had tried and failed to make it through the rising torrent. Nearly a dozen sedans, pickup trucks, and SUVs sat abandoned in the middle to the road. I found myself praying that those behind the wheel managed to make it out okay. As I stood there taking photos, a Dickinson Fire Department truck pulled out into the intersection. Four men in swift water rescue gear stood in the bed of the high clearance vehicle. Dressed in wetsuits and orange climbing helmets, the men scanned the water for any signs of motorists in distress. I watched as a wake spread out from behind the rescue truck in an oddly uniform pattern. It served as a subtle reminder that beauty can be found in the midst of prevalent, unrelenting chaos.

A few miles later I pulled over again and hopped over the outer guardrail along the northbound lane. The deserted highway gave me a perfect vantage point to photograph a flooded neighborhood. The street was doing its best impersonation of Venice, Italy. I took a photo I rather liked of a man standing in red and white speedboat in the middle of someone's front lawn. The scene was equally as absurd as it was heartbreaking. So many homes, vehicles, and priceless possessions must have been lost on this street alone. It was difficult to process so much devastation. The task at hand, however, required the entirety of my attention and emotional energy. I would have to find time to process everything later.

Twenty minutes later I arrived in Texas City. The vast industrial landscape stretched from I-45 to the edge of Galveston Bay. A seemingly innumerable number of condensing towers, gas flares, and emissions stacks jutted skyward from the two refineries. I stuck to public streets and circled the massive refineries, stopping occasionally to take photos through my SUV's window. Oil refineries are notoriously difficult to photograph, in my experience. Over the course of a decade covering the energy industry I can't recall a single time I haven't been harassed by refinery security guards or interrogated by local law enforcement. Once, while shooting a refinery in Toledo, Ohio, overzealous security guards attempted to illegally detain me in a public cemetery from which I was photographing. Much to my satisfaction, when the police finally arrived the responding officer read the private security guards the riot act. The following year in 2017, a Shell Oil security guard tailed me aggressively for miles as I drove down public streets in the refinery town of Roxana, Illinois. The next year a refinery worker screamed at me and accused me of being a terrorist outside a refinery along the Mississippi River in Norco, Louisiana. Two years later, the same man nearly ran me over with his company truck in the same location. To my surprise, I was able to shoot for about an hour unmolested by either refinery security or law enforcement. With the entirety of Texas' Gulf Coast underwater, I figured for once they must have had bigger fish to fry.

One of my favorite things about being a news photographer is the opportunity to rub elbows with friends and colleagues in the field. Covering natural disasters, however, is a notable exception. More so than usual, there is a palpable sense of competition between news outlets on the ground during a natural disaster. Generally, it's every man or woman for themselves. Working without this camaraderie can become rather lonely. Knowing this, I was glad to connect with my friend Jabin Botsford, a staff photographer with the *Washington Post.* It's said that every sensei's goal is to be bested by his own student. I can vouch personally for the accuracy of this proverb.

In the Spring of 2011, I volunteered to be the photo editor of Western Kentucky's student-run newspaper, the *College Heights Herald.* Jabin was one of my star staffers. He consistently knocked his assignments out of the park. Before too long, I realized that he was turning in photos that were more compelling than anything I would have photographed had I been there myself. Not only was he technically proficient behind the camera, he was also loyal, dependable, and hard-working to a fault. On more than one occasion I would call Jabin in a panic with a last-minute photo assignment that I forgotten to assign in a timely manner. Without fail he would take the assignment and bail me out. I once sent him to shoot a performance in the school's concert hall that was scheduled to conclude a mere fifteen minutes later. Jabin dropped everything he was doing, raced to the top of the hill on campus, and snuck in for the last few minutes of the performance. He saved my skin. The kid was a real go-getter.

In the years following, I enjoyed keeping up with his work and watching him achieve professional success in the real world. He made a name for himself during internships at the *Los Angeles Times* and the *New York Times* and eventually landed a coveted staff position at the *Washington Post.* I loved being around the guy and I loved that we were both in Houston at the same time. We linked up north of downtown and shared a bear hug. It had been too long since I had seen him last. We caught up as we edited and transmitted photos to our respective editors. I could feel my tank being filled emotionally as we shared stories and laughed about old inside jokes from our time at Western. With our editing complete, we formed a convoy and set out to find more water rescues.

Unfortunately for us, the situation on Houston's interstates had not improved. In fact, the roads were getting worse. With so many low-lying sections of the highway continuing to flood, we had to get creative. In some cases, this required driving down highway medians to circumvent flooding. Often it looked like utilizing an exit ramp as an on-ramp. Sometimes we were forced to travel the wrong way down sections of interstate that had been severed by flooding. With practically zero vehicular traffic and the entirety of Houston's law enforcement tied up doing water rescues, we simply did what needed to be done.

On a couple occasions we were forced to navigate flooded roads that stood in our way. Eventually we exited the interstate and spent the next couple hours stalking the flightpaths of U.S. Coast Guard rescue helicopters hovering overhead. It stood to reason that the closer we could get to a search and rescue helicopter, the closer we were to a water rescue. Sometime later, we managed to link up with a FEMA boat team that was specially trained to perform search and rescue in urban environments. Many of the locations where rescues operations were underway ended up being unreachable by vehicle. Still, we did our best to make compelling photographs around the periphery. After spending most of the afternoon rolling around in tandem, it was time to split up and each head in our own direction. Before parting ways, I got out of my SUV and gave him another big hug.

"Go get 'em, dude." I said.

I climbed back into my rental car with a full heart, thankful that we were able to meet up. Spending time with Jabin was a reminder that I am not alone, even though sometimes it can feel that way. As iron sharpens iron, so one man sharpens another. I loved this guy like a brother, even if he did usually outshoot me.

The next morning, I awoke from another feverish dream convinced that my hotel room was flooding. Unfortunately, it would not be the last. The stress of newsgathering in the middle of a disaster zone is real. The burden of performance is heavy. I didn't have the bandwidth to make sense of it all at the time. Yet as each day passed, the unprocessed emotional stress compounded. Trying to perform, hit deadlines, stay safe, and keep my equipment functioning was quite the juggling act. When news is constantly happening all around you, it becomes almost impossible to pace yourself and avoid burnout.

Sooner or later, the sight of catastrophic damage becomes somehow commonplace. One can become strangely accustomed to the other-worldly environments that surround them. Indeed, spending enough time in the midst calamity can even make the normalcy of unaffected areas downright jarring in contrast. The longer one spends documenting widespread destruction, the easier it is to become desensitized to it. Trying to chase the dragon and continually one-up yourself has the potential to dehumanize both yourself and the subjects you cover.

I spent my third day in Texas aboard a helicopter shooting aerial photos south of Houston. I met my pilot at the airport in Galveston and boarded the tiny Robinson R-44 helicopter. The R-44 is one of the smallest commercial helicopters on the market. So small, in fact, that I had trouble fitting in the co-pilot's seat with all my gear. After he topped his fuel tank off, we took to the skies and began flying west. Almost immediately, the sheer scale of the Texas' inland flooding became apparent. Hundreds of square miles of Southeast Texas farmland were underwater. We followed a four lane divided highway as it disappeared beneath the muddy water only to reappear a half mile later. Circling over a cattle ranch, I noticed a herd of a dozen cows that had all gathered on a tiny patch of un-flooded pasture. They stood packed in close with one other, staring warily at the encroaching water that surrounded them in every direction. I fired off frame after frame from the right hand seat of the small helicopter.

During our return trip to Galveston, we circled the refineries at Texas City a few times. Much of the flooding had not been visible to me on the ground the day before. My airborne vantage point told a different story. Floodwater filled almost every earthen bunker that surrounded the refinery's oil storage tank farm. If a catastrophic failure were to occur, millions of gallons of oil could spill directly into the Gulf of Mexico. After about two hours in flight, we landed back at the airport. I thanked the pilot for his expert flying and began to send the best of my photos to New York. With my work complete, my editors told me to catch the next flight home. While I was grateful to have been there on the ground in thick of things, I could not wait to get home and see my kids.

A week or so later I would return to the Houston area to photograph cleanup, recovery, and damage assessment in several neighborhoods and commercial properties across the city. Piles of ruined furniture, carpet, and dry wall seemed to stretch endlessly through the city's neighborhoods.

I made a point to drive around some of the neighborhoods that only a week before had been totally under water. In doing so, I reflected on what I had seen during my first day on the ground. I witnessed something incredible in Spring's Highland Glen neighborhood and again at the nursing home. A group of men banded together to protect their community's most vulnerable. They put themselves at risk and willingly entered fast-moving floodwaters. They expertly piloted their boats through an unfamiliar urban environment full of unseen hazards. I returned home from Houston moved, and challenged, after witnessing the events of that day. These were men of action; Men who risked their own wellbeing for the good of those in harm's way.

It took some time for me to shake off the stress that I carried home from Houston. In the weeks following, I found myself feeling uneasy and on-edge during the day. Nor was I sleeping well. I kept waking up in the middle of the night, as I had done in Houston, convinced that my house was flooding.

A few days after returning home to Kentucky, I went to see the director Christopher Nolan's motion picture, *Dunkirk,* before it left theaters. The film re-tells the story of the British Army's frantic retreat from France back across the English Channel to England during the early days of World War II. With The Royal Navy facing a severe shortage of ships, British civilians set sail in their own boats to transport England's war-weary soldiers back across the channel. Miraculously, the armada of fishing trawlers, sailboats, and pleasure yachts rescued more than 300,000 soldiers from certain capture and imprisonment at the hands of the German Army. As the ending credits rolled in the theater, I began to connect the dots between the thrilling motion picture I had just enjoyed, and the heroic rescue efforts of the Cajun Navy during Hurricane Harvey. My nostrils flared, my eyes watered, and a lump appeared in my throat. All the emotions of those few days came rushing back to me. While I had documented only a small part of it all, I was honored to have been there alongside so many courageous, strong, selfless men. Witnessing their decisive action served as a reminder of the kind of man I hoped to become.

There, outside the movie theater, I sat in my car and thought back to those three rainy days in Houston. I remembered the city's normally gridlocked highways eerily devoid of traffic. I could hear the rising floodwaters lapping against the sides of brick mailboxes on residential streets. I felt the never-ending stream of raindrops rolling from my soaked scalp on down my cheeks. I could smell the exhaust fumes of boat motors wafting across the grey, swollen parking lots of Houston's suburbs. I was glad to have witnessed and documented it. I was even more glad to have stepped out from behind my camera.

Scan this code for photos from Chapter 5

6. IN THE EYEWALL

Traffic on the highway was at a standstill. Vehicles sat bumper to bumper, inching their way west to safety. Their roof racks were piled high with luggage, bicycles, and other belongings. I couldn't help but feel bad for the people I saw. They were stuck in gridlock by no fault of their own. Slamming my foot on the gas pedal, I set my cruise control and focused on the empty road ahead. My rental SUV flew down the highway in the opposite direction of the snarled traffic. I was on my way to meet Michael in Panama City, Florida: Michael, the Category 4 hurricane.

A foolhardy part of me loved the fact that while every sober-minded person was fleeing Hurricane Michael, I was driving directly into its path. A couple days earlier, my editors at Bloomberg tapped me to be their man on the ground in Panama City. I prepared for Michael in exactly the same manner that I had prepared for Harvey. The only thing I was missing was a kayak. If the storm surge turned out to be as devastating as forecasters were predicting, a personal water craft would come in handy. "Oh well," I thought to myself. Maybe next time.

As I traveled toward Panama City with a trunk full of provisions and supplies, I indulged my over-active imagination and explored the worst-case scenarios that could be waiting for me over the coming days. The Weather Channel was predicting historic levels of storm surge and devastating hurricane force winds along Florida's Gulf coast. Would the roads be passable after the storm? Would my hotel survive landfall? Did I bring enough extra fuel? Would I be able exfiltrate the disaster zone when the time came? Would I make any good photos? Would I make it back to Kentucky to care for my kids?

I was a newly-single dad and was wrestling with competing desires. On the one hand, I wanted to be a top-performer in my field. I wanted to be known as a photojournalist who could get the job done any time, any place. In addition to my desire for status and accolades, I needed to bring home the bacon, literally, for my two young sons. But I also felt the burden of responsibility to pour masculine, fatherly love into the little hearts of my boys. They needed it from me now, more than ever. I couldn't very well father my sons and chase breaking news at the same time. It didn't matter how great the photo opportunities might be. I was a dad first. My little boys needed me.

Earlier that afternoon, I caught a last-minute flight into Pensacola. The cabin of the Southwest Airlines jet was about as sparsely populated as the eastbound lanes of Highway 98. As my flight taxied to the gate, one of the flight attendants came over the intercom. "We know you have a choice when it comes to air travel, so thank you for choosing Southwest Airlines" she recited in her dutifully cheery tone. "Please, be careful out there. Take care of each other" she added somberly. I picked up my car, the last remaining Chevrolet Suburban on the rental lot, and headed East.

Panama City Beach may hold the record for the most beachfront hotels per square mile in the United States. At least, that's how it looked me as I drove into town: just a series of high rise hotels and resorts constructed one on top of another lining the beach for miles. It was a far cry from the Outer Banks in North Carolina where wild stallions roamed the windswept dunes. Panama City was quite different. Despite the abundance of hotel properties in the area, only a few options showed up in an online search for a hotel room. The vast majority of hotels had shut their doors and heeded the mandatory evacuation order issued by local officials. For perhaps the first time ever (aside from spring break), it seemed like there wasn't a single open hotel room in the entirety of Panama City Beach.

Thanks to a tip from a colleague, I caught wind that the Hampton Inn was renting rooms exclusively to members of the media. It took a few tries, but eventually I was able to get through to the front desk and make a reservation over the phone. I requested an oceanfront room with a balcony. This would be the perfect vantage point to watch the hurricane make landfall. The fourth floor should be high enough above sea level to avoid the crashing waves, but close enough to ground level that taking the stairs wouldn't kill me. Because, as prior experience had taught me, sooner or later the elevators would inevitably lose power.

Super Storm Sandy was the first major hurricane that I experienced as a journalist. It was October 2012, and I had been instructed by the *New York Times* national desk to position myself in Rehoboth Beach, Delaware, ahead of Sandy's landfall. I was 23 years old, single, and eager for adventure. I remember venturing out onto my hotel balcony and watching the angry Atlantic Ocean thrash about as the tempest neared shore. Due to the counter-clockwise rotation of the storm, Delaware was spared much of the damage that forecasters had predicted might occur from Sandy's landfall. The Jersey Shore however, was devastated. The morning after the storm passed, I drove north along the coast to Seaside Heights, a barrier island located across Barnegat Bay from Tom's River, New Jersey. Reports were trickling out that the island had sustained significant damage from the storm.

When I arrived in Tom's River, my progress was halted by a police checkpoint. Only first responders were being allowed to access the Route 37 bridge that led to the island. Multiple squad cars blocked both the inbound and outbound lanes to the bridge. A New Jersey State Trooper walked over to my vehicle as I pulled up to the roadblock. I rolled down my window and identified myself as a member of the press. The officer examined my credentials and informed me that no media were being allowed on the island without the permission of the Ocean County Sheriff. Before I could ask, he pointed me in the sheriff's direction. A line of fellow media members had formed in front of him, each asking for access to the damaged island. I took my place in line to make the same request. Shortly thereafter, the sheriff raised his voice and asked for everyone to gather around for an announcement. I squeezed between two television news crews and made it to the front of the semi-circle that formed around the sheriff. He announced that a bus was en route to take us across the bridge. As many as could fit on the bus would be allowed a few minutes to gather photos and videos of the damage. The timing of my arrival could not have been more perfect.

A few minutes later, a white minibus pulled into the parking lot. Our ride across the bridge was no larger than a small rental car shuttle. A long line of media immediately formed at the entrance to the vehicle. I jostled to snag a coveted spot onboard. By the time I made it on the bus, all the seats had been filled. I opted to stand in the aisle for the short trip. The sheriff slid behind the wheel, shifted into gear, and drove our overloaded transport across the bridge and onto the island. Upon reaching Seaside Heights, he pulled the bus into a parking lot near the island's historic boardwalk. The sheriff turned toward the back of the bus and shouted out our marching orders.

"The bus will leave in exactly fifteen minutes," he announced. "If you are not back on board by then, you will be arrested." With that, he yanked on the draw bar and swung the bus's folding passenger doors wide open.

A stampede of journalists spilled out of the vehicle toward the boardwalk. I grabbed my two cameras and began to run toward the beach. I didn't have much time. As I approached the water line, the sight of the island's famed Star Jet roller coaster stopped me in my tracks.

Sandy's violent surf had collapsed the aging Seaside Heights amusement pier out from underneath it, depositing the largely intact coaster in the middle of the Atlantic Ocean. The scene was otherworldly. I hurriedly composed a photo of the roller coaster and continued on my way. There was no time to linger. Much of the historic boardwalk had been washed out to sea. Entire sections north of the amusement pier were missing. Along with the Star Jet coaster, the pier's iconic Ferris wheel had fallen some twenty feet and now rested on the sandy beach below. Waves lapped at its still upright base. An ornate ticket booth sat askew on top a pile of debris nearby. Other smaller coasters on the pier were reduced to rubble.

With time quickly counting down, I continued to photograph the devastated amusement park. One building full of historic penny arcade games, stuffed animal prizes, and skee-ball machines was missing an entire wall. I poked my head inside as the owner surveyed the extensive damage for himself. The somber scene was interrupted by the shrill noise of the phone alarm I had set for myself. It was time to get back to the bus.

The truth is, I could have spent hours wandering around Seaside Heights. The destruction was so brutally visual and interesting. Covering Sandy taught me valuable lessons that I continue to draw from to this day. One of which being when the sheriff tells you to be back at the bus, you had best get there on time. This was neither the time nor the place to test how lenient law enforcement was feeling toward rogue news photographers.

Back in Panama City, it felt great to check the hotel off my to-do list. With all my logistical concerns taken care of, I could focus on what I was good at: making photos.

All over town, residents who chose to ignore the evacuation order were busy preparing for Hurricane Michael's imminent arrival. My first stop of the afternoon was Home Depot. Plywood, generators, and blue plastic tarps were flying off the shelves of local hardware stores. I spent some time outside photographing customers as they pushed shopping carts full of lumber through the parking lot. People seemed to be in good spirits for the most part. After all, Florida was no stranger to hurricanes.

My next stop of the afternoon was the local supermarket. Other than Home Depot and a Publix grocery store, every other business was closed. Walmart had barricaded their entrances with sandbags, sheet metal, and rows of shopping carts. Even the neighboring 24/7 McDonald's drive thru had gone dark. I grabbed a cart and strolled inside the grocery store. I picked up a couple racks of smoked pork ribs for my hotel mini fridge in case I got tired of beef jerky.

At this stage in the game, the locals were in panic-buying mode. Bottled water and canned food had all but disappeared from the store's shelves. I strolled down the bread aisle and took a few discreet photos of the empty shelves. I watched as a shopper turned her nose up at the few dozen loaves of wheat bread that remained. Apparently, no bread at all was better than wheat bread.

Leaving the supermarket, I cruised around town looking for people boarding up their homes and businesses. Photographs of "the day before" are a staple of good storm coverage, though not quite as enduring as "the day after." The Florida sun shone brightly as I pulled into the parking lot of a local gas station. Two carpenters were boarding up the windows of the station's convenience store. I took photos as they used a power drill to fasten their last two pieces of plywood over the store's entrance. The clear skies and pleasant weather contributed to the cognitive dissonance.

I spent the better part of the next hour photographing storefronts and houses that had been boarded up in anticipation of Michael's arrival. Spray-painted messages left behind by property owners adorned many of the homes.

"Bring it on," read one piece of plywood.

"Rock me like a hurricane," said another.

"Go away, Michael" read a third.

Nearby, a crowd had gathered outside a local bar for one last happy hour before the big storm. Dressed in sleeveless shirts and flip-flops, the bar's patrons joked with one-another and carried on boisterously. The mood was surprisingly lighthearted given their shared knowledge that a monstrous cataclysm was bearing down on their beloved community watering hole. Everyone I spoke with felt confident that they would make it through unscathed. One kind fellow promised to come rescue me in his canoe if storm surge overtook the peninsula. I thanked him for the offer.

"Don't mention it," he remarked before throwing his head back and taking a big swig from the bottle of Bud Light in his hand.

Feeling satisfied with my photos at the bar, I drove over to the nearest public beach access to get eyes on the ocean. On my way to the water, I passed the Hampton Inn. Trucks belonging to NBC News, CBS, and FOX sat parked outside the hotel with their roof-mounted satellite dishes pointed toward the heavens. I arrived at a sand-covered parking lot near the beach and trudged over the dunes toward the ocean. My calf muscles burned as I fought the soft, loose sand in my pair of tennis shoes.

Unsurprisingly, the normally packed beach was more or less deserted. It was a strange sight given the wild popularity of the town as a vacation destination. Without the knowledge that a giant hurricane was coming, the empty beach wouldn't make any sense. The few beach goers there were acted as if it was any other day on the Gulf. A middle-school aged girl did handstands at the edge of the surf as her parents lounged under a beach cabana a few feet away. A shirtless man in a straw hat attempted to launch a kite that resembled a U.S. Navy Blue Angels fighter jet. In the distance, a family of four strolled leisurely along the waterline.

With another half-dozen newsworthy photos under my belt, I climbed into my car and began driving toward my hotel when my phone rang with a call from a local number in Panama City Beach.

"Mr. Sharrett?" the man on the phone inquired.

"Yes, this is Luke." I replied.

"I'm calling from the Hampton Inn. I'm afraid I have some bad news. Our corporate office has instructed us to cancel all our guest reservations and shut down the hotel immediately. I'm terribly sorry."

I let out a groan. "You were right, that really *is* bad news," I said.

He apologized again and wished me luck.

I hung up the phone and immediately got to work finding another hotel. It was far from ideal to find myself without a room this late in the game.

One of my colleagues was staying at the Hilton Garden Inn across the lagoon in Panama City. The woman at the front desk informed me that they were totally sold out. Next, I tried the Fairfield Inn that sat inland on the Panama City Beach side of the lagoon. The hotel manager said he had a handful of rooms left for media only. While the property did not afford a beachfront view, I was nonetheless elated at the news. I headed that direction to check in to my room before the front desk could change their mind.

The parking lot of the Fairfield was full of network satellite vehicles just as the Hampton Inn's lot had been. Those sat trucks meant I was in the right place. I checked in, dropped my bags in my room, and immediately headed back outside. The sun was low on the horizon, bathing everything in dreamy, soft rays of light. It was golden hour.

Crossing Grand Lagoon, I parked at an apartment complex that sat adjacent to a small marina. Residents of the complex were busy packing up their vehicles with personal belongings and groceries. This struck me as a prudent decision in light of the two-story building's close proximity to the water's edge. The western sky turned vivid shades of orange and yellow as the sun descended lazily beneath the horizon. A pair of palm trees stood silhouetted against the evening's sunset. For a moment I stopped to center myself and soak in the scene. I closed my eyes and took a deep breath in through my nose.

The salty air rushed into my lungs and instantly transported me back to beach vacations in North Carolina as a young boy with my family. I felt the warm rays of the setting sun kiss my cheeks. The calm ocean breeze rustled through my hair. I opened my eyes and beheld the glory of creation. Even as the forces of chaos churned through the Gulf of Mexico just over the horizon, beauty had not yet abandoned Panama City. I did my best to enjoy it while I still could. Things would be looking quite different by the time tomorrow morning rolled around.

As night approached, I reached out to several of my colleagues who had also traveled to Panama City to cover the storm. I found an open pizza restaurant in town and began spreading the word amongst my friends. One of the things I enjoyed most about working in Washington, D.C., was the camaraderie between the photographers who covered politics in the District. Since moving back to Kentucky, I had felt the absence of that fellowship.

I claimed a couple booths for us inside Ramon's Pizza, a hole-in-the-wall family owned joint about the size of a Waffle House. Over the course of the evening, some of my favorite photographers stopped by for a slice. The group included Eric Thayer, a long-time legendary freelancer for Reuters. Eric was one of the first photographers on the scene when Captain Sully Sullenberger safely landed his United Airlines jet in the Hudson River in 2009. Brendan Smialowski, a visionary photographer on staff with Agence-France Press in Washington, D.C. also joined us. One of D.C.'s original young hotshot photographers, Brendan had been covering the White House and traveling on Air Force One for more than a decade by this point. Victor J. Blue, a freelancer for the *New York Times*, joined us as well. Vic is a fearless conflict photographer based in Brooklyn who has done more military embeds in Afghanistan than anyone else I know. Scott Olson, a veteran wire photographer with Getty Images, also dropped in to say hello. Based in Chicago, Scott was famously wrongfully arrested by police officers during the Ferguson, Missouri, riots in 2014. Jabin Botsford, my convoy buddy from the Houston floods, helped round out the group that evening.

It was nice to have one last hot meal before all hell broke loose the following day. I polished off a dozen chicken wings as others in our group dug into salads and pizzas. The food was good. The company was even better. Spending time with fellow photographers whom I admired was good for the soul. Their presence motivated me to hone my skills and improve my craft even more. Although none of them ever gave me reason to doubt it, in this group I felt included and accepted as a photojournalist. This gathering helped wither the imposter syndrome that is prone to take root inside me.

The stress and uncertainty of covering this type of breaking news can cause my self-doubt to grow like a weed. For as long as I've been a photojournalist, I've heard the voice of my inner critic accusing me of being a fraud.

"This is the day that you will be found out," it whispers. "This is the time you will return empty-handed from an assignment. You will lose the respect of your peers. Editors will never call you for work again. Your worth and value as a human being are tied solely to your performance. If you're not the best, you are nothing at all."

Lies.

As the night wore on, my colleagues and I swapped stories, laughed together, and shared strategies for covering the hurricane that was slowly chugging our direction. Though we were all technically competing against one another for the best photos, this fact did not diminish the good-natured fellowship shared mutually between us.

Roughly an hour and half after we gathered at Ramon's Pizza, our dinner ended abruptly. We were mid-conversation when an alarm began to sound from my cell phone. A startling tone reminiscent of the emergency broadcast system filled the interior of Ramon's. I instinctively reached to retrieve my phone from the back pocket of my blue jeans. The chatter inside the restaurant halted immediately as virtually every other person in the restaurant did the same simultaneously. I squinted at the message on my home screen.

"The National Weather Service has issued a hurricane warning for your area. Take cover immediately."

Looking up from my phone, I glanced around at the rest of the table. Lest any of us had forgotten, a Category 4 hurricane was scheduled to begin making landfall in less than 12 hours' time. An employee behind the restaurant's front counter called out in a loud voice.

"OK everyone, we're closed for the night."

And just like that, our dinner party adjourned for the evening. Our table boxed up their leftover pizza and filtered out into the parking lot.

"Be safe out there."

"Good luck tomorrow."

I followed Jabin back to the Fairfield Inn across the bridge. We made plans to meet up in the morning and venture out into the storm together. Settling into my hotel room for the night, I took stock of the fact that this would probably be my last night sleeping in air conditioning for a couple days.

The next morning, I woke up before sunrise and drove to the beach to get eyes on the ocean once more. A steady, heavy rain had already been falling for some time. The first of Michael's outer bands arrived earlier that morning from the south. The deep blue pre-dawn sky reflected in the shimmering streets of Panama City Beach as I cruised past row after row of empty beachfront high-rise buildings. Every window was dark, vacated by owners and vacationers alike. Aside from the occasional police car out on patrol, I passed no other vehicles on the road. After some time, I found a good spot to pull over and check out the surf.

I pulled into the parking lot of a tall condominium building and grabbed a long lens from my waterproof Pelican case. The rain was falling at an even steadier rate than it had when I first left my hotel. I sought cover from the elements beneath an exterior staircase of the condo. For the next few minutes, I photographed the heavy surf as it crashed on the beach. A flagpole stood nearby with a pair of red warning flags that blew steadily in the wind. Their edges had already begun to fray in the stiff gale. They signaled to no one in particular that the beach was closed for swimming.

Point taken.

I ran back to my Suburban and sought refuge from the deluge. The streetlights suspended over Front Beach Road danced erratically in the howling wind. As I drove the eerily deserted streets, I began to feel dreadfully exposed. Fear set in as I realized the gravity of the hurricane that was fast approaching. I began to question my competence. Was I up for the task? Was I prepared well enough? Would I find myself in over my head? Save for the gaze of my Creator I felt utterly alone in the midst of the storm.

Soaking wet from the pounding rain, I returned to the Fairfield to dry out. I entered the lobby and weaved through a maze of television cameras, light stands, and electrical wiring. ABC, Fox News, and a handful of local stations had taken up residence at the hotel for the duration of the storm. Upon reaching my room, I flipped on the TV and watched as a correspondent whom I had walked past less than a minute prior delivered a "live hit" on location under the front portico of the hotel.

The experience was quite novel.

As my first batch of photos landed in New York, I stepped into the tub for one last hot shower before the power went out. I tried to savor the last few moments of comfort knowing from experience that some long, sweaty days of news gathering in the Florida panhandle lay ahead. After the shower, I made sure my laptop and camera batteries were fully charged. It wouldn't be long until we were all in darkness and the real work began.

My stomach began to rumble as lunch time approached. I retrieved one of my slabs of smoked ribs from the hotel mini-fridge and hurriedly began preparing what I knew would be my first and last hot meal of the day. Although my car was loaded with 5 days-worth of beef jerky and granola bars, why not take advantage of the opportunity to indulge in some warm grub? I removed the packaging and washed the thick globs of coagulated BBQ sauce from the ribs into the sink. Leaving the sauce on and enduring the inevitable high fructose corn syrup-induced sugar crash this close to game time was not advisable. By the time I was done, the bathroom looked like the scene of a grisly murder. Patches of bright red corn syrup splattered at random across the vanity. As I stood over the sink admiring the mess I had created, I noticed the lights flicker on and off. The power wasn't going to be on for much longer. I hustled over to my room's small microwave and hurriedly nuked my ribs. I crossed my fingers as the numbers slowly counted down from sixty on the appliance's digital screen. Finally, the delightful ding of the microwave reached my ears.

"Success!" I called out to the empty room.

I closed my eyes and sank my teeth into the warm, tender baby back ribs. I reveled in the luxury of a hot lunch in the midst of a hurricane. The Weather Channel played on my TV as I made quick work of the rest of the pork. Colorful doppler radar images shone on the screen.

"If you are still in the Panama City area, this is your last chance to leave," a meteorologist warned. "It's now or never."

For a moment I considered making a run for it and high tailing it back to Pensacola. Should I get out of here? A massive storm was bearing down on me. Again, I entertained the worst case scenarios in my mind. Would I survive? Would I be able to make it out of here to see my kids? I watched the radar depiction of Michael's well-formed eye bearing down on the coast. Something inside me pushed back against the fear. I knew I had spent enough of my life living in fear and backing down from challenges. It was not time for retreat. It was time for courage.

A moment later the power went out. The overhead light cut off and the television screen abruptly went black. Well, it was nice while it lasted. I sat on the edge of my bed in the darkness and listened as my room's air conditioning unit powered down. The hum of the unit faded away into stillness. Only the sound of the falling rain beating against the window remained.

Here we go.

The storm's landfall was projected around 3pm. Before that happened, I wanted to get back out for one last spin around town. Eventually, high winds would force me back to the relative safety of the hotel. Until then I resolved to head back out and shoot more photos. I dressed in my rain gear and texted Jabin to meet me in the lobby. He jumped into the passenger seat of my Suburban and we took off toward the beach. I gripped the steering wheel tightly in an effort to keep the SUV on the road. The streets were completely abandoned as Michael's strong crosswinds ripped across the roadway. The few police cruisers that I encountered earlier that morning had retreated to the county's Emergency Operations Center. Once the winds had reached a sustained speed of

45mph, all emergency services were temporarily suspended until the storm passed. If anything happened to us out here, we would be on our own.

Following a few tense minutes of driving, we pulled into the beachfront high-rise parking lot where I had stopped earlier that morning. Conditions had deteriorated significantly in just a few hours' time. I grabbed my cameras and turned to Jabin.

"Meet me under the stairs at the corner of the building. You ready?" I asked.

He nodded in affirmation. "Let's go!"

We bailed out of the Suburban simultaneously and made a run for the high-rise stairwell. The amount of force it took to crack my door caught me off guard immediately. It felt as if an invisible sumo wrestler was pushing back against me with all his strength. As I struggled to open the door and jump from the driver's seat, the wind caught the interior door panel like a sail and slammed it violently against its hinges in the wrong direction. A loud metallic crunch emanated from my driver's side door.

"That doesn't sound good!" I yelled out loud.

As a journalist covering a hurricane, few things are more important than access to a fully-functioning vehicle. One of my mentors, veteran *New York Times* photographer Doug Mills, always encouraged me to purchase as much supplemental insurance as possible when covering storms in a rental car. It was solid advice that had come in handy a month earlier during Hurricane Florence's landfall in September of 2018. Forecasters were anticipating a direct hit by a fast-moving Category 3 hurricane on the border of North and South Carolina. Florence, however, had plans of her own. The hurricane nearly screeched to a halt in the Atlantic Ocean as it approached the East Coast. As a result, the region saw very little wind damage. Instead, Florence dumped a downright Biblical amount of rain, which caused widespread inland flooding across southeastern North Carolina.

One of my editors at the *New York Times* asked me to cover the storm from Myrtle Beach, South Carolina. I ended up flying into Atlanta, renting a car, and driving the rest of the way to the coast. The only rental SUV I could find at the airport was a black 2019 Cadillac Escalade. I slid into the passenger seat and checked the odometer. It indicated a grand total of 67 miles on the vehicle. I laughed as I realized I was driving into the path of Hurricane Florence in a brand new Escalade.

As Florence's eye moved ashore, I was sitting in my SUV watching the wind blow trash cans around a beachfront access road in North Myrtle Beach. When it became apparent that there would be little wind damage to speak of, I relocated inland toward Lumberton, North Carolina. As the name suggests, the town was settled by laborers who worked in North

Carolina's timber industry. I reached the outskirts of town and pulled off the slick road into the parking lot of a small church. Behind the church stood a sprawling cemetery. Its headstones were inundated by a lake of floodwater from the swollen Lumberton River. I donned a pair of waders and trudged out through a flooded pasture toward the cemetery to make photos.

Fifteen minutes later, I pulled into downtown Lumberton and stopped for dinner at the only restaurant open in the entire town: a Chinese buffet. The dining room was full of U.S. Coast Guard members who were pre-positioned to conduct rescues if needed. Despite having made a handful of compelling photos earlier in the day, I got greedy and went back out for more once darkness fell on the town. I found a few neighborhoods along the river's bank and went to check them out. The massive amount of rainfall throughout that day had overwhelmed Lumberton's storm drains with ease. Subsequently, neighborhood streets quickly turned into rivers. I felt confident enough driving through the foot or so of water that was flowing down the road. That confidence soon betrayed me as I noticed the water level rising up the side of my Escalade.

The thought briefly crossed my mind that I should shift into reverse and back out the way I had come. Something inside me panicked and I decided instead to press on. I gunned the engine and lurched forward even deeper into the flooded street. My white knuckles gripped the steering wheel as I watched water begin to crest over the front hood of the SUV. This was not good. Looking ahead I saw more than 100 yards of watery territory between myself and dry land. I panicked again and pulled left onto a side street. I watched with horror as the water level began licking the bottom of my sideview mirror. Just then, I heard the engine begin to sputter. I slammed my foot onto the gas pedal, but the engine would not respond. My stomach sank even further as I watched the dashboard lights flicker out. The Escalade rolled to a stop. There I was, dead in the water.

I let out a long extended f-bomb. How could I have been so foolish? It was a massive unforced error wrought by a fatal mixture of stubbornness, overconfidence, inexperience, and plain old incompetence. Suddenly, a spark of hope caught fire inside me. What if I had just stalled out? If I could make it to dry ground I might be able to restart the engine. With nothing to lose, I hatched a quick plan. Shifting the SUV into neutral, I rolled down my window, opened the driver's side door and splashed down into chest high water. I was surprised by how deep it was. No wonder my engine had crapped out on me.

I grabbed the driver's side window frame and began pushing as hard as I could. To my surprise the Escalade started rolling.

"Please, oh please, oh please, oh please," was all I could pray under my breath.

I continued to push for about thirty yards. Slowly but surely, my confidence was growing. This plan might just work. As I neared the next intersection it was crucial that I make a right turn out of the water in order to end up on dry land. Reaching inside the driver's side window I tried awkwardly to turn the steering wheel clockwise while continuing to push with my left arm. In the heat of the moment, I misjudged my trajectory and ended up steering the SUV into the road's submerged curb. The escalade ground to a halt. All my momentum was lost at the critical moment when I needed it most. On top of that, my front passenger side tire had become lodged in a storm drain. I pushed and pulled with all my might to free the tire, but nothing was working. It was there, just feet away from dry ground, that I finally gave up hope.

Feeling thoroughly defeated, I climbed back up into the driver's seat and called Jabin on the phone. He was staying 10 minutes away with a U.S. Coast Guard swift water rescue team. I told him my predicament and asked if he would come pick me up.

"Of course," he replied immediately. "I'll be right there."

The cavalry was on its way. I began gathering together all the gear I could possibly carry. My spare gasoline, bottled water, and most of my food would have to be left behind. Holding what little I could salvage above my head, I waded down the road toward dry land. A few minutes later, Jabin showed up and helped me load my stuff into the trunk of his Suburban. Before we left, I snapped a photo of the brand-new Escalade half-submerged in the floodwater.

Being the standup guy that he is, Jabin offered for me to sleep on the couch in his hotel room. I gratefully accepted. As we drove back to the hotel I felt so much shame, embarrassment, and disappointment in myself. The *New York Times* was depending on me, and I was down for the count. It was not a good feeling. That evening I filed a claim with the rental car agency and thanked the good Lord that I had purchased the loss damage waiver. Because of that, I would not pay an extra cent out of pocket for the totaled SUV. The following morning, I hitched a ride with another photographer to the airport in Fayetteville where I caught a flight home. To this day I still feel self-conscious whenever I pass a black Escalade in traffic. Lesson learned, the hard way.

Back in Panama City, I fought the howling wind in a futile attempt to slam the door of my SUV shut. I placed the entirety of my body weight against the door and pushed with all my might. Thankfully, my waterproof hiking boots found just enough traction on the asphalt to muscle the door closed. Fighting against the wind, I turned and sprinted for cover under the stairwell. I pointed up and yelled to Jabin over the roar of the storm.

"Let's go up a few stories. Follow me!" My adrenaline catapulted me up six flights of stairs to a walkway that surrounded the condominium's beachfront exterior.

We reached the third level and stuffed ourselves into a small alcove facing the beach. The arrangement of the high-rise's staircase unexpectedly shielded this small spot from the hurricane-force winds that were swirling all around us. It had been a matter of seconds since we left the dry interior of the Suburban, but both of us were already completely soaked. The amount of rain coming down was akin to standing in front of a firehose. Jabin and I took turns stepping out from the cover of the alcove to make images of the storm surge slamming into the beach three stories below. When it was my turn, I emerged from the alcove and spent a few seconds shooting photos of a lifeguard stand that was completely engulfed by the boiling surf. After a moment out in the elements, I retreated back into the safety of the alcove. I shook the rain from my face and searched for a dry patch of t-shirt to wipe away the water that had accumulated on my camera lens.

I briefly allowed my imagination to run wild. What if I stayed here for the duration of the storm? It was the perfect vantage point to watch as the eye moved in, and the storm surge crested the dunes. The alcove would provide excellent protection, assuming the winds didn't shift. "Hey," I yelled to Jabin. "What if we stayed here for the rest of the Hurricane?" The look on his face communicated that if I chose to stay, he would not be joining me.

"I'm thinking about staying," I reiterated, half facetiously.

Satisfied with our performance from the third story walkway, we retreated back to the safety of the SUV. Somehow, the wind had picked up even more since we made our initial foray to the exterior stairwell. It was long past time to get off the streets and back to the hotel.

We headed back the way we came, ignoring the darkened traffic lights swinging violently in the gusting wind. Sheets of rain pummeled my windshield. The wipers struggled to keep up despite being on their fastest setting. It had become self-evident that spending any more time out and about in these conditions would be far less than ideal.

We made the drive through the abandoned, lawless streets of Panama City Beach in record speed. I felt my stress level begin to fall as we pulled back into the hotel parking lot. The newly constructed Fairfield felt like a well-defended embassy in the midst of the chaos. I found a good parking spot close to the hotel and set the parking brake, just in case the wind tried to sweep the Suburban away. The hotel lobby was just as we left it. The common areas were overflowing with journalists, photographers, and television news crews. There was something oddly comforting about their presence. It was as if this many media professionals in one place signaled that I was in exactly the right spot. We couldn't *all* die. Could we?

Despite the worsening weather outside, I felt a warm sense in my gut that things would be OK. This was where I belonged. There was nowhere else I needed to be right now.

I walked purposefully down the humid hotel corridor toward the stairwell. Illuminated only by the eerie red glow of a battery-powered emergency exit sign at the end the hallway, my eyes did their best to adjust to the darkness. Water splashed from my rain-soaked footgear as I bounded up the carpeted steps to the second story of the hotel. Back in my room, I stripped off my rain gear and sat down to send my most recent batch of pictures to my editors in New York. There was no telling how much longer the area would have cellular service. Actually, given the reality of the winds outside, it was a small miracle that the towers hadn't gone down already.

As I sat on the edge of my bed, I listened to the storm build outside my window. The hurricane's path put our hotel just on the western edge of the eyewall. Due to its counter-clockwise rotation, my room's north-facing window was taking the brunt of the impact. The wind whistling over the small gap between my window and the hotel's stucco exterior filled my room with a constant ghostly howling. This unsettling noise was punctuated by loud, periodic booms as faster-moving wind gusts impacted the window. It sounded as if a lumberjack was outside landing blows on the glass. I set down my laptop and approached the window with trepidation. I imagined that at any moment the glass could shatter from the force of the storm. I instinctively squinted my eyes nearly all the way shut and drew the blackout curtains closed to cover the trembling pane of glass. A curtain would probably do little, if anything, to protect me from the shower of debris if the window did indeed break. But I figured it couldn't hurt. The view through the window was totally obscured by a deluge of rain streaming down the glass. It was as if someone was aiming an industrial-strength pressure washer toward my room.

A short while later, I noticed a steady stream of water seeping through the bottom edge of the window frame. In no time, a puddle formed and began spilling down into the floor-level air conditioning unit. A similar leak in the wall had caused a water balloon of sorts to form beneath the surface of the room's latex wall paint. It grew and grew like a rabid tumor. The place was starting to fall apart.

I retreated from the window at the sound of an incoming text message. It was from Jabin.

"Get down to the lobby," it read. "The eye is almost here."

Donning my rain gear once again, I descended the stairs back to the ground floor and tip-toed back through the maze of TV cameras in the lobby. A handful of other curious media were gathered just outside the hotel's entrance. The portico offered minimal protection from the elements, but it was better than nothing. The fronds of the palm trees that surrounded the parking lot bent ninety degrees in the wind. Raindrops flew sideways through the air, stinging like thousands of tiny needles as they struck my cheeks. I sought refuge from the elements behind an SUV parked under the portico. As the awe-inspiring scene unfolded, I kept an eye on the sheet metal roof of a neighboring Exxon gas station. It flapped violently in the merciless wind. I knew it was only a matter of time before it broke loose and careened through the air like missile.

A single intrepid television journalist was reporting from the outer edge of the portico. Wearing an orange rain jacket and clutching a wireless microphone, the man yelled over the howling wind. I could only imagine what he must be saying.

"We're coming to you live from beautiful Panama City Beach. If you take a look behind me you may be able to see Hurricane Michael making landfall here at the Fairfield Inn. Back to you, Jim.

The eyewall is the single most violent part of a hurricane. It's where power is concentrated and thus where the most damaging winds of a given storm tend occur. As the circular eyewall passes, the intense destruction gives way to a period of eerie calm inside the eye itself. Although I've never experienced it personally, friends and colleagues have described to me the unsettling serenity that permeates the eye of a well-formed hurricane. When the hurricane's eye passes overhead, it's as if someone flipped a switch and abruptly turned off the storm. During hurricanes that make landfall overnight, the stars are often visible in the night sky above. Following the calm passage of the storm's eye, another journey through the eyewall awaits. The winds shift in the opposite direction and complete any unfinished destruction that the first half of the hurricane left undone.

In the case of Hurricane Michael, its path bore directly through Panama City, just across the lagoon to the east of the Fairfield. Subsequently, we didn't experience the trademark calm of the eye. Instead, we spent the majority of the storm in the eyewall itself as it passed directly over us.

The wind and rain started to lessen over the course of the next hour. Seeing the intensity beginning to die down, Jabin and I hatched a plan to venture out and survey the damage on our side of the bridge. We jumped back in my Suburban and drove toward the beach. What I saw confused me. Aside from the odd downed tree and light debris littering the streets, there simply wasn't much damage at all. It didn't make sense given the fact that a powerful Category 4 hurricane had just passed through the area minutes before.

Unbeknownst to me at the time, the worst of a Gulf hurricane's damage almost always manifests on the eastern side of the eye.

During our short jaunt around town, Jabin and I stopped to document downed limbs, a battered gas station, and some light flooding on a low-lying street. What was left of a McDonald's sign caught my eye. It's golden arches stood badly crumpled, barely recognizable as a universally known symbol for hamburgers and French fries. Closer to the beach, we found a partially destroyed boat storage facility that had taken a serious licking from Michael's winds. Before the storm hit, motorboats were stacked neatly inside the four-story warehouse. Now dozens of destroyed boats sat jumbled in a pile some twenty feet high. The ground was covered with razor sharp fiberglass fragments and outboard motor components. So numerous were the destroyed boats that I estimated the financial cost of the damage to be in the millions of dollars, at the least

With Panama City Beach feeling like a bust, we split up into our individual vehicles and caravanned over the lagoon into Panama City proper.

One of the strange paradoxes of storm coverage is that for most intents and purposes the greater the damage to the local community, the better your photos will be. As terrible as it sounds, if a community is spared, there are no dramatic images to be taken. There is no story. There is no reason for audiences to care. No one will buy that newspaper, click that link, or watch that TV segment. Simply put, bad news sells. The worse the news, "the better." Human nature's fascination with everyone else's suffering and tragedy provides a perverse incentive in this line of work. It's appallingly easy to drive through an area with little to no damage and catch yourself saying out loud "well, this sucks." This is an ugly reality of the news business. Unchecked, the appetite to witness destruction can turn you into a heartless vulture.

Entering Panama City was like traveling to another planet. The place looked like a bomb had gone off. Telephone poles were snapped at their bases. Roofs were ripped clean off houses and deposited into backyards. Fast food restaurants and auto parts stores lay in shambles. Feet of rainwater inundated low-lying neighborhoods. Some blocks along Panama City's main drag looked like the aftermath of the Hiroshima bombing in Word War II.

Reprising our convoy strategy that we employed in Houston, Jabin and I navigated our way through the wreckage. Downed power lines draped across the four-lane road, forcing us to detour through parking lots and across medians. All manner of sheet metal, plywood, and lumber littered the roadway. I scanned the road ahead intensely as I kept an eye out for boards with nails protruding out of them. This was not exactly a convenient time to suffer a flat tire. The roads were practically deserted. Even first responders had not yet begun to venture out.

A few blocks into Panama City, we pulled into the parking lot of a dumpy motel turned apartment building. The property was not in good shape. The wind had ripped the entire roof from the building and scattered the complex with shingles and roof truss debris. Residents milled around the outside of the complex, still in shock. With camera in hand, I approached a pony-tailed woman in her early forties. Her oversized t-shirt hung down just above her bare knees as she wiped tears from the corners of her eyes. She paced back and forth as she surveyed the damage to the room she had been renting. Suddenly she burst into tears. Her boyfriend put his arm around her and did the best he could to console her. I took a few discreet photos as the couple embraced. He wore a look of shock and sadness on his face as his girlfriend broke down in his arms. They both had somehow managed to survive the devastating storm.

Not wanting to intrude any further on the emotional moment, I moved on to explore more of the complex. Sections of balcony railing, a satellite television dish, and the odd piece of kitchen furniture littered the parking lot.

A muscular man with tattoos and a shaved head invited me up to his room on the second story. I followed him upstairs as he stepped into what was left of his apartment. The room was missing its roof and was absolutely trashed. It looked like it had been ransacked, the contents sprayed down with a firehose, ransacked again, and then buried under a pile of fibrous attic insulation. The wall's faux wood paneling had been peeled clean from the cinderblock walls. I raised my camera and took photos as he knelt in the middle of the room.

"Everything I own is trashed," he remarked. "My kids almost got sucked up out of their beds into the storm." He gestured toward another room where the remnants of a wooden bunk bed stood devoid of mattresses, sheets, or pillows. He poked around the room looking for anything that might be salvageable. A fresh gauze bandage was taped to his right arm where a piece of debris had sliced open his skin in the midst of the storm. The scene made me realize how grateful I was for the solid construction of the Fairfield. Given the sheer randomness of the storm's path, there was no reason I couldn't have been in his shoes.

Not wanting to overstay my welcome, I wished the man well and told him to hang in there. I knew the local government would partner with the American Red Cross, National Guard, and FEMA to set up shelters for those displaced by the storm. Hopefully the man could find his way there as he figured out what to do next.

Jabin and I pulled back out of the parking lot and continued down Highway 98. The journey was slow and tedious. The sheer quantity of downed power lines slowed our progress considerably. The destruction surrounding the road was total and staggering. It was hard to process. Nothing was left untouched by the overwhelming power of Michael's wind. I noticed a billboard bowed to the ground, its steel I-beam bent and twisted into a U-beam. I turned my attention back to the road and let out a gasp. A monstrous high tension electrical tower lay across an intersection up ahead. Our formidable SUVs were dwarfed by the impressive size of the toppled steel lattice, insulators, and the thick braided-metal transmission lines. The low-lying intersection where the tower came to rest was itself flooded with more than a foot of water deposited there by Michael's storm surge. I held my breath as we plowed ahead through the floodwaters. Thankfully, our SUVs were up for the challenge and made it through without issue.

I pulled onto the soggy grass median of Highway 98 and hopped out of the car eager to document the scene. For the next fifteen minutes I wandered the flooded intersection taking photos. Pickup trucks and sedans sat partially submerged, their rear tires sticking up above the waterline at an angle. I checked one truck's driver seat for passengers. The water came up to the top of its dashboard. Thankfully, it was empty. Whoever it belonged to had hopefully made it to safety.

As I sloshed through the intersection, I looked up at the low cloud ceiling moving quickly overhead. The rain had ceased. The atmospheric rotation had not. As the sun set, the sky turned a preternatural shade of purple. Damaged power lines, mangled pine trees, and blacked out traffic lights stood silhouetted against the ominous violet sky in a thoroughly apocalyptic scene. The only light visible to the human eye came from a line of vehicles attempting to cross the flooded intersection. Before too long, a Panama City Police cruiser parked itself at the edge of the water. Its flashing red and blue lights danced off the reflective lake of storm surge. With ambient light fading fast, Jabin and I decided to head back to the Fairfield.

Aside from the one police cruiser guarding the flooded intersection, there was a noticeable lack of law enforcement on the ground. The complete breakdown of the city's infrastructure compounded with the chaos of the natural order combined to create a wild, lawless vibe. While a part of me wanted to keep documenting the damage, a return to the familiarity of the hotel was a welcomed idea. Complicated by nightfall, our return journey through the devastation took almost twice as long as before. As we continued down Highway 98, we rolled through a law enforcement checkpoint that had sprung up in the middle of an intersection. Bathed in flickering blue light, two Panama City Police officers stood on the muddy median cradling assault rifles. The small show of force sought to deter any would-be looters from taking advantage of the chaos overnight. To my right, I noticed a U.S. Coast Guard helicopter hovering in place over a nearby neighborhood. The helicopter's red strobe light reflected in a flooded parking lot as it flashed on and off.

I felt a wave of frustration set in. Water rescues were happening just a stone's throw away, but it would be almost impossible to get there in one piece. Rather than risk losing my vehicle to floodwater, I reluctantly chose to play the long game. I had a feeling there would be plenty to shoot tomorrow.

After an hour of navigating obstacles along the road, we crossed the lagoon and arrived back at the Fairfield. My pal Brendan Smialowski of AFP met us in the parking lot. His hotel room at the Hilton Garden Inn in Panama City had been severely damaged by Hurricane Michael. Rather than hunker down in the lobby, he chose instead to ride out the storm in his rental car on the second story of a nearby concrete parking garage. Because Verizon's cell towers in the area had been destroyed by high winds, I was having trouble getting photos out. Brendan graciously allowed me to use his AT&T Wi-Fi hotspot to move a handful of frames to the Bloomberg desk in New York. Brendan's generosity saved me an hour in the car and a quarter tank of precious gasoline. If not for him, I would have had to drive west for 25 minutes to find the closest cell signal.

In return, I was glad to let him crash in my hotel room for the night. I booked my room at the Fairfield with two queen beds for just that purpose. Despite the fact that we were working for competing outlets, it felt good to help one another out. Whether someone is having Wi-Fi trouble, suffers a flat tire, or is running low on supplies, it doesn't matter. It could be any of us. Following a late dinner of dehydrated bacon jerky, peanut butter granola bars, and room temperature Lacroix, I crawled into bed, sweaty and exhausted.

My alarm buzzed the next morning before sunrise. I felt recharged from a solid six hours of sleep and was eager to get back into Panama City and document storm damage in the nice morning light. Highway 98 was still a mess, but the previous evening's practice helped me navigate the route in record time. I stuck my camera out the window and fired off a few frames of a National Guard Humvee on the road ahead of me. The rising sun glinted off its armored side panels as I overtook it.

Being surrounded by such widespread destruction presented a challenge. There was so much to shoot. Actually, there was *too* much. It was no easy task discriminating between what deserved to be photographed, and what I should pass up. Along the highway I shot a Ford dealership whose lot was crammed with sedans with shattered windshields. A few blocks down the road, a Waffle House restaurant with broken out windows caught my eye. The individual yellow blocks of its distinctive Scrabble letter sign were all missing, punched out by flying debris. Shards of window glass, laminated menus, ketchup bottles, and miniature syrup pitchers littered the booths and tables inside the beloved 24-hour breakfast joint.

Having documented a good amount of commercial damage, I turned my attention toward a residential neighborhood just south of Highway 98. I photographed a Panama City firetruck as it drove past a palm tree that was bent drastically toward the ground at a 45-degree angle. Nearby, a pair of men stood atop a home whose roof had been impacted by a piece of a fallen tree. They used chainsaws to attack the intertwined jumble of limbs and branches that mangled the roof's brown shingles. People were already starting to restore order.

Further down the block, I encountered a woman and her son who were trying to reach their house a little deeper in the neighborhood. Their family had evacuated inland before the hurricane made landfall. They were desperate to survey the damage and check on their dog who they had left behind inside the house. The route to their home was blocked by countless tall pine trees that had been toppled in the hurricane force winds. I followed behind them as they climbed over fallen tree trunks and lowered themselves down snapped branches. The scene looked like the aftermath of a lumberjack competition gone awry. Anywhere a tree had not fallen, the street was instead covered with pine branches and palm fronds. Search and rescue helicopters buzzed in the sky overheard as we bushwhacked our way toward the family's driveway. Given the sheer number of fallen trees, I didn't have much hope for the woman's house. The chance that her roof was going to be pulverized was very likely, in my estimation. As she reached her front yard, I heard the woman let out a shout of joy.

"It's a miracle," she exclaimed. "Our house is fine!"

The woman and her son rushed inside to retrieve the family dog. The pooch was overjoyed to see them. It bolted out the front door yelping joyfully at the sight of his family. The dog jumped up on its hind legs and began licking the woman's son, its tail wagging up a storm. Witnessing the joyful reunion was a welcomed break from the heaviness of the destruction all around me

I spent the rest of the morning wandering around town photographing downed utility poles, destroyed grocery stores, and similarly damaged fast food restaurants. Traffic on the roads had increased significantly as residents returned to check on their homes and businesses. With the power out, there were no working traffic lights in the entire city. Lines of cars clogged each intersection as they partook in customary post-storm disaster tourism. It was hard to fault them. Human nature is innately curious. I did however, worry about people recklessly burning up their precious gas reserves just so they could rubberneck around town. No doubt it would be many days until power was restored to Panama City. The electrical grid was an absolute mess. Not to mention, most gas stations had sustained considerable damage from either the wind, flooding, or a combination of the two. I felt a sense of guilty privilege knowing that I planned to catch a flight home from Pensacola later that evening.

Around lunch time, I started making my way back west toward Panama City Beach. I passed Ramon's Pizza and was relieved to see that it had been mostly spared from serious damage. Although I would have much preferred a warm pizza for lunch, I again indulged in jerky and granola for sustenance. Before returning to my hotel, I stopped at the small marina where I had enjoyed the sunset two nights before. The two-story apartment complex was in shambles. Debris of every imaginable sort littered the lawn and parking lot. Extensive roof damaged ensured that no one would be living there for quite some time, or maybe ever again. I walked around to the lagoon and took in a wild scene. A huge sailboat lay beached on the grassy shore. Its mast jutted into the blue sky at an angle far off-kilter from the norm. While staring at the boat, a deep voice took me by surprise.

"Do you know how that boat got there?"

I turned and laid eyes on a shirtless man sitting nearby in a white plastic lawn chair. He squinted at me from his chair with a hint of suspicion.

"The hurricane?" I responded with a guess.

"Nope," he said after a short pause.

The sunburned man told me that, apparently, the owner of the sailboat thought he could ride out the storm in the middle of the lagoon. Before too long, he realized he had made a big mistake. He set his course for shore and managed to beach the boat where it rested.

I raised my eyebrows. "Do you know where he went?"

"No idea," the man responded. He turned and pointed toward another large yacht that had crashed into the marina's main dock. "There's a dead family of four inside that boat," he said grimly. "They weren't so lucky."

I turned and spotted the boat where he had pointed. The thought of four dead bodies baking inside the cabin of the craft repulsed me. I thought I might throw up. Slowly, I made my way around the partially-collapsed dock. Half-submerged motorboats and a mass of lumber, Styrofoam, and other flotsam bobbed in the lagoon. I had zero desire to photograph a boat full of dead people. I desperately wanted to doubt the man's story. If four people had died, wouldn't an ambulance be here? Wouldn't there be crime scene tape strung up around the boat?

I finished my walk around the marina with a knot in my stomach. I could barely focus on making photos as the wrecked boat invaded my thoughts. The jarring reality of death and tragedy had awakened me from the journalistic trance I had occupied for the past 3 days. Hiding behind a camera was a very effective way to insulate myself from the emotional toll of everything going on around me. I climbed back into my Suburban sobered, shaken, and more ready than ever to get back home and hug my two little boys. In addition to the emotional and physical stress of hurricane coverage at the present moment, I was in the middle of brutal divorce proceedings back in Kentucky. I was mourning the loss of my own family of four.

I ran into Jabin on the way back to my hotel and gave him my supply of extra gasoline. The *Washington Post* wanted him to stay for a few more days, he told me. With my return to civilization imminent, I knew that he would make much better use of the extra fuel than I would. We hugged and I told him to stay safe. At the Fairfield, I retrieved the rest of my stuff from the room and packed up my car. The parking lot of the hotel had already started to empty out. NBC's satellite truck was gone. I got the feeling that the national media was already moving on to other stories. "That was fast," I thought to myself.

As I pulled out of the parking lot, an amber warning light caught my eye on the dashboard. The low tire pressure indicator was illuminated.

"Shit!" I exclaimed loudly.

I was going to have a flat tire soon. I thought back over the course of the morning. There were any number of places where I could have driven over a nail. I was actually kind of surprised it hadn't happened sooner. With a flight to catch and the power still out in Panama City Beach, I decided to try and make it back to Pensacola on the leaking tire. I said a quick prayer as I merged and accelerated onto the highway. I checked the tire pressure obsessively as I drove. It seemed to be holding air as long as I drove at high speed. Any time I stopped for a red light, however, the tire pressure gauge on the dashboard lost another couple pounds per square inch.

Half an hour later, I made it back into cell coverage. My phone blew up with 2 days-worth of texts, emails, missed call notifications, and voicemails. Despite the stress of my slowly leaking tire, it was good to be back in civilization. Somehow, I managed to nurse my Suburban with the punctured tire back to the Pensacola Airport. Against all odds I pulled into the rental car return lane in one piece. This Suburban had paid its dues and successfully transported me through Michael, a hurricane for the record books. While stressful, dangerous, and emotionally exhausting, covering these storms is without a doubt an adventure.

Strangely enough, the act of leaving a disaster zone is by far the hardest part for me. On the one hand, I'm more than eager to return home to my two sons. By day two of storm coverage, I'm already missing my favorite parts of being a father. I miss the wrestling, the Nerf gun wars, bedtime stories, and goodnight kisses. Selfishly, I also miss air conditioning, hot showers, and warm food. But on the other hand, I feel as though I'm abandoning a community that I've formed an emotional bond with in a short period of time.

However fleeting and cursory my presence in these communities may be, I seem to form a kinship with those I come in contact with before, during, and after the storm. I deeply admire the EMS, firefighters, police, and National Guard members who stand ready to respond in the wake of the disaster. Rather than flee to safety, these first responders routinely choose to stay and fight for their communities. They sleep on cots in gymnasiums and eat dehydrated meals for days at a time. They are in it for the long haul.

Skipping town before the dust has even settled can be quite jarring. It leaves me feeling a sense of guilt for failing to stand by the communities that I become attached to. In some ways it feels like a betrayal. Regrettably, this is the nature of the job. News photographers parachute into the middle of a disaster, find story-telling images in the midst of the chaos, then send their photos to the outside world. The attention spans of Americans and those in the national media can be very short. With the exception of disasters like Hurricane Katrina, national news organizations tend to move on to other stories by the first or second day after landfall.

As I flew home from Pensacola, I experienced a number of conflicting emotions. I was grateful to have emerged from such a monster storm in one piece. The opportunity to be a journalist and tell stories to the world is a real privilege. I felt a sense of accomplishment having completed my mission successfully. My photos were appearing in publications all around the nation and the world. My fellow Americans were being made aware of the needs of their countrymen.

I also felt guilty.

While the storm itself had passed, I was leaving just as the going was about to get tough for Panama City and Florida's Gulf Coast. I was only one man, but I wish I had the means and the time to stay behind and help out in some way.

I arrived back to my house in Louisville and collapsed into bed. As I drifted off to sleep, my thoughts turned to the good people of Panama City. They would endure months of rebuilding and restoration. A long, hard road lay ahead of them. Despite the challenges, I knew that the community had what it took to get the job done. With hard work, determination, and patience, they would rebuild.

Scan this code for photos from Chapter 6

7. THE HEARTLAND

We landed on the surface with a crash. The helicopter fuselage began rapidly taking on water. In a matter of seconds, the water level had risen from my feet to my knees, and then up to my neck. The navy-blue coveralls I was wearing clung to my skin as they quickly became saturated. Tilting my head toward the ceiling, I took one last gasp for air as the fuselage filled completely with water. I opened my eyes and took in the scene inside the dim interior of the helicopter. The passenger cabin was completely submerged. To make matters worse, I began to feel the fuselage list onto its starboard side. I felt the uncomfortable sting of water as it rushed up my nose and into my nasal cavity. The compartment had rolled 180 degrees and was floating inverted. My heart continued to pound out of my chest. There I was, strapped into a seat, upside down in a submerged, confined space. I reached instinctively to unbuckle myself from the aviation harness. As my hand grasped the metal seatbelt buckle, I remembered my classroom training. In the unlikely event of a water landing, do not attempt to free yourself from your safety restraint until you've secured a path of egress from the aircraft. Over-riding my innate survival instinct, I let go of the seatbelt and instead yanked on the emergency exit handle of the window beside me. Using my still-buckled seatbelt as leverage, I bashed out the window with my shoulder. The clear acrylic pane dislodged in one piece and floated lazily away outside the fuselage.

I was starting to run out of air. My body's demand for oxygen was heightened by my pounding heartbeat. I was in fight or flight mode and needed to escape this death trap as soon as humanly possible. My lungs started screaming for breath. They were sending desperate signals to my brain.

We need oxygen, my lungs demanded.

Overruled.

Giving in to the reflex to take a deep breath would drown myself in no time. I fumbled with the three-point restraint for a moment as I tried to free myself from the seat. At last, I felt the gratifying click of my seat belt coming loose. The thick nylon belt that kept me strapped firmly into my seat at impact gave way. My body started to float toward the middle of the fuselage like an astronaut in orbit. I looked around me and noticed that my fellow passengers were all conscious and working to free themselves in a similar manner. Our classroom training had paid off.

Grabbing for the windowsill beside my seat, I pulled myself through the small opening and escaped the submerged tomb. I paused for a second to try and get my bearings. With the helicopter fuselage having flipped upside down on impact, I needed to make sure that I didn't mistakenly swim the wrong way to the surface. To dive deeper into the depths in which we had already submerged would be a huge mistake. Normally, I would swim *up* to reach oxygen. But because we had inverted, I needed to swim in the opposite direction. I swam down.

Again, I had to overpower my instincts and trust my rational faculties. I kicked my legs violently and swam down, toward the surface. With a final kick I rocketed out of the water and took a gasp of sweet, sweet oxygen. I gasped again, filling my deflated lungs with air.

YES! I nearly yelled out loud.

I made it out. I continued to breathe greedily and started treading water. Looking around me, I noticed a few of my fellow passengers from the helicopter cabin had made it out ahead of me. A few others broke the surface of the water as I watched. We took a quick headcount, calling out numbers that had been assigned to use before we buckled ourselves into our seats. All present and accounted for. A blaze orange survival raft bobbed in the water a short distance away. My soaked coveralls clung to my limbs and weighed me down as I swam for the octagonal life raft. I swung a leg over the side and managed to pull myself up and out of the water. Another passenger climbed aboard. Together we helped pull our fellow swimmers into the craft. Once safely in the life raft, we sat with our backs to the gunwales and attempted to catch our breath as we bobbed up and down.

"Good job, everyone" our instructor's voice called out from the side of the pool deck. "Well done."

I nodded my head in agreement and looked around the raft as the others broke out into big smiles. We all had just passed the final phase of Helicopter Underwater Egress Training, or HUET.

With the test complete, I climbed out of the pool and back onto dry ground. I toweled off and watched as the course instructors began to winch the dummy helicopter fuselage, from which we had just escaped, up from the bottom of the pool. My training had taken place at the Shell Oil

Training Center in Robert, Louisiana. I changed out of my soaked coveralls and back into dry clothes before receiving my HUET certification card. The next day I would board a real helicopter and fly 120 miles out to the middle of the Gulf of Mexico on assignment for Bloomberg News. My destination was Jack/St. Malo, one of Chevron's largest deepwater oil platforms. Passing HUET was a prerequisite before I could make the ninety-minute trip from New Orleans to the floating platform.

The following morning, I drove to the heliport at New Orleans International Airport and boarded a Red, White, and Blue AgustaWestland AW139 transport helicopter for our nearly 250-mile roundtrip flight between New Orleans and the Gulf of Mexico. The AW139 is a 17 seat, twin engine, 1530 horsepower helicopter capable of flying some 776 miles on a single tank of fuel. We lifted off from the helipad and turned south toward the coast. I watched out the window as our flight path followed Bayou Lafourche toward the Gulf. Commercial shrimping boats motored up and down the bayou, coming and going from port. Upon reaching Port Fourchon, the Gulf of Mexico appeared on the horizon. We passed over the port where dozens and dozens of oil industry support ships sat docked. I noticed that many of the vessels had their own helipads onboard and took note in case we needed to make an emergency landing. As soon as we passed Grand Isle we were "feet wet" over the Gulf. My thoughts returned to the HUET training course I had completed in the pool the previous day. I felt a sense of calm confidence replace any anxiety I had previously felt about my long helicopter flight. Thanks to my training, I knew exactly what to do if we ended up ditching in the Gulf of Mexico.

I watched out the starboard window as modest sized oil platforms began to appear close to shore. A vast network of oil pipelines converges along the southern coast of Louisiana. These pipelines bring crude oil in from the Gulf and transport it to refineries further inland. According to NOAA, some 3200 active drilling rigs, production platforms, and other structures stand in the Gulf at present day. Undersea drilling began in the Gulf of Mexico in 1942. Because the oil deposits closest to shore have long since been tapped, oil exploration has been forced further and further out into the Gulf. We spent about an hour over the water and passed a handful of resupply ships on their way to and from various platform operations. The helicopter began a steady descent as we drew near to our destination. Soon, the Jack/St. Malo platform came into view on the horizon. At altitude, the platform seemed dwarfed by the expanse of the Gulf of Mexico that stretched as far as the eye could see. I remember initially feeling underwhelmed by my first impression of the structure. The closer we got, however, the more I began to appreciate the scale of the behemoth vessel. The helicopter pilot's voice came over my headset and informed me that he would circle as many times as I needed in order to get good aerial photos. I covered all my bases with a collection tight, medium, and wide shots of the platform both backlit and in full sun. Content that I had made some nice frames, I clicked on my headset microphone and told the pilot that we were good to land.

"Roger that," he replied.

We descended toward a pair of octagonal helicopter pads, each marked with a big uppercase letter H in the center. The impressive platform sat on four enormous pylons that kept the vessel afloat. A red and white scaffolded metal structure reminiscent of a television broadcasting tower jutted away diagonally from the platform. An oil flare burned brightly at its apex. Atop the platform sat what was essentially a miniature refinery that pumped crude oil up from the bottom of the ocean and prepared it for its journey back to Louisiana through an undersea pipeline. A small yellow crane used to load and unload supply vessels jutted out from the side of the platform opposite the oil flare. I continued to shoot out the window as our pilot skillfully landed us on one of the helipads. The rotors of the helicopter spun lazily and eventually came to a stop as the aircraft's twin engines powered down.

A group of men wearing hard-hats and dressed in blue coveralls emerged from a doorway and made their way toward our helipad. One of them grabbed the door of the helicopter and slid it open.

"Welcome aboard Jack/St. Malo," he called.

"Thank you, it's good to be here," I replied as I removed my aviation headset and hopped out onto the helipad.

My reporter and I were led toward the door from which our welcoming committee had emerged. The first order of business was an extensive safety briefing and power point presentation in a small, windowless boardroom. We stepped inside and descended a flight of stairs to the main deck. Most of the platform's interior consisted of long fluorescent-lit corridors plastered with signs, safety bulletins, and corporate wellness initiative posters.

Following our initial briefing, the platform manager led us on a tour of the vessel's key production areas. Our first stop was in the platform's control room. A large bank of computer monitors supplied information about the platform's vital systems in real time. Next, we poked our heads inside a bunk room in the platform's living quarters. With two people living in each room, it reminded me of my freshman dorm at Western Kentucky University. Offshore workers typically worked 14 days on, and 14 days off and were handsomely compensated for their work. Similarly, supply vessel workers pulled shifts of 30 days at sea, and 30 days off. *I could get used to that.*

After departing the living quarters, our tour group headed topside. For the next forty-five minutes, we were lead through a dizzying maze of pressurized pipes, pumps, boilers, valves, walkways, staircases, and cranes. The sheer amount of infrastructure that was crammed into such a small footprint amazed me endlessly. Near the edge of the platform, I peered over the railing down at a huge support vessel that was floating a few yards away from the southeastern pylon. A steady wake emitted from its stern as the boat's captain utilized the vessel's propulsion to prevent it from smashing into the towering platform. I marveled as a crane operator onboard the platform picked up corrugated shipping containers full of food, supplies, and other required materials from the deck of the ship below.

The overcast skies that hung low over the ground during our helicopter ride had since dissipated, bathing us in warm sunlight. The deep, clear saltwater of the Gulf radiated a brilliant color blue that I had never before witnessed. Its rich hue was foreign to me, but all at once familiar at the same time. It was as if I was witnessing the truest shade of sapphire that could exist in the natural world. As if every blue river and sky was pointing to this previously unseen glorious shade of ultramarine.

I stood transfixed by the Gulf. The surface of the sea practically boiled with marine life. The water was teeming with schools of fish, tuna, dolphins, and the occasional shark. I felt as if I was witnessing what the natural world would look like if human beings, the apex predators that we are, suddenly ceased to exist. I tried in vain to capture the brilliance of the scene below me with my camera. It started to become apparent, however, that this was one of those moments in life that a camera simply couldn't capture. I hung my camera back on my shoulder and tried my best to soak in the scene. With the sun on my face, I took a deep breath of salty air, and feasted my eyes on the glorious biodiversity of the scene ten stories beneath where I stood.

Our tour continued around the top deck of the oil platform. In turn, I continued to be amazed by the engineering spectacle all around me. The tour descended to a lower deck where we were afforded a view of the suspension lines that tethered the platform to the bottom of the ocean floor. The steel cables extended some seven thousand feet below the surface of the water. Upon reaching sediment, the pipeline extended another staggering 19,500 feet to the Jack and St. Malo oil deposits. Chevron's petroleum engineers had managed to extract natural deposits of crude oil an additional four miles beneath ocean floor. I marveled at the fact that a gallon of petroleum could travel such an incredible distance from the earth's crust, up to the platform, across a pipeline, through a refinery, and eventually end up at a gas station. All the while costing me less than $2.50 per gallon after taxes.

We ascended back upstairs to the top deck. The next stop on our tour found us observing a pair of Chevron engineers as they collected a sample of crude oil for scientific testing. Throughout my time above deck, two platform workers shadowed me with air quality instruments in hand. They constantly measured the atmosphere around me for any sign of irregularities that might indicate a methane leak or other such occupational hazard. If we happened upon on accidental discharge of flammable gas, there was a chance that the electrical circuits inside my two cameras could ignite the cloud of gas and trigger a devastating explosion. My thoughts turned to the Deepwater Horizon disaster that had occurred in 2011. It would be best to avoid a repeat, if possible.

With the noonday sun beating down on us, we retreated inside for lunch in the galley. A cafeteria style buffet featuring BBQ pork, potato salad, and coleslaw awaited us as we filed in to dine with the rest of the platform's day shift. Television screens mounted on the galley walls beamed in reminders of home in the form of cable news, ESPN, and Discovery Channel programming via satellite dish. After lunch, it was time to fly back to New Orleans. My reporter and I bid farewell to our hosts and made our way back to the helicopter. Thankfully, it was right where we had left it a few hours earlier. As much as I had enjoyed my visit, I had no interest in sticking around for an additional 13 days like the rest of the crew would be doing.

I shook hands with the platform superintendent and climbed back aboard the AW139. As the helicopter's main rotor spun up, our tour guides disappeared back inside the same door from which they had emerged during our arrival. Shortly thereafter, we were airborne. The behemoth oil platform quickly shrunk in size, eventually fading from view completely over the horizon. An hour later we passed back over Port Fourchon and Grand Isle. Some 30 minutes later we touched down at New Orleans International and taxied to the heliport at the northwest corner of the airport. It was good to be back on terra firma.

The following morning, I stopped to top off my rental car with gas on my way back to the airport. I waited impatiently for the pump to fill my gas tank, already taking for granted the dizzying amount of infrastructure required to extract, transport, and refine each gallon of fuel flowing into my vehicle.

While some of my assignments in the heartland took me a thousand miles away from Louisville, others were practically next-door, across state lines. Such was the case in the summer of 2016 when I traveled to West Virginia to photograph a *New York Times* business section story about the future of the state's struggling coal industry. My first stop was one of the largest surface mines in The Mountain State.

I sat in the front passenger seat of a Ford Super Duty pickup truck. The vehicle's diesel engine growled as it battled gravity up and down the winding mountain roads. Its tires kicked up thick clouds of dust that coated the exterior of the pickup, effectively transforming its factory paint job from glossy white to a flat brown color. My tour guide, the superintendent of the Hobet surface mine, sat in the driver's seat. Named for its original owners, Homer and Betty Nutter, Hobet was easily West Virginia's highest-producing coal mine in its heyday. These days, however, coal production had slowed to little more than a trickle. The sprawling strip job located near Danville, West Virginia, was so extensive that it took us more than half an hour to drive across the property. The coal deposits closest to Route 119 had been mined out decades earlier. For much of the drive, we rumbled along bumpy haulage roads wide enough for massive dump trucks to pass one another on their way to and from the facility's railroad load-out. With production declining steeply, it was determined to be more economic to transport what little coal was still being mined via conveyor. A network of covered material handling belts stretched for miles across the facility before finally descending to the load out located on the Little Coal River.

We passed an empty single-cab pickup that guarded a gravel road near the summit of the mountain. The words on the side of the decoy truck read "Security." It looked like even the guards had been laid off along with almost all the facility's miners. The superintendent's truck crawled up above the tree line and into the area of the mine that had been most recently stripped of its coal. Remnants of the demolished mountain top, referred to in the industry as "overburden," stretched to the horizon. Years of mountaintop removal had flattened the peaks into an otherworldly mesa. Pulverized boulders filled valleys and hollows. Miles of sheer rock face, called highwall, lined the top of the mountain. Countless tons of valuable coal had been stripped from the summit over the years. With the dynamite blasts having long since faded, an eerie stillness sat over the barren moonscape. Across a valley of boulders sat a derelict dump truck still wearing its original grey Hobet Mine paint scheme. The heavy mover's paint was slowly disintegrating and chipping away to reveal an ever-growing patchwork quilt of rust. The once proud earth mover's tires sat crumpled and deflated, causing the truck to lean mournfully to one side. Even without fully inflated tires to boost its profile, the vehicle stood about the same height as a two-story house. Surveying its sad condition, I wondered to myself if the machine would ever make it off the mountain in one piece. It was much more likely to be carted away little by little at the hands of illicit mountain scrappers looking for a quick buck.

The only other piece of mining equipment that remained behind was a massive dragline nicknamed "Big John." Standing some 18 stories tall, the towering electric shovel overlooked one of the valleys it had just filled and smoothed over with excess overburden. The dragline's power cable was thousands of feet long. Its thick electrical line was suspended fifteen feet above the ground by a series of metal poles cemented into worn-out dump truck tires. Having spent many years demolishing mountain peaks, the mighty dragline was now tasked with putting things back in their place as best it could. Big John's crane-like boom extended far into the air. Beneath the boom hung a ginormous steel excavating bucket. This attachment, which was designed to scoop 80 cubic yards of earth inside its toothy metal mouth, seemed to be large enough to park a UPS delivery truck inside.

The superintendent stopped his pickup and let me hop out beside the dragline. I peered up toward the side of the massive structure. Big John certainly lived up to its name. My six-foot three frame was dwarfed by the contraption. The fact that human beings could design, construct, and transport such a gigantic machine was a marvel to me. Any time a dragline needed to shift its position, a pair of hydraulic legs would spring into action and move the machine a few inches at a time. With permission from the superintendent, I climbed up a set of staircases that ascended the side of the superstructure. After traversing multiple flights of exterior steps, I stopped to photograph the former strip mine laid out in front of me. The sun was setting on the vast un-reclaimed desert of stone.

I took a few photos of the altered landscape and descended back down to the ground. A new startup coal company had purchased Hobet as a part of a bold plan to kickstart a renewal in environmentally conscious coal mining. For every ton of West Virginia coal that the company mined, a tree would be planted here on the former surface mine to offset the carbon dioxide emissions of the coal that was sold. Most of the coal in West Virginia was steam coal used to generate electricity at power plants situated up and down the nearby Ohio River. The southern coal fields' black diamonds were regularly transported to customers outside the region by rail, truck, and barge. With Big John's tenure at Hobet finally ending, the dragline had been put up for sale. An international buyer in Morocco had expressed interest in purchasing and disassembling the dragline piece by piece for shipment overseas. If the deal fell through, however, Big John's survival would be in question.

The foreman and I drove back toward civilization as the sun ducked below the few surrounding mountaintops that hadn't been flattened for coal's sake. Soft rays of pink sunlight, diffused and filtered through layers of humid summer air in the atmosphere, bathed the unnaturally smooth grass hillsides of Hobet's reclaimed areas. I watched as Big John faded from view in the rear mirror. The dragline was well into the twilight of its many decades of productivity. Like it or not, this vast area had been a workplace for hundreds of miners over the years. It had produced paychecks every two weeks for households all over southern West Virginia. Its economic impact spread out to supporting industries, local retailers, gas stations, restaurants, and bars. Outside the mine office I watched as a family of five deer ascended in a row to the top of a coal pile. Despite the surface mine's devastating effect on the natural landscape over the years, nature was beginning to reclaim what was once hers.

A week prior to setting foot on Hobet, I visited another mine, this one a few hours' drive away in northern West Virginia. My route took me along a winding two lane road through the mountains. Thick banks of fog filled the valleys. My headlights fought to pierce through the dense clouds of condensation that hung suspended in mid-air. The route roughly paralleled Dunkard Creek, a tributary of the Monongahela River west of Morgantown. Occasionally the road would cross paths with a set of rusty railroad tracks that traveled to the handful of coal mines that still operated deep in the hollows. The railroad line crossed a meandering stream via girder plate bridge and made a sharp curve to the south. Just down the line was one of the region's last functioning underground coal mines: Federal No. 2.

I followed the railroad until it arrived at the historic deep mine near Fairview, West Virginia. Nestled in a valley between two hills, the mine portal and prep plant were built adjacent to one another. An empty coal train sat parked underneath a loadout tower in the middle of the mine. Beneath a maze of blue-painted tubular steel conveyor belts sat towering mounds of freshly-mined coal. The jet-black stockpiles contrasted against the morning's blue skies and the lush green vegetation of the valley. As evidenced by the soaring peaks of black diamonds outside the prep plant, finding and extracting the coal was not the hard part. The challenge, instead, was securing buyers for the fuel source. With many steam-generated power plants in the region switching to natural gas, the market was saturated with unwanted Appalachian coal. Even within the industry, coal from the Illinois basin in the Midwest and Powder River basin in Wyoming was significantly less costly to excavate in comparison. With the help of massive excavators, companies out west were able to simply peel back the shallow layer of topsoil to reach massive coal deposits buried just under the surface.

The miners at Federal No. 2 did not have such luxury. Instead of accessing the coal from above, they had to tunnel down thousands of feet and then attack coal seams from the side. This dangerous and time-intensive method naturally drove up the cost of each ton of coal that they mined.

I pulled into the parking lot outside the mine office for my safety orientation. It was full of big pickup trucks, many customized with huge tires, lift kits, and other after-market accessories. My reporter and I were given a simple overview of the long wall mining process and instructed what to do in the event of an explosion or collapse. Following the briefing, we suited up in our protective gear. I stepped into a pair of coveralls and pulled the front zipper up to my neck. Long strands of fluorescent yellow and silver reflective material had been stitched along the arms and legs of the coveralls for maximum visibility. After lacing up a pair a steel toed boots, I donned a sturdy reflective belt with an emergency breathing apparatus hanging from one side. Housed inside a hard plastic protective case, the breathing mask would theoretically supply me with enough oxygen to escape from underground in case of an emergency. On my way out the door, I slipped on a pair of safety glasses and placed a white miner's hat on top of my head. The low-profile hard hat had a flashlight fastened to the front to aid visibility in the mine. A thick-gauge rubber power cable ran from the flashlight over the top of the hard hat and down the back of my coveralls to a battery pack mounted on my reflective belt.

The day's schedule called for us to meet up with the CEO of the mining company and descend into the mine to see its operations firsthand. It would be the new CEO's first time in an active underground mine, as well as my own. My reporter and I approached the group of men who would be taking us beneath the surface. The veteran miners stood in a semi-circle near the entrance to the mine shaft. One by one, the men looked me in the eye and greeted me with a firm handshake. The intentionality of their greeting inspired a sense of confidence in me that these men knew what they were doing. In contrast to my own attire, these miners' coveralls were broken in, faded and worn from many 12-hour shifts underground harvesting coal. Their hardhats were plastered with stickers broadcasting their love of God, country, and of course, coal. The cleanliness of my equipment and the two cameras hanging from my left shoulder clearly broadcasted my status as an outsider. Still, I was grateful to be in the company of such experienced miners for this journey toward the center of the earth.

After our handshakes were complete, we moved as a group toward the massive mine shaft elevator that would be transporting us 734 feet underground. I stepped into the large industrial lift and turned to face the entrance through which I had just come. One of the miners slammed a metal door shut and pressed a glowing button on the elevator's well-worn control panel. With a jolt, we began to descend through the shaft at a steady pace. I watched as the sky disappeared from view, and darkness enveloped the elevator car. One by one, our guides reached up and flipped on the headlamps mounted to their miner's hats. Following their lead, I reached up to do the same. After fumbling in the dark for a few seconds I finally managed to click my own light on as well. The concentrated beam of light emitting from my forehead appeared on the elevator wall in front of me. Some time passed as we continued our descent down into the mine. A second jolt signaled that we had arrived at our destination some seventy stories underground.

Our group filed out of the elevator and into a dimly lit horizontal mine shaft. The air temperature was noticeably cooler than it had been on the surface. The constant 57 degrees sent a shiver up my spine as my body acclimated to the new environment. I did my best to resist the natural urge to look others in the face, so as not to shine my flashlight directly in their eyes. To alleviate this problem, I mimicked the veteran coal miners by tilting my miner's hat slightly askew and glancing out of the side of my eyes when I needed to look at someone. Waiting outside the elevator shaft was a small mine train, or "man trip" as the miners call them. The train's cars were a little longer than a golf cart and hugged the ground. A catenary pole near the operator's seat extended up at an angle to an electrical wire that ran the length of the mine's ceiling. We piled in, and the self-propelled man trip rolled forward down the narrow-gauge tracks. Sparsely spaced wooden crossties kept the skinny rails aligned as we zipped along the route.

The height of the shaft's ceiling decreased ever so slightly as we put distance between ourselves and the elevator shaft. Every few feet, thick bolts anchored metal plates into the roof and walls of the mine. This reinforcement formed a spiderweb support network that was successful in preventing roof cave-ins and similar calamities. In addition to our head room decreasing, the wall-mounted electric lamps soon ceased as well. The train's pair of small headlights would provide our only illumination for the duration of our journey. Every inch of rock was covered with a thick layer of limestone dust. This federally-mandated practice helped prevent combustible coal dust from hanging around the air inside the mine. The whiteout effect of the dust paired with the natural chill of the air reminded me of careening through the snow atop my family's flexible flyer sled as a young boy. In addition to the ubiquitous limestone, a steady flow of ventilated air permeated the shaft. Massive fans back on the surface pushed fresh air down into the mine while others sucked the used air back out.

The man trip continued its way over the rickety track system. Along the route we passed many side tunnels on our left and right that lead to other seams that had long-since been mined out. Given Federal No. 2's relative old age as a mine, her miners had to endure a 45-minute man trip journey down the shaft to reach the nearest coal seam. Just like us, the coal also had to make the same trip back to the shaft where we started.

Another tunnel ran parallel to the man trip tracks. It housed a conveyor that transported tons of coal along heavy-duty rubber belts. Once the coal had completed its journey back to the elevator shaft, it was loaded into a giant bucket, or skip, and hoisted up to the surface. From there the coal was fed via another set of conveyors to the prep plant adjacent the mine portal. The massive, windowless building towered some fifty feet over the mine property. Three sets of tubular conveyors fed in and out of the plant. One belt brought the raw, unprocessed coal in from the mine's skip. Another transported rock, sediment, and waste material culled from the coal to an enormous retention pond located atop one of the nearby hillsides. The third conveyor transported processed coal to a set of tipples that sat elevated over the coal yard. Beneath each tipple sat an enormous pile of coal waiting to be sold on the market. Tracked bulldozers climbed methodically to the top of each stockpile and pushed the newly-dumped coal down the pile to make room for more. Once the coal was sold, it was loaded into open-top railroad hopper cars via a system of underground conveyor belts and gravity-fed load outs that straddled the railroad tracks. Inside the prep plant, several different processes prepared the coal for market. First, it was separated from any excess non-coal geologic matter that made the trip up to the surface. Next, the coal would be cleansed of any impurities with the help of chemicals. Finally, it would be run through a crusher and pulverized into smaller pieces for shipping.

Our ride continued deeper and deeper into the mine. Aside from the occasional twist and turn in the track, it was hard to differentiate where exactly we were. Judging by our rate of speed, I guessed that we must have traveled at least five miles since we boarded the man trip. Occasionally, the power cable above us would end and a new electrical circuit would begin. A shower of sparks flew as the operator guided the catenary pole from one power cable to the next. Upon each successful transition, the man trip would lurch forward and accelerate back up to top speed. We passed many side shafts with track spurs that led into the various dark tunnels. Reflective red emergency signs marked refuge and escape shafts in case of a cave in or explosion. I tried to make a mental note of these locations in my memory in case there was a disaster. Each escape shaft was stocked with a stash of first aid kits, food, water, and spare rescue breathers.

Eventually, we reached the coal seam that the company was relying on to keep the mine financially viable. I exited the man trip and ducked down to avoid hitting my head on the low ceiling of the mine. Just down a corridor from the main shaft stood the long wall mining machinery that so effortlessly stripped coal from the underground seam. Huge metal teeth rotating in a circular motion dug into the soft carbon and deposited the mineral onto a conveyor belt. A hefty steel roof above the machine's control panel kept any collapsing rock from injuring the miners below. As the long wall machine moved along the seam, the tunnel behind it methodically collapsed with the coal layer now missing from its strata. The technical challenge of making clean photographs underground was far outweighed by the novelty of witnessing the mining operation firsthand. We spent a good amount of time observing modern coal mining up close.

One of our guides went into detail explaining the ins-and-outs of the process as another pair of miners turned the man trip around for our return journey to the elevator shaft. The men stood next to the car, silhouetted by the train's headlights. Their headlamps glinted off the metal tracks on the mine floor as they waited to take us back to the elevator shaft. I took a photo and captured the proud posture of these men at work.

The ride back on the man trip seemed to pass a bit quicker than before. Perhaps because anticipation has a way of stretching out time. The novelty of the experience began to wear off as we retraced our earlier path. For the first time that morning, I started to really consider just how much rock lay between me and the surface. It was hard to wrap my head around how far underground I was. The distance between myself and the surface was roughly equivalent to the height of the Golden Gate Bridge. If a cave-in or explosion were to occur, it would likely be days before help would arrive. I thought about what it would be like to scramble for safety toward one of the pitch-dark rescue shafts. I imagined sheltering in place trusting that help was on the way, sitting, waiting, praying, and thinking of my two sons back home. Eventually, I emerged from my worst-case scenario fantasy and came back to reality. Despite being an un-naturally far distance below the surface of the earth, I was comforted by the competency of the men around me.

On the afternoon of April 5, 2010, I was sitting at the *New York Times'* desk in the White House briefing room. President Obama had no more public events for the day, but the press pool still stuck around in case that were to change unexpectedly. A small TV in the White House briefing room was tuned to CNN to monitor any breaking news. I looked up from my computer as the mid-day anchor's words caught my attention. A coal mine explosion had occurred at an underground coal mine in south-central West Virginia. Preliminary reports from local media outlets estimated that up to a dozen miners were trapped. Their conditions were unknown.

Images on the screen showed a mine rescue truck accelerating up a steep gravel road toward the entrance of the Upper Big Branch mine in Montcoal, WV. I pried my eyes away from CNN in time to see an email pop up in my inbox. One of my photo editors from the national desk was asking how soon I could get to West Virginia. I immediately began packing up my things and abandoned my post at the White House. I caught the Metro back to Arlington, threw a few changes of clean clothes in a backpack, and set out for West Virginia.

I listened to the radio over the course of my 5-hour drive across Interstate 64. As the miles passed, the news out of Montcoal got worse and worse. Some 31 men had been working the day shift when the incident occurred. An initial search-and-rescue mission into the mine had turned up only handful of bodies. Many were still missing and unaccounted for. My stomach churned at the news. By the time I crossed the West Virginia state line, the sun had set. Darkness enveloped the rolling foothills of the Appalachian Mountain range. The closest hotel to Montcoal was in the city of Beckley. The town is located along I-64 and acts as a commercial hub for those who live and work in the coal fields surrounding it. I spent the night at a motel near the interstate and awoke early the next day. Although Montcoal was only 25 miles away as the crow flies, it took nearly an hour to reach by car. The two-lane road twisted and turned sharply as it followed ridge lines and creeks down into the Coal River valley. Having lost cell service shortly after I left the hotel, the drive to Montcoal felt increasingly isolating. Sometime later, I pulled into the Marsh Fork elementary school. The local community had asked media to stage there in order to receive updates about the ongoing search and rescue operations in the mine. The fledgling elementary school sat precariously beneath a massive coal refuse pond on the mountaintop nearest to it. A grassy earthen damn held back tens of thousands of gallons of rock, sediment, and toxic chemicals from spilling into the valley below.

By the time I arrived, the school parking lot was overflowing with media satellite trucks from all the major networks. The trucks sat parked with their broadcast dishes pointed skyward. ABC, NBC, CBS, CNN, and Fox News were all there along with numerous local affiliates from Charleston, the state capital. I stepped inside the school and found a large gathering of reporters being briefed by local law enforcement officials in the cafeteria. Local residents had stopped by to drop off food, drinks, and snacks as a welcome gift for the steady stream of media that continued to arrive on the scene. By the end of the day, the lunchroom tables were overflowing with bags of chips, cookies and the like. I was struck by how welcoming the community was to a bunch of strangers like myself. The hordes of media that usually descend upon vulnerable communities in the days following tragedies like this one are generally disdained, and for good reason. People who have lost loved ones want to be able to mourn in peace. No one wants a camera shoved in their face by a bunch of outsiders from New York and Washington. Yet, here they were, a long-forgotten community extending an olive branch to a group of people that are often seen as vultures.

Leaving the elementary school, I drove toward the mine entrance where search and rescue crews had been entering the Upper Big Branch portal. Many miners were still unaccounted for. Family members held out hope that their husbands, fathers, brothers, uncles, and nephews would be counted among the survivors. A West Virginia State Trooper sat parked outside the entrance to the mine with his lights flashing. The law enforcement presence acted as a deterrent to any over-zealous journalists who might try and sneak a closer look on mine property.

I continued driving toward the little town of Whitesville. Not far from the mine entrance sat a small country church with a humble white steeple. A vintage illuminated sign sat in front the rustic church. Its customizable black letters spelled out a simple, desperate plea: "Pray for our miners." Rows of mostly identical coal camp houses lined State Highway 3 along the way into Whitesville.

In the early 1900's, coal companies constructed entire towns around their mining operations. Often named for the companies themselves, they were complete with homes, schools, and company stores. Many of the surviving towns in West Virginia's coal fields grew out of these coal camps. Whitesville was no exception.

The main drag was lined with two story brick buildings that had been there since coal's heyday. A small Chevrolet dealership sat nestled between two such buildings. Brand new Chevy Silverado pickup trucks painted red, white, and blue were displayed for sale prominently on the car lot. The trucks called out to the young men of the Coal River valley. A deeply held cultural tradition compelled a great many boys to graduate high school, get a job at the local mine, and use their first paycheck as a down payment on a brand-new truck. It was a rite of passage for the young men who lived and worked in coal country.

I continued to explore Whitesville and shoot scene-setting photos of the town. In all likelihood, the readers of the *New York Times* would never step foot in a place like this. It lacked cell reception, boutique stores, and brunch spots. The town was so small that it didn't even have a McDonald's. Instead, a humble Dairy Queen occupied the region's fast-food throne. A single traffic light hung suspended from a wire across Main Street. Despite there being little to no cross traffic, it continued to govern the intersection in the sleepy downtown. In addition to reporting the news, part of my job was to paint an accurate portrayal of a place that most Americans had forgotten. Even worse, I suspected, most members of America's middle and upper-class had simply stereotyped and written off the region completely.

While the coal that came from the region may have fueled the power plants that generated the electricity with which they charged their iPhones and Priuses, to them Appalachia was little more than a community of truck driving, camouflage wearing, gun toting, toothless hillbillies. I didn't come here to perpetuate that stereotype, however solidified it may have been in the minds of some. After a few hours of shooting scene setters around town, I drove an hour back toward Beckley until I found cell reception. I sat in the parking lot of a Family Dollar store and sent my first batch of photos back to New York.

As the agonizing days wore on, families of the missing miners began to lose hope. The death toll continued to climb until the bodies of every missing miner had been recovered and identified. 29 of the 31 miners on the day shift had been killed in the explosion. Miraculously, two men had somehow managed to survive the devastating blast. Dangerous conditions lingering inside prevented search and rescue teams from penetrating deeper into the mine in the hours immediately following the explosion. Investigators with the Mine Health and Safety Administration, or MSHA, came to determine that insufficient ventilation, high methane levels, and excess coal dust in the air created a perfect storm for the blast. All it took was a single spark to ignite the deadly cloud of combustible gasses. The company that owned the mine, Massey Energy, would eventually declare bankruptcy after facing stiff fines and penalties. The company's CEO, Don Blankenship, would also be indicted on federal charges relating to the disaster.

The community's churches filled with mourners in the days following the blast. As the sun set, a crew of a few hundred locals gathered at a little league baseball diamond downtown for a candlelight vigil. An elderly woman caught my eye as she sat alone in the bleachers. Wearing coal miner's pants and an American flag T-shirt, she sat slumped over with a single wax candle in her hands. Its wick flickered in the blue light of the Appalachian dusk. She wore a forlorn expression on her wrinkled face. I followed the group as it marched by candlelight in a solemn procession along the sidewalks of downtown Whitesville.

Slowly, the media circus fizzled out and left town. Residents would do their best to return to some semblance of life as usual before the disaster. However, no number of memorial gatherings or CNN interviews would be able to fill the hole left in the community. Even as the town mourned the loss of so many of their men, mining continued at other complexes in the area. Coal trucks still rumbled through downtown. The sound of locomotives spooling up and coupling onto long strings of loaded coal cars echoed through the valley's wooded hills. Even in the face of tragedy coal was a way of life here, and the surviving miners would carry on.

Over the course of the next decade, I would return to Whitesville a handful of times. On my first trip back, I discovered a handsome black granite memorial that had been erected downtown. Life-size silhouettes of the 29 men lost at Upper Big Branch adorned the memorial along with their names. A few miles down the road, a makeshift memorial sat at the base of an elevated coal conveyor. 29 black miner hats sat atop 29 red wooden crosses. A laminated photo of each man lost in the mine was taped to a steel support beam at the base of the coal conveyor. Flowers and wreaths left by well-wishers fluttered in the breeze. Over the years the photos on the makeshift memorial began to fade. Piles of wilted, sun-bleached flowers were scattered about the memorial when the occasional thunderstorm rolled through the valley.

In time, the Dairy Queen eventually closed its doors. It's building remains vacant and overgrown with weeds as of the publishing of this book. More of the storefronts along Main Street became vacant as local businesses stopped being able to turn a profit. The town's only streetlight has gone dark. Whitesville was hollowed out. Coal exports in the valley have slowed to a trickle as several large mines were forced to idle production or close altogether. The sun may be setting for good on Whitesville and the other small communities located along the Coal River. Even so, I won't forget them and the work ethic that their coal miners embodied.

My eyes squinted as they adjusted to the daylight that was pouring in through the elevator shaft. We had finally reached the surface after spending some two hours underground inside the Federal No. 2 mine. I flipped off my headlamp and relished being able to look the other miners in the eye once again. I said goodbye and exchanged handshakes once again with our tour guides. In doing so, I reflected on the lengths that these men went to provide for their families. It was both convicting and inspiring at the same time. These men did real, hard, backbreaking work. Coal mining was by no means a safe profession. Each year miners lose their lives in accidents above and below ground. The type of work I did couldn't quite measure up to theirs.

The expressions of pride these men wore on their coal-blackened faces said it all. They loved being miners, despite its hazards. They would be back the next day, and the next, to descend once again into the depths of the earth on behalf of their wives, their children, and their communities. So too did the petroleum engineers and oil field workers who lived on the Jack/St. Malo platform. They were men who knew how to think on their feet, problem solve, and bring home the bacon for their families who lived back on shore.

As I drove through the hollows of West Virginia on my way back home, I reflected on my role as a provisioner for my own family. I realized how blessed I was to be able to take photos for a living. While I was grateful for all the adventures and unique experiences photojournalism had provided me, what mattered most to me now was providing for the future of my two young sons. Whether I accomplished that with a camera in my hands, or someday behind the wheel of a delivery truck, it didn't matter to me. The miners with whom I had spent the day and the offshore workers in the Gulf of Mexico reminded me of a central tenet of masculinity: a man protects and provides for his family. I bit down on my lower lip and prayed for the strength and tenacity to be that kind of man for my kids.

Scan this code for photos from Chapter 7

8. ROSWELL

William "Mack" Brazel strolled through the grassy pasture toward his flock of sheep. A July thunderstorm had just swept across the desert, not an uncommon occurrence in that part of New Mexico, near Roswell. As the familiar bleating of sheep reached his ear, an unfamiliar sight caught his eye: Debris lay strewn about the land in front of him. The year was 1947. A few days later, on July 8, a surreal headline appeared on the front page of the *Roswell Daily Record* newspaper. It said the military had captured a "flying saucer" on a ranch outside of town. The next day the Army corrected its news release. A weather balloon had crashed, not a flying disc. From that day forward the sleepy little town of Roswell would no longer be known simply as the dairy capital of the Southwest.

On the eve of Roswell's annual UFO festival, I rolled into town on assignment for the *New York Times* opinion section. My goal was to compile a photographic record of the town and their curious claim to fame, known the world over. At first glance, the main drag leading into the center of Roswell is not unlike the suburban sprawl found in most American towns. Fast food restaurants, car washes, and big box stores line the boulevard. Upon closer examination, however, it became apparent that many of the town's local businesses have run with Roswell's claim to fame. The local Arby's displays an "Aliens welcome" sign beneath its familiar ten-gallon hat logo. A few blocks away the town's McDonalds was cleverly constructed in the shape of a flying saucer. The streetlights that line the sidewalks of Roswell's downtown sport pairs of slanted, almond-shaped eyes that transform the pointed glass globes into alien heads as dusk falls.

A few minutes after 10pm, I pulled onto the grounds of the former Roswell Army Airfield. During World War II, the airfield was the site of a bombardier school. Wave after wave of enlisted airmen cycled through Roswell for training during the war. It was here that they learned the art of accurately dropping bombs from altitude. Later in the war, a B-29 training squadron took up residence at the dusty airfield. The same bombers that dropped the atomic bombs on Hiroshima and Nagasaki plied the airspace over the humble town of Roswell. The sleek, silver, streamlined airplanes were a common sight in the airspace above Roswell's neighboring cattle ranches. Once the U.S. Air Force ceased operations at the base in 1967, a local community and technical college took up residence in the former installation's many structures. Even as recently as 2017, little of the airfield's architecture looked to have changed since the early post-war years. The short, boxy control tower still stood along the flight line. A navigational light located on the roof of the tower rotated steadily on its axis, mournfully signaling its existence to any stray aircraft who might have accidentally wandered into Roswell's airspace. Many of the original hangars still stood as well. That night, I was searching for a specific hangar. One steeped in extraterrestrial folklore: Hangar 84.

According to local legend, remnants of the Roswell wreckage were transported to an empty hangar on base. Armed military police officers stood watch outside the entrance to hangar 84 in the days following the crash. All except the highest-ranking officers on base were refused entrance. Where exactly the debris was eventually moved remains shrouded in mystery.

As luck would have it, hangar 84 was still standing. Now occupied by an aviation services company, little more than a tall privacy fence separated the hangar from a nearby street. When I stumbled upon the hangar, thick slats of diagonal plastic occupied the open spaces of the chain link. There was no possible way to shoot through the fence. If I wanted to make an acceptable photo, I would need to gain some elevation. I clambered up onto the roof of my rental car with my camera. I rose to my feet and froze. There I was, face-to-face with the hangar in all its glory. The storied structure's semi-circular roof curved gracefully down to each of the building's four corners. The hangar's tall accordion-style doors were stretched out end to end, blocking any available line of sight inside. Surprisingly, the hangar doors' patchwork quilt of rectangular glass windowpanes stood mostly intact. No lights were visible inside the structure. It was buttoned up tight for the night.

Somehow, the otherwise unremarkable hangar felt different to me than the other buildings on base. I tried to focus on making photos but couldn't shake the strange feeling that I was being watched. Although seven decades had passed since the Roswell wreckage was allegedly housed in hangar 84, it felt like this corner of the airfield had been imprinted with a bizarre, anomalous energy. Try as I might, I couldn't put my finger on it. A plethora of stars hung suspended in the night sky above the eerie hangar, adding to the otherworldly mood of the moment. Despite doing my best to think rationally, I was thoroughly creeped out. I made a few more quick frames and then drove to my hotel to turn in for the night.

The following morning, I drove to Roswell's historic downtown. A handful of two-story shop buildings more than a century old, dotted Roswell's central business district. Their brick construction and tall windows were reminiscent of many small towns I had explored during my college years in the mid-south. I found a parking spot, slung a camera over my shoulder, and walked half-a-block to the International U.F.O. Museum and Research Center. Housed in an old movie theater complete with a vintage art-deco marquee, the museum has long been a hub for all things alien-related in town. In addition to boasting an extensive gift shop, the museum's interior walls are covered with photos of suspected UFO's captured on camera. Hand-drawn sketches of alien life forms were displayed along with eyewitness testimony of those who claim to have been abducted. In the middle of the museum, a facsimile of a flying saucer emits clouds of smoke as if it had just landed to check out the museum itself. The highlight of the museum is a life-size diorama of an alien autopsy. A mannequin clad in a white surgical gown, hat, and mask is positioned at the head of a vintage hospital gurney. A government agent dressed in a black suit and fedora stands ominously in the corner of the operating room, keeping a watchful eye over the proceedings. A lifeless, child-sized alien corpse lays on the stretcher behind glass, the centerpiece of the grotesque scene. Teenaged museum goers posed for selfies in front of the display flashing peace signs. Children of a younger age stared wide-eyed, unsure what to make of the disturbing scene housed behind the thick pane of glass before them.

While wandering around the museum, I struck up a conversation with a relic hunter who was seated behind an exhibit table. He claimed to have scoured the original 1947 crash site multiple times and retrieved several curious artifacts from the supposed scene. These included a button from a World War II era military uniform, various soil samples, and a few small pieces of mysterious metallic debris. Much of the scrap he had discovered using a metal detector. Over the decades since the crash, scavenging ants and other small critters had stashed this peculiar chaff inside anthills and insect colonies beneath the surface of the soil. The metal shards had been sent to a lab for metallurgical analysis. According to him the results returned as inconclusive. Whatever materials comprised the metal debris were apparently unidentifiable. I asked the man if he had any tips for finding the crash site. While he didn't seem interested in giving me directions to the spot, he did share with me a helpful tidbit. The crash site that most tourists end up traveling to is not the true spot of impact. In the 1990s, a sign was erected along a highway outside of town. "UFO crash site, 1947" it read. Was the sign placed there as a decoy to throw the masses off the trail of the true crash site? Was it part of a failed scheme to somehow capture tourism dollars? It was hard to say, exactly.

Since the early '90s, a steady stream of tourists have passed through Roswell each year in search of the truth and a few souvenirs. Downtown Roswell is now home to half a dozen alien-themed shops located a stone's throw from the center of town. In 2017, the town of Roswell turned out to commemorate the 70th anniversary of the crash at their annual UFO festival on Main Street. Prominent ufologists, including the nuclear physicist Stanton Friedman, gave lectures on the latest theories surrounding the Roswell incident. Families donned costumes alongside their pets in matching outfits and marched in the festival parade. Tourists plundered gift shops of alien-shaped coffee mugs. Most locals would agree that government cover-ups are very good for business. Next-door to the museum a kitschy tourist-trap beckons the less academically inclined. One of the many UFO-themed dioramas inside inexplicably portrays a pair of grey aliens occupying space in a human living room. One of the aliens watches TV in nothing more than a pair of purple boxer shorts. A second sits slumped back lethargically on a ratty couch, an opened beer bottle within reach. The more I thought about it, the more I realized that it was a frighteningly accurate depiction of how extraterrestrial visitors might adapt to the human lifestyle. Having had my fill of Roswell's museum district, I walked back toward my car and prepared to venture out into the wilderness to find the crash site. Thanks to some internet sleuthing I believed that I had narrowed down the general area of the 1947 crash.

As I set out to confront the unknown, I noticed an all too familiar sensation settle in the pit of my stomach. I felt fear clenching tight like a fist in my gut. Questions started swirling around inside my head. What would I find out in the desert? What would I encounter? What lurked out in no-man's-land? Extraterrestrials? Maybe. In reality, an even more terrifying prospect could be waiting for me just over the horizon: failure. I was afraid to fail. I feared that despite putting forth my best efforts, I would come up short. I was terrified I didn't have what it took to get the job done.

My fear could be absolutely debilitating, and it had the potential to grind my forward progress to a halt. But I knew I had a choice. I could let my fear stop me in my tracks, or I could harness it and allow it to motivate me. I could choose to let it push me to the edge of my comfort zone. That was the answer. I resolved to muster up whatever courage I could find and press into the fear. The solution was not to be less afraid, but instead to embody courage in the face of the challenge.

I left the town of Roswell behind and merged onto the open road, setting my rental car's cruise control a generous amount above the posted speed limit. The flat desert expanse stood in contrast to the rolling, wooded landscape of the Ohio River valley that I had grown accustomed to since moving to Kentucky. Punctuated only by the occasional billboard, the novel terrain stretched to the horizon for most of the two-and-a-half-hour drive.

Nearing the fledgling village of Corona, New Mexico, I pulled my car off the smooth asphalt highway. The rest of my journey would be on dirt country roads. My tires kicked up a thick cloud of dust as I turned westward off the highway. During my drive, the landscape gradually transitioned from flat and sandy to more rugged, rocky terrain. Rusty windmills spun lazily in the breeze as herds of cattle grazed nearby. A short time after turning off the highway, I spied a man in a cowboy hat and sunglasses tending to a cattle gate.

Not wanting to be a stranger, I hopped out of my car and introduced myself. The cowboy's name was Mark Sultemeier. He and his family were long-time ranchers in the area. While friendly enough, the man's no-nonsense demeanor left me feeling a bit self-conscious. I somewhat sheepishly explained what I was doing driving through his neighborhood. I told him what I'm sure he had instantly gathered: I was searching for the Roswell crash site. Mark nodded as if he had heard the same explanation every day for the past two decades.

"There's nothing out there but a bunch of rocks," he said matter-of-factly as he returned to tending his herd of cows.

We parted ways and I continued down the dusty county road. A mixture of self-conscious pride and embarrassment had prevented me from working up the courage to ask him where exactly the crash site was. *That's ok.* I resolved to find it on my own.

Yet as the time ticked by, I started to regret my decision. Nothing that I saw around me looked familiar or seemed to match the photos I had found while doing research on the internet. I began to contemplate defeat. What if I spend all afternoon out here and come up empty-handed? How am I going to turn in a project to my editor without crash site photos? I'm not out here on assignment for some college newspaper. I'm here for the *New York Times.*

Forging ahead down the road, I noticed, unsurprisingly, that I no longer had cell reception. There would be no calling in the cavalry or scouring Google Maps for hints. I was on my own. As I drove, I uttered a short prayer. *God, please help me find this crash site. Please.* In retrospect, it seems like a silly thing for which to pray. But I wanted to do my best. I wanted the finished product that appeared in the *New York Times* to reflect maximum effort on my part.

A few minutes later, I spotted a pair of dusty pickup trucks parked along the shoulder of the road. I slowed down and threw a friendly wave to two men who were out mending a barbed wire fence. As I passed by, I heard my gut tell me to pull a U-turn.

You should turn around and talk to those guys, I reasoned to myself. *Go introduce yourself and ask to take their photo.* For a few seconds I fought the urge.

"It's too late," I countered to myself. "It will look weird if I turn around. What if they're jerks? What if they tell me to get lost? What if they tell me I'm trespassing? Am I trespassing? I'm probably trespassing." Despite my own persuasive counter-arguments, I knew that a good journalist would go back.

Remember, Luke, you are the New York Times. Start acting like it.

That did the trick. I whipped my car around and returned to talk to the two ranchers.

Ever since my first day working for the *Times* in 2009, I have felt the weight of what it means to represent America's newspaper of record. Upon arriving in Washington, my personal identity quickly became inextricably entangled with the storied newspaper. Perhaps it was a function of my own emotional un-health and immaturity at the time. Perhaps it was a symptom of the toxic professional atmosphere so prevalent in the District of Columbia. I was no longer "Luke." I was "Luke, with the *New York Times*." In Washington, one's worth and value as a person seem to depend solely upon the prestige of the organization for whom you worked. Leaving Washington at the conclusion of my second year in the *Times'* D.C. bureau afforded me this bitter revelation. I went from being somebody, to being just another undergraduate on campus at Western Kentucky University. The severity of this abrupt transition highlighted a painful personal reality that I continue to wrestle with. Being a well-known freelancer for the *New York Times* was something that would not, and could not, fill the hole in my heart. It was just a job. I fear that some people spend their entire careers working their way to the top only to encounter this soul-crushing realization. It's never as fulfilling or exciting as they imagined it will be. By God's mercy I learned this lesson before I had the chance to potentially sacrifice my family, friendships, and personal wellbeing to reach the pinnacle of photojournalism.

Doing my best to overcome my social anxiety, I parked my car near the two ranchers and hopped out. I approached the men and introduced myself.

"Howdy, gentlemen," I began. "My name is Luke Sharrett, and I'm working on a story for the *New York Times* about the 70th anniversary of the Roswell incident."

The rancher closest to me was leaning on the gatepost of a rusty metal cattle guard. A lit cigarette hung from between two of his wrinkly, sun-spotted fingers. He wore a faded red button-down shirt tucked into a pair of working-man's jeans. Tufts of silver chest hair protruded from his half-buttoned shirt. A pair of sunglasses sat askew on the bill of the cattle-rancher's baseball cap that he wore atop his head. The man's name was Sandy Proctor.

Just like Mark Sultemeier, his family had been tending to their herds outside Corona for generations before him. Yet unlike the rancher I had encountered a few minutes before, a strange, perplexing energy emanated from Sandy's persona. Missing was the dismissive amusement I had sensed from the previous rancher. As I introduced myself a hint of a smile began to form on his leathery face. Pulling his baseball hat low over his eyes, the cowboy turned and looked down the length of the barbed wire fence. He raised the lit cigarette to his lips and inhaled slowly.

"Mama seen the wreckage," he uttered with conviction.

Failing to keep a good poker face, my eyebrows raised.

"Really?" I replied with a mix of skepticism and excitement.

"Mmhmm," he responded with a slight nod. With his gaze fixed down the road where I had pulled the U-turn, he recounted childhood memories of his late mother Loretta. It had been a stormy night when word began to spread amongst the local homesteads. Something unusual was forced down by the storm onto a nearby ranch. Local ranch hand Mack Brazel had discovered it and began spreading the word amongst his neighbors. According to Sandy, Brazel had even brought some of the mysterious wreckage over to Loretta's house before he alerted the military of his findings.

The demeanor with which Sandy spoke struck me as sober, and sincere. There was no talk of UFO's or little green men, simply a crash in the desert. That much was indisputable, even by the U.S. Government's own admission. What exactly had crashed, however, was the question.

"Our government hides things from us," he concluded as another puff of cigarette smoke escaped his lips. His words hung heavy in the moment of silence that followed the remark, ominous as it was self-evident. I watched silently as the tobacco smoke dissipated into the desert air. Without another word Sandy returned his attention to the barbed wire fence post beside him. Then, as if he had read my mind, he offered up some unsolicited directions.

"Keep driving down this road for about 15 minutes and take your first left. That's where you'll find the crash site."

Energized by the news, I said thank you, bounded back to my car and drove deeper into the desert. My excitement built steadily as I approached the previously mentioned left turn. At the intersection I spotted a small shack set back a few dozen yards from the dirt road. The structure felt strangely familiar. From the look of it, the outbuilding dated back to the 1940s, at least. Then, it hit me. I had seen depictions of the humble four-walled structure in various artwork relating to the Roswell crash. My heart began pounding. I was close. I could feel it. Across from the shack was an overgrown two track dirt road. It climbed a slight incline to the top of a grass meadow directly to the west. To my delight, the property was not posted. There was no "private property" nor "no trespassing" sign to conveniently ignore. I pulled my car off-road with a clean conscience and began to slowly climb the hill. The 4x4 path paralleled a dried creek bed that looked as if it had not seen rain in years. I wasn't completely sure, but I had a strong sense in my gut that I was heading in the right direction.

In my research leading up to the trip, I discovered a set of photos taken during a university-sanctioned archaeological dig on the crash site. One of the photos depicted a vintage windmill along a dirt two track, not unlike the one I was currently traversing. I held my breath as I crested the grassy knoll. Gripping the steering wheel, I leaned forward with anticipation. There, a few hundred yards away, was a windmill. *Could it be?* I thought to myself. I hurriedly retrieved the photo from the archaeological dig and compared to the two. *Bingo. I made it.* I found the crash site.

A wave of excitement washed over me. I drove a few more yards until I could no longer resist. I hopped out of the car and planted my feet on the soil. The grassy field did not look the least bit remarkable to the untrained eye, but I knew I was standing in a storied spot. I took a moment to center myself and soak in the scene. Feelings of satisfaction, accomplishment, joy, and wonder abounded. The tall grass of the serene pasture swayed in the gentle afternoon breeze. Crickets droned in the distance. The veil between the cosmos and the terrestrial felt strangely thin in that place. In my imagination I pictured William Brazel arriving to the site on horseback exactly seventy years prior. Turning around 360 degrees, I imagined what the debris field must have looked like. I could almost see the hundreds of shreds of reflective metal strewn every which way across the landscape. I imagined a convoy of headlights approaching in the distance as the U.S. Government descended upon this very field. I could practically hear the shouts of the Army officers directing their men in the cleanup effort. I could nearly feel the vibrations of the enlisted men's boots pounding the ground as they jumped from the back of Jeeps and olive drab deuce-and-a-half trucks.

I grabbed my camera from the car and spent some time photographing the scene. I focused on the two-track dirt road, a nice visual element and leading line that ran through the middle of the pasture. The road's two dirt tire tracks stretched toward the distant horizon. Switching to my telephoto lens, I took a couple photos of a herd of cattle grazing nonchalantly some distance away. They were oblivious to everything other than their next mouthful of grass. As I composed and took pictures, I felt the atmospheric conditions begin to shift.

A line of severe weather was racing into the area. Ominous clouds, black with rain, appeared out of nowhere on the horizon and moved swiftly across the desert. In no time they had obscured the blue New Mexico sky above me. The wind picked up and began to gust forcefully, blowing the tall grass of the crash site violently to one side. Spooked by the sudden shift in the weather, the herd of cattle skedaddled to seek shelter from the impending storm. The sun hung low in the sky behind the approaching thunder clouds. A fiery orange strip of sunset peaked through the sliver of unobscured sky just above the horizon.

I retreated to my car as the first raindrops began to fall. The sky grew darker still. Popping the rear hatch of my rental car, I climbed into the trunk and photographed from relative safety inside the car. I raised my camera and shot a frame of the pasture and the jet-black storm clouds that now filled the sky. At that moment a bolt of lightning struck nearby. The ear-splitting thunderclap that accompanying the lighting echoed across the plain. I ducked instinctively as the flash of electricity traced a disjointed, circuitous route from sky to ground.

At the first thunderclap, the clouds opened up. Buckets of rains pelted the roof of my car and the field around me. With conditions deteriorating rapidly, I faced a decision. Should I leave now, or try and wait out the storm? I imagined the worst-case scenario If I chose to stay. My car could easily become bogged down in the soggy field with no avenue of escape available. If I tried to seek help on foot, I could be struck by lightning or swept away in a flash flood, never to see my two beloved sons again. Staying put would also likely mean spending a spooky, restless night in my rental car at the crash site. Glancing out the window, I noticed that the dirt two track had transformed into a pair of fast-moving streams. Question answered. This might be my only window to make a clean getaway.

Despite having spent so much of the afternoon searching for the crash site, my time there was being cut short. I closed the trunk hatch and shift into four-wheel drive. My tires spun in the mud as the car's wheels grasped at the pasture for traction. I made my hasty retreat along the now-mud two track. The landmark windmill spun in the wind like the propellor of a World War II bomber's engine. The bone-dry creek bed that paralleled the two-track on my drive in was now overflowing its banks with rain. The massive amount of water that had fallen from the cloudburst was threatening my escape. A knot of stress and panic formed in my stomach. *Lord, please help me make it out of here in one piece*, I prayed. I managed to make it back to the dirt county road, but knew I wasn't yet out of the woods.

With the sun already setting before the storm blew in, the ambient light was fading fast. I flicked on my high beams in an attempt to increase my visibility. Frustratingly, the headlights only served to illuminate even more of the falling rain occupying the space in front of my windshield. I abandoned my brights and went back to navigating the road with my normal headlights. My rental car crashed through deep puddles that had formed out of nowhere on the muddy road. I increased my speed just a bit to reach the paved highway before the roads became completely impassable.

Suddenly, through the onslaught of rain, my headlights caught a shadowy shape moving across my path in the darkness. My already elevated heart rate skyrocketed as I jumped out of my seat.

"What the hell was that?" I blurted out to no one in particular.

My fight or flight impulse kicked in as fear took hold of my brain. A moment later my headlights caught a pair of large reflective eyes staring back at me. I slammed on the breaks of my car and skidded to an abrupt stop through the mud.

"Mooooooo!" exclaimed the black Angus cow blocking my path in the middle of the road. Relieved, I let out a loud laugh. The herd of cows in front of me walked lazily across the road from one pasture to another, ambivalent to my incessant honking as I unsuccessfully tried to shoo them out of the way.

After what seemed like an eternity, I reached the paved highway. The rain finally began to let up just as I turned to the south and again set my course for the city of Roswell. During the drive I reflected on everything I had seen and experienced on my trip. For some reason, I do some of my best thinking behind the wheel. Something about watching the asphalt lane markers pass by in hypnotic intervals as I chased a perpetual horizon was conducive to self-reflection. How can we make sense of America's widespread fascination with UFO's and aliens? What was it exactly about the subject that captures our collective imagination? The longer one is in Roswell, the harder it becomes to avoid trying to answer the question: Did an alien spacecraft really crash to earth 70 years ago? Are we all alone in the universe? Does any of this even matter? Perhaps the more meaningful question is deeper and more pressing. In Roswell, some of humanity's foundational yearnings hide in plain sight. Look no farther than the tourist-trap T-shirt rack: "The truth is out there." Absolute truth exists. "I want to believe." Our souls long for something to believe in. "Aliens please abduct me." Things here on earth are not as they should be. The T-shirts know. We are desperate to find meaning in our lives. We search for answers to the tough questions. Who are we? Why are we here? Who will descend from the heavens and rescue us from the terrible suffering and mortality of life?

What had drawn me out into the desert on a wild goose chase? What was I doing here? I can't say I reasonably expected to uncover any new information about the already exhaustively researched events of 1947. Yet, I did feel a strong urge to travel to Roswell and check things out for myself. To come and explore. There was something for me to discover out there in desert. Even if I had never found the crash site and turned up empty-handed, there is merit in forging a new path. There is treasure to be found pushing to the edge of our comfort zones and confronting the unknown.

Scan this code for photos from Chapter 8

9. THE PARACHUTE SCHOOL

I watched with anticipation out the front windshield of the old pickup truck. A lone airplane hangar came into view just over the horizon. The structure, visible for miles around, towered above the grassy plains of south-central Oklahoma. Earlier that afternoon, I squeezed myself into the backseat of the pickup with two other World War II buffs about my age. My legs had long since gone to sleep as the three us spent the three-hour drive crammed into a bench seat meant for two. It didn't matter. We were on our way to learn how to parachute.

By the time we neared the hangar, the last of the setting sun's rays bathed the top half of the structure in soft, pink light. The harsh summer sun had just dipped beneath the horizon, leaving behind only a pale glow in the hazy summer sky. As the pickup pulled into the hangar's gravel parking lot, I noticed a hand-painted sign posted at the entrance of the driveway. "Welcome to Frederick Army Airfield, est. September 1942." I had arrived at the home of the Parachute School.

Based in Frederick, Oklahoma, the World War II Airborne Demonstration Team is a nonprofit, all-volunteer organization dedicated to remembering, honoring and serving the memory of our ever-dwindling World War II veteran population. The team accomplishes this mission by performing low-altitude round canopy parachute jumps dressed in authentic World War II equipment at air shows and veterans' events around the United States and Europe. Three times a year they run a parachute school for new members, like me, who wished to try out for the jump team.

With a population of only 3600, Frederick became the unlikely home to the team thanks to a story in the town's local newspaper. Some years ago, the fire department in the sleepy cattle ranching town was planning to torch a derelict airplane hangar at the small Frederick Regional Airport. Doing so would provide much needed practice for the town's fledgling fire department. It would also rid the community of a dilapidated eyesore that plagued the citizens of Frederick for years. The hangar was constructed in the early 1940's for the purpose of training U.S. Army Air Corps pilots during World War II. It had long since fallen into a state of disrepair.

Around the same time the Frederick fire department was preparing to set the structure ablaze, the jump team was looking for a permanent home somewhere in North Texas. Their numbers had grown steadily, and it was time to find a permanent base of operations. One of the team's members happened to hear about the proposed fate of the hangar just across the state line from Wichita Falls, Texas. The team reached out to the Mayor of Frederick and managed to halt the destruction of the historic structure, just in the nick of time. The leaders of Frederick made a deal with the team. If the non-profit parachute organization would commit to helping maintain the hangar, the city would agree to rent it to the team for $1 annually. They had a deal.

The night before my flight from Louisville to Oklahoma, I double checked my packing list and deposited all my gear and clothing into a vintage canvas G.I. deployment bag that I picked up at a local antique store. Inside the bag I had packed my camera and a week's worth of plain white T-shirts. After an uneventful flight down to the Sooner State, I met up with a handful of other jump school students in the Oklahoma City airport. We gathered our luggage from the baggage carousel and met our ride down to the hangar on the outskirts of Frederick.

The pickup sent a cloud of dust into the air as it ground to a halt in the gravel parking lot. I hopped out and grabbed my luggage from the bed of the pickup. With bags in hand, I paused and looked back up at the impressive structure towering some forty feet above me. I swore I could feel actual butterflies in my stomach. A hint of dread settled in my gut. *What was I getting myself into?* I wondered what I might encounter over the course of the next ten days. Having paused for a moment, I gathered my courage and charged ahead. Mimicking so many Americans who marched off to fight in World War II, I slung my vintage deployment bag over my shoulder and crossed the threshold into the hangar. With my head held high, I stepped forward into the unknown and embarked upon a journey toward membership in the World War II Airborne Demonstration Team.

Just inside the structure, a team member dressed in an authentic World War II military uniform welcomed our group and directed us upstairs to the student barracks to drop our bags. I ascended a flight of creaky wooden steps and proceeded along an elevated catwalk that ran the length of the hangar's second story. U.S. military flags bearing the insignia of airborne units past and present fluttered lazily in the evening breeze that wafted through the building. I turned my gaze toward the middle of the hangar. The hair on the back of my neck stood on end. Two airworthy C-47 Skytrain transport planes sat parked nose to tail inside in the front half of the cavernous hangar. Both aircraft were coated in olive drab paint and wore distinctive black and white invasion stripes on their wings and fuselage. The team's two planes, named Boogie Baby and Wild Kat, both saw action in World War II and had been painstakingly restored by jump team volunteers and aircrew members who lived a few hours away in Tulsa, Oklahoma.

As I thought about the massive volunteer effort required to restore these vintage transport planes, I reflected upon a restoration of my own. In the spring of 2017, I purchased a beat-up World War II era Willys Jeep on Craigslist. This particular model—a Willys CJ-2A—was the first civilian Jeep model produced at the end of World War II in 1945. Willys Overland assumed that their popular all-terrain general purpose military vehicle would be a hit with civilian ranchers, farmers, and postal service mail carriers after the war. Right they were.

Despite lacking confidence in my ability to restore a vintage motor vehicle, I hired a flatbed truck to ship the Jeep to me from its previous owner's house in Fayetteville, NC. A few days later, the venerable old workhorse arrived in my driveway. The Jeep was quite rusty. Her paint was chipping. Under the hood, however, she was in good mechanical condition. I knew that I had neither the tools nor the know-how to mechanically restore a 70-year-old antique automobile. What I did possess were the skills to handle a cosmetic restoration. I set an ambitious goal to finish the project by Veteran's Day. It was time to get to work.

The summer prior to my Jeep restoration I had restored an old railroad signal to its former glory. Following an exhaustive online search, I located the perfect candidate: a Norfolk and Western color position light signal. A few weeks later, I fished it out of a scrapyard at the N&W Historical Society in Roanoke, VA.

"Fix me!" the venerable sentinel practically called out from the scrap heap.

This type of antique signal featured three pairs of cast-iron lamps. Both the color of the lamps (red, yellow, and green) and their arrangement (horizontal, diagonal, and vertical) combined to form a redundant signaling apparatus to railway crews. When illuminated, the lights shone through six small circular holes stamped into a larger sheet metal target some five feet in diameter. Following months of sanding, painting and rewiring I proudly erected the 100-year-old signal on a pole in my backyard outside Louisville. The finished product wasn't museum quality, but it passed the "ten-foot rule." If one was standing a moderate distance away, it looked pretty good. The small imperfections weren't immediately noticeable. While not perfect, it was a step in the right direction. If I could restore a railroad signal, how much harder could a Jeep be?

Despite my Jeep having no legitimate military heritage to speak of, it wouldn't take much work to make it at least *look* like it did. An angle grinder helped me take off all the rust and chipping paint that I could find on the exterior surfaces.

In the shadow of my recently-restored railroad signal, I set up a crude paint booth in my backyard. With the help of a compressor and spray gun I managed to coat the entire vehicle in classic olive drab paint. Much of my free time that summer was spent working in the backyard on the Jeep. From time to time, my two toddler-aged sons, Truman and Calvin, would join me. I found age-appropriate tasks for them as I worked to install new seat cushions, re-wire headlights, and apply historically accurate stencils to the Jeep's hood and bumpers. With only a few days to spare before the Louisville Veterans Day parade, I put the finishing touches on the vehicle. The feeling of pride and accomplishment far outweighed my perfectionist fixation on all the minor flaws that likely no one other than myself would notice.

Having completed my Jeep, I realized that I was missing only one thing: period-correct military attire. I certainly couldn't drive the vehicle around town dressed in my civilian clothes. My love of history simply wouldn't allow it. A couple days later, a reproduction World War II paratrooper uniform, web gear, steel pot helmet, and a pair of leather jump boots arrived in the mail. My 101st Airborne impression was complete.

On the morning of November 11th, 2017, I fired up the Jeep and made the 35-mile trek into downtown Louisville for the parade. Despite bundling up like a militarized Michelin man, the frigid 29 degree29-degree temperature chilled me to the bone. Along the way I received plenty of friendly honks and thumbs up from passing motorists. Reaching downtown, I pulled onto the parade route and slowed to a stop beside an organizer holding a clipboard.

"Mr. Sharrett, please proceed to the head of the parade," the organizer said. "You are our lead vehicle." The man with the clipboard informed me that the parade's grand marshal, the commanding general of Fort Knox, would be riding with me in my Jeep. A tidal wave of self-doubt and insecurity rose up inside me.

"Lead vehicle?" I half-stuttered. "Are you sure?"

While I was plenty proud of my restored Jeep, I was not yet a proficient operator of manual transmission vehicles. Nonetheless, I agreed to transport the general in my Jeep. As the general approached the vehicle, I explained that I was still learning how to drive a stick shift.

"I'm sure you'll do fine," he encouraged me as he climbed into the back seat of the Jeep with his young daughter. I shifted into first gear as the parade kicked off down Main Street. Crowds thronged the sidewalks on either side of the boulevard, waving small American flags. Then, it happened. My jeep stalled and stuttered to a stop.

"Oh no," I groaned. I shifted back to neutral, popped the clutch and cranked the engine. To my relief she revved back to life. *Phew!*

I tried to shake off the embarrassment of the hiccup as we continued down Main Street toward the parade's grandstand. I forced a smile and waved to a group of school children watching from the sidewalk. Then, it happened again. Another stall-out. My blood pressure spiked and my cheeks flushed with color.

"What am I doing wrong?" I asked myself. "I just drove 35 miles here and didn't stall out once. What gives?" Thankfully, I managed to get the Jeep started up a second time. I stepped on the accelerator and caught up with the rest of the parade.

Then, a third and final time, my Jeep stalled out again. My face turned beet red. Beads of hot sweat appeared on my otherwise frozen face. This time, try as I might, I simply could not manage to get the flooded engine restarted. Again and again, I cranked the starter. Nothing worked.

"We might get out and walk," the general explained apologetically from the back seat.

"Good idea, sir." I replied. I didn't blame him one bit. A group of soldiers marching behind us broke formation and helped push me to a rolling start. Thoroughly embarrassed, I sped past the front of the procession and proceeded down the parade route at four times the normal pace of those marching. As I reached the end of the route, I pulled over to the side of the road and waited for the rest of the parade to pass by.

Over the course of the next half-hour, I stood up in the back seat of my Jeep and did my best to enjoy the parade.

"Luke, it's OK. You did your best. No, it didn't work out like you wanted it to. But you will do better next time," I preached to myself. Besides, the parade wasn't about me or my Jeep. It wasn't about looking cool or competent. It was about honoring the veterans of our armed forces. It was about remembering the sacrifices of our World War II veteran population. It was about memorializing the service of my cousin Dave, whose date of birth doubled as my Jeep's hood-borne serial number.

The crowd began to disperse as the last of the parade procession trickled by me. Before I could turn to leave, several other Willys Jeep owners pulled alongside me and extended an invitation to join them for lunch at a barbecue restaurant across town. I did not feel worthy of the invite, but decided to accept it nonetheless. Their plan called for everyone to caravan across town in our historic military vehicles. Another wave of anxiety hit me. What if I stall out again? I would be even more embarrassed than before. I resolved to face the fear head-on. The only thing I could do was shove down my anxiety and accept the invitation. I slid back into the driver's seat of my Jeep and prepared to crank the engine. It was then that I noticed what had been the cause of my embarrassing parade performance. I completely forgot that I had employed my Jeep's parking brake when I first arrived downtown.

I disengaged the infernal brake with a frustrated groan. The reason I kept stalling had been staring me in the face the whole time. I just hadn't realized it. Pulling out onto Main Street, I followed the other historic vehicles down the boulevard. The distinct chorus of a dozen Willy's Jeep engines reverberated off the towering office buildings in downtown Louisville. We honked gratuitously as we passed beneath highway underpasses, enjoying the echoes of our vintage horns as they bounced off the concrete. The shame and embarrassment I had felt earlier began to melt away. I was in a convoy of fellow Jeep owners who had braved the frigid cold to honor our veterans. These were my people. It felt so good to be included.

Falling in with this column of Jeeps was a risk. Agreeing to lead the parade was a risk. Even restoring a Jeep in the first place was a risk. Yet, I was far better off for having taken those risks. The inevitable discomfort of pushing toward the edge of my comfort zone was well-worth it. The possibility of pain and failure is linked inextricably with the glory and satisfaction of overcoming a challenge. One cannot exist without the other. I pulled into the barbecue restaurant and found a parking spot beside the rest of the convoy. With my head finally clear, I realized all was not lost. I had a pound of beef brisket and next year's parade to look forward to.

Back at the hangar, I picked out a bed in the student barracks and unpacked my clothes. The long bunkhouse was modeled after a typical World War II sleeping quarters. It was filled with two rows of vintage metal frame beds. Each was covered neatly with thick, green wool blankets. It was the perfect bedding for a toasty Oklahoma summer. An old wooden footlocker sat at the end of each bed. After I unpacked, I met our drill instructor for the next 9 days, USMC Master Sergeant (Retired) Jon Tehan. Reminiscent of Sgt. Slaughter from the 1980's G.I. Joe cartoon series, Msg. Tehan was the very definition of squared away. He dressed neatly in a crisp white t-shirt, green army fatigues, and a "Smokey Bear" drill instructor's hat. His direct manner of communication, muscular physique, and well-manicured pencil mustache communicated a level of discipline that was a hallmark of a veteran who had spent most of his adult life in the United States Marine Corps. While I personally found him to be more than a little intimidating at first, I would soon come to realize that Msg. Tehan genuinely wanted us to succeed and become valued members of the team. It was his job to teach us how to march, wear our uniforms, stand in formation, salute properly, and take care of ourselves physically throughout jump school. Doing everything he could to help us succeed was his goal.

Each morning we were expected to have our beds made to exacting standards. Most of us slept on top of our covers to save time and avoid having to make our beds every morning. My first night in Frederick I stayed up past lights-out to polish my boots. I felt a wave of fear and self-doubt rise up inside me. *What am I doing here? Am I detail-oriented enough to succeed? What If I don't pass my tests?* I sat on the edge of my bed in the dark, buffing the last bit of polish from my jump boots. Before I turned in for the night I said a quick prayer for peace and confidence. The next morning, my classmates and I woke before dawn and started preparing for our first full day of training. By the time morning formation was called at 0600 (six o'clock in the morning) we were expected to be clean shaven, in-uniform, and have our jump boots polished to a shine. Msg. Tehan called us to attention on the hangar floor and gave us a quick rundown of the day's schedule. He seemed to be in a more amicable mood than the night before, which was an encouraging sign.

My first few days at Frederick were spent learning the fundamentals of static line parachuting. My classmates and I practiced emergency procedures, navigation under canopy, and, most importantly, how to avoid injury when landing. The proper landing technique for a round canopy is the parachute landing fall, or PLF. A properly executed PLF distributes the impact of landing from the balls of your feet up the side of your calf, thigh, hip, and finally onto your pushup muscle. For hours we practiced PLFs jumping from a three-foot platform into a sand pit. Between jumpers, the cadre would help us examine the indentations we left behind in the sand and offer guidance on how we could each improve our form. To be declared eligible for jump operations, we had to perform four satisfactory PLFs before a panel of judges.

Another training exercise I became intimately familiar with was nicknamed extended misery. In this evolution, each member of my class was strapped into a parachute harness and suspended approximately 4 feet above the concrete floor of the hangar. For the next thirty minutes, cadre members quizzed us on what to do in response to different emergency procedures. Each of us was expected to be able to recite the appropriate course of action from memory, step by step. These emergency situations included high speed malfunctions of a main canopy, mid-air collisions with other jumpers, emergency deployment of a reserve chute, as well as power line, tree, and water landings. Following our practical tests, we also took a written examination. On our third day of training, we were ordered to the office of the team's commanding officer, or XO. One by one, my classmates disappeared across the hangar to receive the results of their written and practical evaluations. I sat quietly, waiting my turn.

"Sharrett, Luke." An instructor called out.

Hearing my name, I leapt up from my chair and walked tepidly across the width of the hangar toward the small office that the XO inhabited. The fifty-yard walk dragged by. I felt my pulse elevate. I had worked so hard to get to this point. The XO held the fate of my mission in his hands. *What would the verdict be?* The sound of my thick jump boots impacting the concrete floor echoed throughout the hangar. *Had I passed?* A positive answer meant continuing to the jump phase of the parachute school. A negative answer would mean an early trip home. I imagined changing my flight home and bumming a ride back to the airport in Oklahoma City. There was no way I was sticking around to watch my teammates make their jumps without me. With my mind still racing, I knocked on the door of the office.

"Enter," came a muffled voice from inside.

I stepped into the office, removed my green fatigue cap, and snapped to attention with my back straight, feet together, and hands at my side. Photos of the team's two C-47 Skytrain aircraft adorned the walls.

"Mr. Sharrett," The commander addressed me from behind his wooden desk. A pregnant pause filled the small space as I waited for him to finish the rest of his sentence. "You've passed your training. You are now on jump status. Congratulations." I returned his salute, overjoyed by the good news. I felt a huge weight lift off my shoulders. Now all I had to was jump out of an airplane five times. How hard could that be?

The next morning, those of us who had achieved jump status gathered in the hangar's main classroom for our morning briefing. Our jump master walked with purpose to the head of the classroom and clipped a satellite photo of our drop zone to a whiteboard. He reviewed relevant details such as wind speed and direction, altitude, and any obstructions we should be aware of on the ground. From there we were instructed to draw our main and reserve chutes from the rigger shop and begin suiting up. Experienced team members helped each of us don our parachutes and strap on our reserves securely. From there we underwent two redundant safety checks called Jump Master Parachute Inspections, or JMPIs. I stood with my arms and legs spread wide, much like I did in order to board Air Force One a decade prior,. The jump master in front of me inspected the integrity of each strap and buckle on my harness. Upon completion of our safety checks, my classmates and I formed a large circle and held hands for a team prayer. COL Ray Steeley, a retired Vietnam-era Special Forces officer and our team recruiter, led us in a prayer for fair winds, good canopies, and soft landings. My sweaty palms tightly gripped the hands of those on either side of me during the prayer.

"Please bring our jumpers safely back to Earth. We ask these things in Jesus' name," COL Steeley concluded. "AMEN," the circle responded in unison. I looked around the circle at my teammates and thought back to my first encounter with the organization.

With my Jeep restoration complete, I began to look for events where I could employ my passion for World War II. Seeing as I already owned much of the necessary gear, re-enacting was a natural next step. One of my first re-enactments was at the Thunder Over Michigan Airshow in Ypsilanti, Michigan. Located 30 miles west of Detroit, the airshow takes place each summer. It features flyovers by vintage warbirds in addition to performances by teams like the Blue Angels. While I have long been a fan of military aviation, my main reason for attending was to participate in the World War II re-enactment that took place on the airfield between aerial acts.

Instead of showing up with a weapon, I opted instead to carry a camera and take photographs during the mock battle. To do that, however, I needed to disguise my modern Canon digital SLR to look a little more retro. Military photographers employed the use of 4x5 Speed Graphic box cameras during the war. My buddy from Washington, Getty Images photographer Mark Wilson, generously gifted me a U.S. Army Signal Corps speed graphic from the Korean War. Its olive drab paint and white "U.S." insignia stenciling made it look right at home on the battlefield. With a few modifications, I was able to effectively hide my digital camera inside the vintage Speed Graphic housing.

Satisfied with my camera's disguise, I loaded up my re-enacting gear and set course for Michigan. After six hours on the road, I arrived a little past midnight and slept in the trunk of my Subaru hatchback for the rest of the night. I woke with the sun, dressed in my gear, and set out to find re-enactor check in. Once I was squared away at the registration tent, I linked up with a group of re-enactors from the St. Louis area who were kind enough to let me join their squad and answer my myriad of questions about the hobby. As is commonplace at living history events, the group who welcomed me in had set up a period-correct encampment complete with army cots, sleeping bags, and canvas tents where they spent the night.

The weekend's battles took place in a vast soybean field between the airport's runways. Three restored Sherman tanks, a pair of half-tracks, and a few Jeeps transported us from the Allied encampment to the battlefield. Fellow re-enactors with an interest in the German military played the bad guys. To add as much realism to the battles as possible, participants were using authentic World War II-era weapons modified to shoot blank ammunition. Using real weapons allowed for big muzzle flashes and loud gunshots on the battlefield. The pungent smell of burnt gunpowder also really helped elevate re-enactments to the next level. Not only would it look and sound like combat, it would smell like it too.

During one engagement, re-enactors portraying American soldiers moved alongside the trio of restored Sherman tanks before being ambushed by a squad of German troops. A cacophony of gunfire, smoke bombs, and pyrotechnic explosions went off all around me as I took photos with my camouflaged camera. Vintage Allied fighter and bomber aircraft made low passes directly overhead, trying in vain to turn the tide of the ground battle in the Allies' favor. In reality, the organizers of the re-enactment had decided ahead of time that the Germans would win round one. Rather than surrender to Axis forces, I decided to "take a bullet" and go down in dramatic fashion in front of the large crowd of spectators.

Laying lifeless in the grass, I caught my breath until an announcer came over the loudspeakers asking the audience to give us all a round of applause. I rose to my feet and shook hands with several nearby German re-enactors who had survived the battle unscathed. For the next few minutes, I gathered up a handful of spent rifle shell casings from the grass and made my way over to the crowd. I handed out shell casings to the younger members of the audience, shook hands with a few veterans, and posed for a couple photos with attendees. I quickly found interacting with the general public to be the most rewarding aspect of re-enacting.

Later that afternoon, the airshow's grand finale called for us to sneak through the soybean field and ambush a German position alongside one of the airport's taxiways. Just before the ground battle kicked off, a flight of vintage C-47 transport planes took off from the airport with civilian parachutists onboard. The planes circled the airport and then dropped their jumpers over a drop zone at the far edge of the airfield. Dressed in World War II-era uniforms and helmets, the static line jumpers floated to the ground under dozens of dark green jellyfish-shaped parachutes. Static line differs from traditional skydiving in both altitude and method of chute deployment. Skydivers typically free-fall from high altitudes and deploy their parachute manually via ripcord. Static line jumpers, on the other hand, typically jump from a much lower altitude and utilize chutes that deploy automatically as soon they clear the aircraft.

Dozens of jumpers under canopy filled the sky as I watched, awestruck. It felt like I was on the set of a Hollywood blockbuster. If I thought running around taking photos in this soybean field was hardcore, how much more so was jumping out of an airplane? These folks were next level. Following the conclusion of the mock battle, I split off from the other re-enactors and made my way over to the tarmac where the transport planes had returned from the airdrop. Adjacent to the line of C-47s was an information table staffed by members of the World War II Airborne Demonstration Team.

I approached one of the team members who was manning the table. Dressed in a jump uniform with aviator sunglasses and an olive-green airborne garrison cap, he struck me as a commanding presence on the flight line. I introduced myself and congratulated the team on a successful jump. Through our brief conversation I learned that the team was planning a trip to Normandy, France in 2019 to participate in the 75th Anniversary of D-Day. Preliminary plans called for the team to transit the English Channel in a formation of vintage warbirds and jump into an historic drop zone in Normandy. On my drive home to Kentucky that evening, I realized what I needed to do. I was going to join the WWII Airborne Demonstration Team and make that trip to Normandy. I was going to help recreate the D-Day jump and document the entire thing for a national news outlet. I had no choice.

Later that week, I fired up my laptop and applied for a slot at the team's July 2018 summer jump school. To be eligible for the Normandy trip, I needed to successfully navigate through the team's training pipeline and accumulate at least 10 jumps. Jump school would afford me my first five, assuming I successfully passed the rigorous training.

I immediately began planning for the logistics of the trip to Oklahoma. I would need to save up the money for jump school tuition. In addition to preparing financially, I had to lose a minimum of fifteen pounds to make weight. There was also equipment that I needed to buy such as a proper steel helmet rated for jumping. The next ten months flew by as I started training to accomplish the first step of my new goal. To shed pounds, I cut sugar and carbohydrates out of my diet completely and forced myself to go to the gym every day. I cut un-necessary expenses from my budget and began saving to cover the cost of plane tickets, lodging, and team membership dues. I even started to forgo air conditioning in my apartment in an attempt to acclimate myself to the extreme heat that was waiting for me in Oklahoma, come July. The sense of anticipation I was feeling grew steadily as my departure date approached. It was becoming ever more apparent to me that I had not chosen this goal. On the contrary, it had chosen me.

Back in Frederick, it was time to board the airplane for my first jump. I turned my attention to Boogie Baby, the majestic C-47 that would act as our jump platform. The first hints of sunrise silhouetted her sleek form against the deep blue hues of the dawn sky. The aircraft's proud nose tilted ever so skyward, as if to point out where she knew she really belonged. My classmates and I made our way single file from the hangar toward the venerable taildragger's door. Her twin radial engines roared to life. The scent of aviation fuel exhaust transported me back to my days traveling aboard Air Force One. Unlike the presidential aircraft, there were plenty of parachutes aboard this plane.

Upon reaching the door of the C-47, I exchanged fist bumps with a cadre member and proceeded to climb inside. My heavy parachute weighed me down as I awkwardly ascended the ladder in my leather jump boots. Our jump master stood in the entrance and gave me a hand up. One by one, my teammates and I filed in and took our seats on two metal benches that ran the length of the interior of the aircraft. We sat with our backs to the fuselage and faced inward toward one another. I settled into my seat and studied the faces of my fellow teammates seated across from me. I could only assume that my face bore a similar expression of subdued internal terror. It's a strange feeling to board a plane with the knowledge that you won't be onboard when it returns to the ground.

With everyone aboard, Boogie Baby lurched forward and taxied toward the runway. The pilots turned into the wind and revved the RPMs of both engines. They performed one last pre-flight check of the engines, oil pressure, flaps, and other vital systems. Everything was in order. The engines roared once again, and we took off down the runway as the first rays of sunlight began to peek above the horizon. The sound of the powerful radial engines reverberated inside the unpressurized aluminum cabin. Kneeling in the open door through which we would soon be exiting en masse, our jump master watched as the plane's landing gear lost contact with the landing strip.

"Airborne!" He yelled in our direction.

"Airborne!" We responded in unison over the rumble of the engines.

I craned my neck over my right shoulder and watched through one of Boogie Baby's small rectangular windows as we quickly gained altitude.

On our preliminary pass over the neighboring drop zone, the jump master threw two wind drift indicators out the open door. The pair of red and yellow streamers were visible to our spotters on the ground as they fluttered gracefully ward the drop zone. The indicators were a useful, if low-tech, tool to determine whether the winds at altitude had shifted in terms of direction or speed. As we circled back around, I prayed to God under my breath.

"Please help me remember my training, and please keep me safe."

A few minutes later I followed the jumper in front of me toward the door and stepped out into thin air, 1500 feet above the Sooner State.

My chute deployed flawlessly. Apart from the sound of Boogie Baby's engines fading away in the distance, the atmosphere at 1500 feet above ground level was remarkably quiet. I took in the crystal-clear view for a moment. A patchwork of corn and cotton fields stretched for miles in every direction. I looked around at my classmates who were also experiencing their first ever parachute drop. Before long, it was time to prepare for my landing. I clenched my feet and knees together and did a PLF onto the drop zone. I had made it to the ground, uninjured. It all happened so quickly. I moved off the drop zone and stacked my parachute in the truck bed of the team's surplus deuce-and-a-half. My teammates and I posed for a team photo. Each of us held up a hand with a single index finger extended, signifying the completion of our first jump. With our group photo complete, we returned to the hangar to watch GoPro footage of our door exits and identify areas where we could improve.

High winds kept us grounded the following morning, but team leadership saw a window of opportunity to squeeze in a pair of jumps later in the afternoon. I suited up in my parachute harness and climbed back aboard Boogie Baby with a newfound confidence. This time I was the first jumper in the second stick. We took off, circled the drop zone, and discharged our first stick of jumpers over the drop zone. As the C-47 turned to make another pass the second stick of jumpers stood up and hooked our static lines to the plane. The jump master gave me the command for which I had been waiting:

"Stand in the door!"

I extended my arms and gripped the outside of the fuselage at hip level. The tip of my right foot protruded just outside the plane. I locked my eyes on the horizon and listened intently for the jump master's next command as I stood in the open door. My adrenaline spiked as the 120mph wind shear whipped past my face.

"GO!" yelled the jump master.

I launched myself out from the plane and into the air. A second later, I felt the jolt of my parachute deploying. Looking above my head, I was pleased to find another good canopy slowing my rate of descent. I turned into the wind and prepared to land. Unlike my first jump, I failed to keep my feet and knees together and impacted my tail bone upon landing. I performed a maneuver called the "foot to butt" and allowed my posterior to absorb the entirety of my body's force of impact. I screamed in agony as waves of excruciating pain shot up my spine and into my brain.

Our team's Drop Zone Safety Officer, or DZSO, watches each jumper's landing through a pair of binoculars. If you hit the ground and don't rise to your feet immediately, the DZSO scrambles the team medic in your direction. As I writhed in pain on the ground, I briefly considered staying down. I had never felt pain this intense in my entire life. Had I broken my back? Would I need to be hospitalized? Was I paralyzed? I considered the extreme embarrassment I would feel being carted of the drop zone on a stretcher. Wanting desperately to avoid an ambulance ride to the local emergency room, I resolved to stagger to my feet. Upon doing so I bent over at the waist, placed my hands on my knees, and let out a single angry F-bomb from the top of my lungs (Sorry, mom).

With the pain still shooting up my back, I gathered my parachute as best I could and hobbled off the drop zone with a severe limp. My classmates assembled on the edge of the field for another group photo, each of us holding up two fingers to signify the completion of our second jump. Wearing a tormented scowl, I made a peace sign for the photo and then limped gingerly over to the old deuce-and-a-half. I did not remember the dirt road back to the hangar being so bumpy on our previous trip. My tailbone felt every single pothole and imperfection in that dirt farm lane.

Awash in anger, pain, embarrassment, and disappointment, I kicked myself for flubbing my landing. As I rode back to the hangar in the bed of the truck, my anger turned quickly to fear. What if this happens the next time I jump? I can't do that again. I don't know if I can handle experiencing that level of pain twice in one day. In that moment, I considered quitting. I pictured walking up to COL Steeley and letting him know that I was washing out. I envisioned packing up my belongings in the empty barracks and leaving the hangar with my head hung low in shame. I imagined nursing my bruised tail bone on the flight back to Kentucky and living the rest of my days knowing that I quit because I was too afraid to jump again.

No.

No way.

Quitting was not an option. I had come too far to turn back now. I needed to make it to Normandy for the D-Day anniversary. But I was *so* afraid. Downright terrified. As the truck pulled back up to the hangar, I sought out the venerable COL Steeley for a pep talk. I pulled him aside and explained in hushed tones about my bruised, possibly fractured tailbone, and how fearful I was.

The grizzled old former Green Beret looked at me with a neutral expression.

"Luke, you know what to do. Just remember your training." With that he walked off to help unload chutes from the truck.

While I was expecting something a little more rousing and emotionally charged, the colonel wasn't wrong. He skipped the emotional fluff and gave me the facts. I knew exactly what I needed to do. I prayed for God to give me courage in the face of my third jump.

With the sun starting to set and the winds picking back up, a sense of urgency filled the hangar.

"Students, don your parachutes and get your JMPI's done," a cadre member yelled. "Our window of opportunity is closing. Let's go!"

I checked out another main chute from the rigger shop and began to put my harness on. A sense of fearful dread followed me through my two JMPI's. There was no time for another group prayer before our second jump.

"Damn," I muttered. "I could really use another one of those right about now."

Boogie Baby sat idling on the tarmac waiting for us to board. As I walked toward the door of the airplane, I felt a connection through space and time to the airborne troopers of old. While admittedly there were no Nazis waiting to try and kill me on the drop zone, I still felt a deep, terrifying fear; a fear that those brave men must have felt twentyfold before they jumped into Normandy on D-Day. With my aching tailbone reminding me all too clearly of the dire consequences of failure, I climbed back aboard Boogie Baby to attempt jump number three.

The twenty minutes that elapsed between boarding the aircraft and my third time through the door felt like an eternity. All I could do was try and combat my overwhelming sense of fear and dread with prayer and positive thinking. As I sat there listening to those awful engines roar, I practiced visualizing a perfect exit out the door and a smooth landing.

"You can do this, Luke. You've got this," I reassured myself. I took a series of deep breaths in through my nose and exhaled out my mouth. "Jesus, please keep me safe," I prayed.

A few minutes later I crossed the threshold again for my third jump. My prayers were answered with a smooth exit, good canopy, and incredibly soft landing. It was a textbook jump. I packed up my chute and made it back to the truck for a celebratory third jump photo. In contrast to the previous picture, I wore a huge smile across my face as I held up three fingers. That night I drifted off to sleep with a sense of deep satisfaction in my heart. I had faced down my fears and emerged intact.

The following day, jumps four and five went off without a hitch. Following our fifth and final jump, my fellow classmates and I gathered in a circle on the drop zone and sang *Blood on the Risers*, an airborne folk song set to the tune of the *Battle Hymn of the Republic*. I belted out the chorus with gusto, "Gory, Gory, what a helluva way to die!"

I was now what they call a "five jump chump." The next day we had our class graduation ceremony and open house for members of the local community. I was honored to have my bronze jump wings pinned to my chest by an 82nd Airborne veteran who made a combat jump during the Korean War. In attendance were several other airborne troops from World War II. They were honored guests in Frederick and treated as such. We all knew that without them we would most likely be speaking German.

Later that night, the team threw a big party in the hangar to celebrate the end of summer jump school 2018. One of our members, renowned World War II historian Mark Bando, showed up for the party with a worn leather case containing an ornate silver chalice. He took the stage and explained that the cup was on loan to him from a 101st Airborne vet who had fought through France and Germany during World War II. The silver cup belonged to none other than high-ranking Nazi leader Hermann Goering before it was liberated by American paratroopers and brought to its new home in the United States. Team members passed the goblet around and took turns taking sips as we toasted all the airborne troopers who came before us.

"To the drop zone!" One member cried out.

"I wish I was there!" We thundered in response.

Early the next morning, I bid farewell to the hangar and caught a ride back to the airport in Oklahoma City. On the drive, I reflected back upon the lessons that I learned during the week prior. My still-aching tailbone reminded me of how I had overcome an injury to accomplish my goal. Seven years earlier I found myself facing a similar set of crossroads. Back in college I chose to shelve my dream of joining the Navy due to an injured knee. I gave up instead of pressing on. This time was different. I had no interest in limping down that same path. Regret and self-doubt were not companions that I intended to invite along with me on this journey. Because I had mustered the courage to face down my fear on the drop zone, I was able to savor the sweet satisfaction of overcoming a challenge.

Along with this sense of accomplishment, I also noticed a newfound confidence radiating from within me. This was an enduring reward for choosing to dive headfirst into my training. Again and again, I practiced my PLFs in the pit until I emerged looked like a sugar cookie, covered in sand. Over the course of the week, I rehearsed door exits until they become muscle memory. Each night, I stayed up past lights-out and used a flashlight to review my notes on emergency procedures. Despite having no prior experience when I arrived at jump school, I was now a qualified parachutist. I walked through the Oklahoma City airport terminal with a spring in my step and my head held high. I was extremely proud of what I had accomplished.

While I waited for my flight to begin boarding, I looked around the gate area. A group of fellow team members was sitting nearby waiting for their own flights. They wore handsome leather bomber jackets adorned with WWIIADT team insignia. A long sought-after sense of belonging settled in my heart. That week, I had proven myself. I had earned my jump wings and had become an official member of the World War II Airborne Demonstration Team. No longer a student, my new friends now referred to me as "teammate." Soon, I would be sewing a team patch of my own onto a leather bomber jacket. I belonged.

I watched out the window as my Southwest Airlines jet throttled up and accelerated down the runway. The 737 was much quieter than

Boogie Baby, perhaps because this aircraft had all its doors attached. Our landing gear lifted off the runway and we climbed gradually into the air.

"Airborne," I whispered to myself and the clouds just outside the windowpane.

Scan this code for photos from Chapter 9

10. NORMANDY

Waves of anxiety came over me as the tiny, single-engine Cessna barreled down the grass runway. I sat uncomfortably with my knees pressed tight against my chest. My six-foot frame barely fit inside the small plane. We quickly reached altitude some 10,000 feet in the air. With my back to the aircraft's control panel, I popped open the airplane's starboard hatch. My legs quivered as I looked down toward the green Earth nearly two miles below. This was not my first time staring out of an open airplane door in flight. Our current altitude, however, was *considerably* higher than the 1500 feet from which I was accustomed to jumping. I fought hard to overcome my natural instinct to remain safely inside the plane. Gathering my courage, I swung my feet out the open door.

It was time to jump.

I reached out and grabbed hold of the diagonal strut that secured the Cessna's wing assembly to the bottom of its fuselage. With my parachute's static line clipped securely to a metal ring on the floor of the airplane, I shimmied up the strut until I was hanging from the wing like a kid on a set of monkey bars. I felt my baggy orange skydiving jumpsuit ripple in the 100mph wind and took a moment to reflect on the pure insanity of my current predicament. How exactly had I found myself here? What in the world was I doing dangling from the wing of an airplane at 10,000 feet above ground level?

I turned my head back toward the Cessna and caught the gaze of my jump master for the day. He gave me a nod. That was the signal. I looked back at my two hands that clung desperately to the wing strut. My knuckles were white. There was no turning back now. *Three. Two. One.* I released my grip from the wing. Gravity took hold of me as my 220-pound frame fell toward the grassy drop zone below me. I extended my arms and legs in a jumping jack position as the little Cessna shrunk quickly from my field of vision. My brain froze in shock. I was all alone, free-falling backwards through the atmosphere like a ragdoll.

After what felt like an eternity, my parachute deployed with a violent jolt. My body absorbed the impact of its sudden deceleration as the RAM-air canopy above me filled with air and assumed it's rectangular form. Unlike the MC1-Bravo round canopies I had grown accustomed to jumping in Frederick, this particular chute was smaller and rectangular in shape. It was highly responsive and infinitely more maneuverable compared to the mushroom-shaped military surplus chutes that my team jumped in Oklahoma.

The previous summer, I joined the World War II Airborne Demonstration Team and successfully graduated from their parachute school in July 2018. Shortly thereafter, I signed up to travel with the team to Normandy, France. In order to qualify for the trip, team leadership decreed that any member wishing to jump in Normandy would need a minimum of ten jumps under their belt. Many of my fellow teammates had dozens, if not hundreds of jumps recorded in their jump logs. I, on the other hand, did not. It was safe to say that I had my work cut out for me.

I completed my first five jumps as a student during jump school at the organization's hangar in Frederick, Oklahoma. Right off the bat, I was halfway to my goal. My next pair of jumps would come as a newly-minted team member at subsequent jump schools the following October and April

I accomplished another two jumps in Virginia's tidewater area. In preparation for the Normandy trip, the WWIIADT East Coast platoon organized a jump day at Skydive Suffolk, a well-respected drop zone at Suffolk Regional Airport in southeast Virginia. While our team prefers to jump from vintage C-47 aircraft whenever possible, sometimes we are forced to adopt whatever alternative jump platforms are available to us. Our jump day in Suffolk was one of those cases. With no C-47 available, we jumped from a skydiving plane called an SC-7 Skyvan. Affectionately nicknamed the "flying shoebox," the inside of the civilian aircraft was plastered with stickers left behind by U.S. Military special operations units who had made their own training jumps from the quirky plane. The U.S. Navy Leap Frogs, U.S. Army Golden Knights, and other elite parachute teams had all left their mark inside the jump platform.

Additionally, Skydive Suffolk serves as the venue where the east coast-based Navy SEAL teams conduct much of their free-fall parachute training. Between jumps I reveled in the opportunity to do pull-ups on the same exercise equipment utilized by the SEALs on their jump days. While I had ultimately opted not to join the Navy after finishing college, it was a treat to hang from the same pull-up bars and jump from the same aircraft that I would have had I found myself in the SEAL training pipeline.

By the time May rolled around, I was sitting at nine jumps. Despite taking advantage of every opportunity to get under canopy, my tally was still one jump short of the ten required to qualify for the Normandy trip. To miss out on the trip of a lifetime because I was one jump short of the threshold was unacceptable. I simply was not content to have come this far and be disqualified on a technicality. With time running out, I contacted a nearby drop zone a few hours from me in Ohio. As it turned out, the crew at Skydive Cincinnati would be happy to take me up for my tenth static line jump. With less than a month left before my scheduled departure for Normandy, I drove up to Ohio and underwent their training course. Although I passed the class handily, the weather that day chose not to cooperate. I would end up spending a gloomy afternoon waiting around for the low cloud ceiling to dissipate. The clouds, however, had other plans. There would be no jump that afternoon. I drove back home to Louisville discouraged, but still determined to visit again the next weekend.

My second try at Skydive Cincinnati yielded much more favorable atmospheric conditions. The blue sky was dotted with only a few puffy white clouds. These were pristine jumping conditions. I donned a fluorescent orange jumpsuit and strapped a pair of clear skydiving goggles to my face. This outfit was *much* different attire than I was used to jumping in. Feeling more like a convict than a parachutist in my bright coveralls, I trudged across the grass landing strip toward the tiny Cessna 182 that would soon take me airborne.

The jarring drop from the Cessna paired with the jolt of the chute's opening left me shaken under canopy. I couldn't decide whether I wanted to vomit or pass out. Neither option would be ideal at the moment. I said a prayer and started taking short breaths in through my nose and out through my mouth in an attempt to regain my composure. It worked. The impromptu breath work allowed me to begin navigating my chute in for what I hoped would be a soft landing.

As I approached the ground, I yanked down on the two toggles that I had used to navigate my sport canopy in toward the drop zone. My chute flared, slowing both my forward and downward momentum. I extended my legs parallel to the ground and slid gently onto the grass runway on my bottom.

For all its downsides, the experience of exiting that Cessna at 10,000 feet helped me truly appreciate the comparative luxury that is jumping from a C-47. Everything about it was vastly superior. The exit, the drop, the chute deployment. Everything. I vowed never to take another C-47 jump for granted again. It was a downright treat in comparison to that dinky little airplane at Skydive Cincinnati. Despite the unpleasantness of the day, I was overjoyed to have my qualifying tenth jump under my belt.

A few days after my adventure in Cincinnati, I listened as the sound of my alarm clock echoed through my apartment in the pre-dawn darkness. I was already awake out of pure anticipation but felt oddly compelled to stay in bed until my alarm went off. Rolling out of bed, I jumped to my feet and began getting ready to leave for the airport. It was June 1, 2019, and I would soon be on my way to Normandy, France, to help commemorate the 75th anniversary of D-Day.

On June 6, 1944, wave after wave of American, British, Canadian, and French military personnel descended upon northern France's coast by air and sea. D-Day was one of the largest military operations in history, and a tipping point for World War II. June 6, 2019, would mark the 75th anniversary of this momentous event. There was no better way to commemorate the anniversary than by parachuting into Normandy with the World War II Airborne Demonstration Team.

I departed from Louisville in the morning's pre-dawn darkness. Two flights and three train rides later, I found myself at JFK International airport ready to board a transatlantic flight from New York to Paris. My mood was electric as I made my pilgrimage to the hallowed shores and hedgerows of Normandy. I couldn't wait to pay my respects to the brave men who cracked Adolf Hitler's Atlantic Wall. With my Delta Airlines flight barreling down the runway for takeoff, I reflected back upon all the hard work I had undertaken to get to that point.

During the flight to Paris, I spent some time creating a checklist of photos that I planned to take on the day of the big jump. A few weeks prior to departing for France, a photo editor at National Public Radio, or NPR, agreed to publish my photos from the trip. In addition to the pictures I would shoot, I planned to write an accompanying essay that explored my motivation for recreating the historic jump. If all went according to plan, my piece would be published on the NPR website the morning of June 6th. A gut feeling told me that this might be the single most-meaningful photojournalism project I had ever undertaken during the course of my career.

Checking my watch, I realized we would be landing in a short 4 hours. During World War II it took American soldiers more than 2 weeks to cross the treacherous North Atlantic by convoy. Bad weather and German U-boats threatened their survival. My flight was like the blink of an eye in comparison. With another long day of travel ahead of me, I decided to try and get some sleep for the rest of the flight.

I woke from my nap just as our plane touched down gracefully at Charles de Gaul International Airport. I collected my carryon luggage from the overhead bin and proceeded toward the French customs checkpoint in the airport's international terminal. While waiting in the lengthy port of entry line, I decided to seize the opportunity to practice my French with the customs official who would be checking my passport. Finally, it was my turn. I approached the checkpoint and greeted a middle-aged officer in his native tongue.

"Bonjour," I said.

"Bonjour," he replied.

"Je m'appelle, Luke. J'habite aux Etats-Unis," I explained in French as I handed over my passport. The customs official looked up at me with surprise and launched into a long interrogatory.

Having exhausted the extent of my Franco vocabulary much earlier in the conversation, the only reply I could muster was a confused "Um?"

"Parlez-vous France?" he countered.

"Non," I replied sheepishly. He switched to English and eventually gave me an entry stamp in my passport.

"Merci," I responded, placing a hand over my heart in gratitude.

I picked up my luggage from the baggage carousel and proceeded through a gauntlet of airport police who were performing random screenings of passengers exiting the terminal. My large green duffel bag stuffed full of airborne gear apparently caught an officer's attention, so he pulled me aside for extra screening. A group of officers gathered around to watch as my kit was unloaded from the bag piece by piece. I rather enjoyed showing off the historically accurate gear that I had compiled over the past year. A short time later the officer who singled me out zipped up my duffel and wished me good luck on my jump.

"Merci," I replied as I handed him a WWIIADT team patch. Along the way I had enjoyed handing out team patches and challenge coins to the various flight crew members, and train conductors that I had encountered during my travels up to that point.

Outside the terminal, I met up with approximately 78 of my fellow team members. As the last of the stragglers trickled in, we took a head count, loaded our luggage into our rental vans, and set out for the coast. The drive from Paris to Carentan took a little over three hours. When we arrived in Normandy our team split into two groups: one group who would be participating in the cross-channel jump, and another who would remain behind in Normandy and provide support on the drop zone. Those of us in the cross-channel group drew our parachutes and set out for the port of Ouisterham near the city of Caen. Immortalized in the 1962 war film *The Longest Day*, the seaside village was the site of a fierce battle between soldiers of the No. 4 French Commando unit and hardened German defenders who lay in wait inland from Sword Beach. The first boots that landed on the beaches of Normandy belonged to the French commandos; a symbolic gesture of liberation.

Our team's plan called for us to cross the English Channel by overnight ferry. If everything went according to plan, the next morning we would arrive in Portsmouth, UK and convoy to the Imperial War Museum in Duxford. It was there that we would prepare for our cross-channel jump. As we waited to board our boat in Ouisterham, a group of incoming passengers disembarked through the ferry terminal. Among them was an American World War II veteran arriving in Normandy for the week's festivities. Our team lined up on either side of the terminal exit and broke out into sustained applause and cheers as the veteran came into view. Walking slowly with a cane, he stopped to shake each of the hands extended to him in appreciation of his service. Feelings of pride and gratitude filled my heart as I watched the man treated like a returning hero. A group of French school children and their chaperones joined in with us to congratulate the old vet. After a grueling 36 hours of international travel, the spontaneous celebration in the ferry terminal provided me with a much-needed morale boost. This is what it was all about.

With two 30-pound parachutes in tow, plus my own luggage, I shuffled up the long gangplank and boarded the cruise-ship sized ferry. After stowing my things, I set out to explore the ship. Dressed in crisp khaki trousers and maroon polo shirts bearing the WWIIADT team logo, our teammates were easily recognizable as they spread around the boat socializing and having drinks. I made my way above deck and watched from the stern as we steamed out of the harbor and into the channel under starry skies. The distant city lights of Ouistreham slowly faded away into the darkness. As I surveyed the inky water of the English Channel, my thoughts turned to the shipwrecks and crashed aircraft that littered the ocean floor beneath us.

Between 1939 and 1945 the deep, frigid, channel waters would become the watery graves of many an Allied sailor, soldier, and airman. With my eyelids drooping, I decided to give in to my jet-lagged body's yearning for slumber and turn in for the night. I retraced my steps back to our team's quarters and slipped quietly inside the pitch-black sitting area where many of my teammates were already asleep. I collapsed into the first unoccupied seat that I could find. Feeling too exhausted to even unlace my jump boots, I caught a few hours of much needed shut-eye below deck.

The first rays of the rising sun woke me the next morning, June 3rd. I stood up from my seat and stretched my arms toward the ceiling of the cabin. Many of my teammates were still curled up asleep under their leather jump jackets. My morning stretch routine was interrupted by a loud growl from my stomach. I joined a few other early risers from our team and walked to the ferry's restaurant for a full English breakfast. The perfectly poached eggs, ripe tomatoes, savory bacon, crispy fried potatoes, and syrupy baked beans on my plate really hit the spot. Say what you will about the rest of their food, the English at least knew a thing or two about breakfast. With the ferry passing the Royal Navy base at Portsmouth it was time to disembark in the United Kingdom. Our team descended another long gangplank with parachutes in tow and queued up to pass through yet another customs checkpoint. Despite the jetlag and short night's sleep on the ferry, I stood in line feeling grateful that I needn't rely on my scant grasp of the French language like at the airport in Paris. A teammate in front of me stepped up to the checkpoint to present his documents.

"What brings you to the United Kingdom?" An officer asked as he examined my teammate's passport.

"We're here to invade France," my friend replied.

"Excellent," replied the customs official as he stamped the passport with an entry visa.

Our group walked to board a pair of charter busses and in doing so ran into a second American World War II vet who was making his way to Normandy for the 75th. We gathered around the old warfighter for a group photo outside the ferry terminal. A few dozen handshakes later we parted ways and loaded onto our busses for the three-hour trip to the Imperial War Museum at Duxford.

Crossing the threshold onto the museum grounds felt like going back in time. The original wartime concrete and barbed wire fence still encircled the base. Our charter busses came to a stop outside a massive hangar at the western end of the runway. Parachutes and jump gear were promptly transferred from our motor coach to the interior of the hangar. While waiting in line to check in with the event organizers, a sudden thunderous roar turned my attention skyward. A formation of three vintage C-47 aircraft flew low over the horizon. Each was painted olive drab with black and white invasion stripes on their wings. For a moment, the sun broke through the otherwise overcast sky and bathed the trio in angelic golden light. A huge smile spread across my otherwise sullen, exhausted face. I noticed goosebumps rise on my forearms as the roar of the warbirds' six radial engines enveloped the airfield. As suddenly as they had appeared, the planes were gone. I stood frozen in awe along with a dozen of my teammates who had witnessed the stunning flyby. We turned to look at each other, eyes wide with wonder. Welcome to Duxford.

During World War II, Duxford was home to the Royal Air Force's 19 Squadron. Flying the famed Supermarine Spitfire, RAF pilots fought valiantly to repel wave after wave of German air raids during 1940's Battle of Britain. The Spitfire pilots, many hailing from the upper echelons of British high society, would lounge in the grass beside their brown and green camouflaged aircraft while waiting for the next missions to come down from headquarters. The hours often crawled by as the RAF men tensely awaited the inevitable. Without warning, a shrill telephone bell would break the silence.

"Scramble, scramble, scramble!" An operations officer would bellow to the lounging aviators. Already dressed in their flying gear to save precious seconds, the intrepid pilots sprinted for their fighters and took off to face the impending Luftwaffe attack on Great Britain's critical infrastructure.

While no longer an official RAF fighter command base, most of the original hangars and buildings from World War II were still standing and were now under the care of England's renowned Imperial War Museum. Each hangar was brimming with historic aircraft and vehicles from the Second World War, including a German Bf109e Messerschmitt that had crash landed along the coast in Sussex. The plane came to rest miraculously intact in a farmer's field where the pilot was quickly apprehended by members of Britain's civilian Home Guard. Another hangar contained an impressive collection of U.S. Army Air Corps fighters and bombers that operated from bases in Southern England later in the war. Every allied airplane that I had read about as a boy was crammed inside that blessed hangar.

To mark the occasion of the 75th, the Imperial War Museum played host to the largest modern gathering of surviving Douglas DC-3/C-47 Dakota aircraft in recent memory. In 1944 approximately 830 C-47s took to the skies on D-Day to deliver some 24,000 airborne personnel, gliders, and equipment onto the drop zones in Normandy. Around 30 surviving C-47s made the trek to Duxford from around the world. Fifteen of the thirty planes followed the historic North Atlantic route on their way over from North America. Along the way, the warbirds made stops to refuel in Nova Scotia, Greenland, and Iceland. These venerable aircraft would serve both as our rides across the channel and jumping platform into Normandy.

After checking in and dropping our parachutes in one of the base's largest hangars, we made for our team hotel near the Cambridge International Airport. I checked into my room at the Holiday Inn Express and crashed for my first good night's sleep in three days. The next morning, I awoke and partook in my second consecutive full English breakfast.

The day's schedule called for an afternoon practice jump on the airfield at Duxford. Much to the disappointment of the thousands of onlookers who had gathered for the concurrent air show, high winds and a low cloud ceiling forced a last-minute cancellation of the practice jump. Still, we donned our parachutes and loaded onto the aircraft for a photo-op, despite being unable to make the jump. A half-dozen historic planes took flight, circled the skies above Duxford, and eventually landed. We disembarked our planes and made our way over to the waiting crowd to shake hands, answer questions, and pose for photos. With the day winding down, we returned to the Holiday Inn to rest up for the next day's cross-channel jump.

Waking early on the morning of June 5th, I polished my boots and made sure the rest of my gear was squared away. Our team met in the parking lot of the hotel to put the final touches on our paratrooper impressions. Following the lead of my teammates, I pulled a handful of wine corks from my pocket and started to burn their edges with a vintage Zippo lighter. I smeared the charred cork on my face in a crude attempt to camouflage my facial features. One of the most recognizable photos from the D-Day invasion depicts Supreme Allied Commander General Dwight D. Eisenhower giving a motivational speech to troopers from the 101st Airborne Division, 502nd Parachute Infantry Regiment, Company E. Their pockets bulging with combat gear and faces blackened with char, the men exude a quiet confidence as they interact with Ike. A short time after the famous photo was snapped, the men would load onto their C-47s and cross the channel for Normandy. I examined my reflection in a car window. Thick streaks of charred cork spanned the width of my face, darkening it like the complexion of a West Virginia coal miner.

A short bus ride later, we arrived back at Duxford and began the arduous wait for our departure that afternoon. Periodic weather reports from the drop zone across the channel in Sannerville did not inspire confidence. Throughout the day, gusting winds and sporadic rain showers plagued the area where we planned to jump. It was too late in the game to find an alternate drop zone. Nor was postponing the jump a viable option. French aviation authorities had granted us a narrow window to execute our mission. Airspace would be shut down for the duration of the sixth due to heads of state traveling into the region. Much like the men of the Airborne 75 years earlier, we were at the mercy of the weather. I shuddered at the thought that we would come all this way only to be stymied by cloudy skies. Our team passed the time milling about the cavernous hangar, triple-checking our gear, and trying to catch short naps here and there. After hours on edge, good news came down the pipe from team leadership. We had a green light. The jump was a go.

"Thank you, God" I said under my breath after many prayers.

On the tarmac outside our hangar, we ran through our pre-jump commands and practiced each step of the process from hook-up to door exit. Finding ourselves in need of an elevated spot from which to practice our parachute landing falls (PLFs) we borrowed the tailgate of a British Army truck and cycled through a few rounds of practice. A crowd of curious onlookers gathered around as we hurled ourselves off the dark green truck, or "lorry" as they call them across the pond.

With our pre-jump exercises complete, it was time to get suited up for the big jump. I slipped my arms through a pair of khaki suspender straps and buckled my web belt around my waist. In 1944 airborne troopers fed their suspenders thorough thick chunks of felt to help pad their shoulders from the taxing weight of their combat gear. With an eye for historical accuracy, my teammates and I had done the same with ours. From my belt hung a canteen, Carlisle bandage, leather pistol holster, and a six cell Thompson submachine gun magazine canvas pouch. A musette bag stuffed full of my personal effects from the past 3 days hung from my suspenders. The complicated logistics of our trip dictated that everything we brought with us on the ferry be jumped back into France on our person. Fastened to the bottom of my musette bag was a coil of white "let-down" rope in case I landed in a tree or atop a barn roof. Strapped to my left thigh was a rubberized gas mask bag. Much despised by the troops, most gas masks were immediately ditched by their owners upon landing. The rest of my pockets bulged with dirty laundry, my toothbrush, boot polish, and spare camera batteries.

Next, I turned my attention to my helmet. The steel pot, an original from WW2, was covered with a hand-knotted fishing net, as most Allied helmets were by mid-1944. Long strips of dark green and brown burlap snaked through the net. The intertwined helmet scrim accomplished two things: it broke up the distinctive outline of the helmet and resembled foliage from a distance. The utilization of these burlap strips was unique to the 101st Airborne Division during the airborne portion of the Normandy invasion. A white heart, the symbol of the 101st's "Five oh Deuce" regiment, adorned either side slightly above the ear. I slipped my helmet's leather chin cup strap beneath my jaw and tightened the steel pot firmly on my head.

Overtop of my web gear I wore a faded yellow Mae West life vest. Named colloquially for the well-endowed movie star of the 1940's, the life jacket inflated via Co2 cartridge. When expanded, a large chamber of air protrudes out from the chest of the person wearing it, providing ample buoyancy in the water. Officially known as the type B-3 life preserver, it was worn by U.S. Army Air Corps pilots, aircrew, and paratroopers during the war. Mine was an original, manufactured by the Goodyear Rubber Co. in 1942. On the back of the vest the name of its original owner, LT. Urban H. Bowdin, was stamped in faded black ink. Bowdin was a native of Minneapolis, Minnesota who graduated from the United States Army Air Forces Advanced Flying School in November of 1943. He went on to fly airplanes in the Pacific theater before returning safely back to the States after V-J Day.

While I adored my vintage life preserver and its back story, I couldn't rely on it to save my life if we ended up ditching in the English

Channel. I stuffed a modern life vest beneath my Mae West just in case we developed engine trouble on our flight to Normandy. I briefly entertained this worst-case scenario in my head. If our jump master gives us the order to abandon ship, will I have time to deploy my chute, chuck my helmet into the channel, remove this ancient life jacket, and deploy my modern one?

Boy, I sure hoped so.

With my personal kit squared away, I found a teammate to pair off with. In turn we helped one another don our parachutes and clip on our reserves. As our team jump masters double and triple checked our chutes, I felt my stomach begin to rumble with nervous anticipation. The next time I took this parachute off I would be in a different country. With our chutes donned, our team filed out of the hangar toward the crowded tarmac. Each jumper wore upwards of 70 pounds of gear on their person. As we drew near to the flight line, the multitude of air show spectators parted before us like Moses and the Red Sea. Those without a smart phone or camera in their hands broke out into spontaneous, sustained applause. An older gentleman extended his arm to wish us well with a handshake.

"Good luck, lads. Good luck." he repeated as we filed past him. "Godspeed."

Snaking single file through the crowd, I was energized by the presence of the adoring well-wishers. A minute or two later, our column of jumpers came to a brief halt at the gated entrance to the tarmac.

I turned and noticed a woman and her young daughter who were clutching miniature U.S. flags. We locked eyes. The woman clasped my hands in hers and spoke to me with tears welling from her eyes.

"Thank you. Thank you for what you are doing," her voice cracked through her thick British accent.

"It's an honor to be here," I replied. "Thank you for coming out to support us." The line started moving once again and I continued on my way.

We emerged from the crowd out onto the flight line. Dozens of taildraggers sat parked in a uniform row along the tarmac. Their respective air crews buzzed around them as they performed last minute pre-flight checks. The stick of jumpers to which I had been assigned split off from the larger group and approached our ride across the channel. Stepping out of line, I stopped to study the noble C-47 Skytrain parked in front of me. A shade of dark green paint covered all but the underbelly of the vintage airplane. The moniker "Placid Lassie" adorned her nose in hand-painted yellow letters. The same cursive script could be found on both of her engines. The left motor was named "Idling Ada" after her crew chief's wife. Her right was named "Eager Eileen" in honor of her radio operator's wife. Seventy-six years earlier, in July 1943, she rolled off an aircraft assembly in Long Beach, California before eventually flying the North Atlantic passage to England. Less than a year after arriving in Europe, Placid Lassie saw action on D-Day. She dropped paratroopers behind enemy lines in the opening assault of Operation Overlord. The airplane would go on to participate in Operation Market Garden in Holland in September of 1944, and later drop supplies over Bastogne, Belgium during the Battle of the Bulge.

Placid Lassie wore distinctive black and white invasion stripes on her wings like many of the other taildraggers on the flight line. During the airborne invasion of Sicily in 1943, scores of friendly C-47s were shot out of the sky by allied anti-aircraft gunners on the ground who mistook them for enemy aircraft. Following a spate of similar friendly fire incidents leading up to the Normandy invasion, Allied high command decided that something must be done to help differentiate friendly planes from those belonging to the enemy. It was ordered that an alternating pattern of three white and two black stripes be painted on the wings of all aircraft participating in the imminent invasion. Legend has it that all the white paint in England was consumed in order to accomplish the task. Some aircrews had so little time to follow through on the order that brooms and mops were used to hastily apply the stripes prior to the invasion. In a few cases, planes took off for Normandy with wet paint still dripping from their wings.

A member of Placid Lassie's crew stood in the rear door. He gave each jumper ahead of me a hand up as they scrambled up the plane's detachable metal ladder and into the belly of the C-47. When it was my turn, I reached for his hand and tried to keep my balance as I hoisted myself up off the tarmac. The seventy pounds of equipment strapped to me served to complicate what would normally be a fairly straightforward task. I was the second-to-last jumper to climb aboard. My former drill instructor at jump school, Jon Tehan was the last man to board and subsequently would be the first man to jump. A USMC vet of nearly two decades and a natural born leader, Tehan had seen action in both Somalia and Iraq along with numerous other deployments around the globe. I could think of no other teammate I would rather follow through the door over the drop zone.

Unlike most of the other C-47s in the D-Day squadron, Placid Lassie did not have the typical aluminum bench seats installed along the sides of her fuselage like Boogie Baby did back in Frederick. We piled into the plane and sat in a row on the floor with our backs facing the cockpit. Taking my seat inside, I extended my legs until my boots occupied the space in front of the curved door frame. We would be making our nearly two-hour journey to France without a rear door. Placid Lassie's engines roared to life along with a dozen other taildraggers on the airfield. The smell of engine exhaust transported me momentarily back to Oklahoma where my journey had begun almost a year earlier. Shortly thereafter, the control tower at Duxford gave our formation permission to move out. I watched through the open door as neighboring C-47s peeled off one by one and motored away from their parking spots on the flight line. The prop blasts from each plane's engines blew the airfield's blades of grass in a mesmerizing pattern.

Soon it was our turn. Placid Lassie began to roll forward as we taxied toward the end of the runway. Our pilots turned the C-47 into the wind and revved the RPMs of both engines. While we were still on the ground, the crew performed one last pre-flight check of the engines, oil pressure, flaps, and other vital systems from the cockpit. Idling Ada and Eager Eileen roared to life once again as we accelerated down the runway. I felt my stomach leap as we defied gravity and slipped the surly bonds of earth.

"Airborne!" we all yelled in keeping with our team tradition.

As we gained altitude above Duxford, I unclipped my static line from my reserve chute and placed my thumb in the metal opening of the hook. It was prudent to be ready to hook up and bail out at a moment's notice. If, in the event of an emergency, we were given the choice between bailing out or crash-landing, it was far preferred to jump and take your chances outside the plane. While these beautiful C-47s were lovingly maintained they were also three quarters of a century old. It was best to be prepared, just in case.

Placid Lassie climbed to 1,000 feet, the invasion stripes glistening on her wings. We set our course for Normandy with a dozen C47s and other vintage warbirds acting as escorts. Soon we were joined by other restored troop transports with names like D-Day Doll, Aces High, and Betsy's Biscuit Bomber. Leading the pack was That's All Brother. During the D-Day invasion, she had dropped the first stick of pathfinders into Normandy in advance of the airborne armada. It was only fitting that she take the place of honor at the front of the formation. Pathfinders were a group of specially-trained paratroopers whose job it was to jump into enemy territory and mark drop zones with lights and radio equipment ahead of the main airborne assault. Despite the Pathfinders' best efforts, most paratroopers landed nowhere near their designated drop zones. Withering anti-aircraft fire from German ground units forced most C-47s to break from their pre-determined flight paths. In the midst of the chaos, most never recovered their navigational bearings. Entire sticks of jumpers were dropped from such low altitudes that their chutes barely had a chance to open before they hit the ground. Some even landed in the English Channel.

Tehan and I craned our necks toward the door in order to catch a glimpse of the ground. The surface roads surrounding Duxford were lined with cars. Appearing from altitude as a sea of colorful ants, thousands of locals had turned out to watch the formation take off. They stood along the shoulders of the roads taking photographs and waving. We returned their waves and marveled at the incredible turnout that stretched for miles around Duxford. Our formation banked to the south as we flew over the bucolic countryside of southern England. The farm fields and meadows formed a lush patchwork quilt of green that stretched to the horizon. D-Day Doll, a fellow veteran of the original invasion, flew in formation just off our wing on the port side. I framed up a photograph of her through the door as she paced alongside us.

With the excitement of takeoff behind us, I settled in for the duration of the flight. I looked around the interior of the riveted aluminum fuselage at the dozens and dozens of names and signatures of World War II veterans had been scrawled on the walls of the aircraft. Many of the veterans were former airborne. My thoughts turned to the more than 13,000 paratroopers of the All-American 82nd Airborne and 101st Airborne "Screaming Eagles" divisions who had flown this same course before me 75 years earlier to the day. On the morning of D-Day, more than 1,600 paratroopers would be killed or listed as missing in action. Another 900 or so would be wounded in the jump or subsequent combat. Forty-two C-47s and many of their crews would be shot down by German anti-aircraft fire. It was the courage and sacrifice of those men that helped guarantee the success of the Normandy invasion. Without the strategic foothold provided by the airborne, a German counter-attack would likely have pushed the Allied troops off the beaches and back into the English Channel. The paratroopers prevented what could have been a disastrous repeat of Dunkirk in 1940.

I turned my attention away from the ribbed walls of the fuselage back to the open door. The green farmland of Hampshire suddenly give way to a chalky, white cliff face. Our formation had reached the English Channel. We were finally "feet wet." I looked down at the choppy waves in the English Channel below and felt a surge of relief when I remembered the modern life vest around my neck.

About that time, an escort of smaller World War II fighter planes joined us from Duxford. The shiny silver planes appeared alongside us as the southern coast of England faded from view. A restored P51 Mustang fighter descended down alongside us on Placid Lassie's starboard side. Dubbed "little friends" by American bomber crews during World War II, fighter escorts protected American bombers from menacing German fighters. As the Luftwaffe was beaten into submission later in the war, raids of up to 1,000 B-17s would depart airfields in Southern England en route to industrial and military targets around Berlin. The little friends would accompany them as much of the way to Germany as their fuel tanks allowed. I marveled at the graceful curves and distinctive glass bubble cockpit of the Mustang fighter flying along beside us. Its powerful Rolls-

Royce Merlin engine had no trouble keeping up with our lumbering C-47. The P-51 was so close that I could make out the whites of the pilot's eyes.

Once again, I felt goosebumps appear on my arms and legs. There was nowhere else in the entire world I would rather be at that moment. I closed my eyes for a few minutes and took some deep breaths. I meditated on how far I had come and how proud I was to be on this jump team, on this aircraft, and on this mission of remembrance. I relived everything I had sacrificed to be afforded a spot on this plane; the hours I had spent on the treadmill getting ready for jump school, the meals I had skipped to save money for the trip, the intense fear I overcame to earn my jump wings, the 24 hours of exhausting travel. It was all worth it. Every single sacrifice and moment of discomfort. *Enjoy this, Luke.* I fought to be present and soak in the glory of it all, even as anxiety surrounding my imminent jump started to manifest inside me.

Our two-hour flight from the outskirts of Cambridge across the English Channel afforded plenty of time for soul-searching. I grew up idolizing the men whose names were written all over Placid Lassie's interior walls. Who were these men who had volunteered for such a dangerous job? They were farm boys, auto mechanics, school teachers, and steelworkers. When their nation asked for volunteers to step forward and fight, they answered the call and said, "Here am I. Send me."

Their descent down into the dangerous unknown in the early morning hours of June 6, 1944, was a feat worth imitating in more ways than one. They jumped to confront the tyranny and evil of the Third Reich. What darkness and malevolence did I need to confront in my own life? They stepped from order into pure chaos to accomplish their mission. In what areas did I need to abandon safety or comfort and take a risk? Upon landing in France, they searched one another out in the darkness and attacked the enemy in small but lethal groups. Who were the men in my life that I needed to stand with and form my own band of brothers alongside? The paratroopers who jumped left behind girlfriends, wives, and children. Was I living a life worthy of their sacrifice?

I marveled at the bravery of the paratroopers who had filled this same space so many years earlier. *This* is the kind of man I want to be. I want to be a courageous man who sacrifices for the good of those around him. I resolved to make the veterans who had jumped on D-Day proud of my actions on that day. As I sat deep in thought, I recalled the woman who grabbed my hands on our way to the flight line back in Duxford. I pictured the tears welling up in her eyes. What had I done to merit that kind of emotional outpouring of gratitude and support? Go to jump school? Dress-up in WWII gear? Take time off from work and travel to Europe? None of these things alone, nor any combination of them, merited her reaction. I looked down at the Mae West hanging from my neck and thought about Lt.

Bowdin's name stenciled in faded ink on the back of the yellow canvas life preserver.

Then, it hit me. It wasn't about anything *I* had done. It wasn't about the depth of my training or the accuracy of my uniform. It wasn't about the hours I had spent impregnating my jump jacket with bars of wax to achieve an authentic soiled look. Nor was it about the painstaking lengths I had taken to ensure my web gear and equipment were historically accurate down to the last detail. It was not about me. I was not a hero. I was simply a living, breathing embodiment of a group of astoundingly heroic men.

While the ranks of those who survived D-Day continues to decrease in number with the passage of time, the myth surrounding them, and their exploits lives on. More and more people have never had the opportunity to say "thank you" to those who cracked Hitler's Atlantic wall and liberated a continent. My presence gave these people the chance to shake a warm hand, make eye contact, and connect to the past. Rather than saying thanks to me, they were saying thanks *through* me. They were expressing their gratitude to the men who willingly stepped from order into chaos at great risk to themselves.

Before I knew it, the deep, grey waters of the Channel merged with a sandy stretch of coast. We had made it to France. For the first time in my life, I beheld the beaches of Normandy with my own two eyes. I peered down on Sword Beach and wondered what it must have looked like 75 years earlier. In my imagination I could see hundreds of Royal Navy ships and landing craft anchored off the coast. I visualized thousands of British Army soldiers scrambling across the beach carrying rifles, ladders, bicycles, and bagpipes. God bless those chaps who braved that machine gun fire and faced certain death all those years ago.

As we crossed Sword Beach, the formation banked inland toward the tiny village of Sannerville. Nearing the drop zone, our jumpmaster initiated pre-jump procedures.

"Six Minutes," he yelled to us over the thunderous clamor of Placid Lassie's two engines.

"Six minutes!" I belted out with the rest of my teammates.

"Stand up!" He yelled.

We repeated his command and staggered to our feet.

"Hook up!" he ordered, making a hook with his index finger and gesturing toward the static line cable above our heads that ran the length of the C-47's fuselage. I attached my metal hook to the cable and ensured that it locked in place.

"Check your equipment!" came the next command. I made sure that the static line belonging to Tehan in front of me was not tangled. The jumper behind me did the same for mine.

"Sound off for equipment check," the jumpmaster yelled. Each jumper replied in order.

"Nine, OK!"

"Eight, OK!"

"Seven, OK!"

"Six, OK!"

A few more teammates counted off their numbers. I felt the jumper behind me slap my upper thigh to signal that my static line was in good shape.

"Two OK!" I yelled at the top of my lungs. I slapped Tehan's thigh ahead of me.

"All OK, jumpmaster," he yelled. The two men shook hands. Minutes ticked by while our formation navigated inland to the center of the drop zone.

I glanced over my left shoulder through one of Placid Lassie's windows and spied Pegasus Bridge come into view below us. Just before midnight on June 5th, 1944, the British Army's 6th Airborne Division, the Red Devils, occupied this same patch of airspace. Strapped into Horsa gliders made of wood and fabric, the men descended silently onto the banks of the Orne River and proceeded to fire the opening shots of the D-day Invasion. A savage firefight ensued as the Paras battled to wrest control of the small bascule bridge from its German defenders. The Brits fought off multiple counter-attacks until their own reinforcements arrived from Sword beach in the late morning. They were famously ordered to "hold until relieved." They did just that.

In the split second that Pegasus Bridge remained visible through the window, another C-47 flying at a lower altitude came into view. *This is the coolest damn thing I've ever done in my life*, I thought. Not wanting to distract myself from the task at hand, I pried my gaze away from the window and focused my attention back to the impending jump.

"One minute!" The jumpmaster warned.

My nervous system coursed with adrenaline and testosterone. I vividly experienced the physiological war that rages between my body and my mind in the seconds leading up to a jump.

"Don't do this! Don't you dare jump out of this plane. What the hell are you doing?" my gut screamed to my brain.

Shut up. We're doing this, my brain countered. *I would rather die than not make this jump with my teammates.*

I said my customary pre-jump prayer under my breath. "Please help me remember my training, and please protect me. Amen."

I repeated the silent prayer again and again in my mind. But the fear inside me refused to abate. My left hand trembled ever so slightly as I held my parachute's metal static line hook out in front of me. Fear gripped every part of me. *Luke, don't do this.*

"Stand in the door!" Called the jumpmaster. Tehan complied and took his position in Placid Lassie's open door. I stood at the ready to take his place. Any second now I would be following Tehan out the door. I dialed in my concentration and stared at the jumpmaster. The seconds ticked by at an agonizingly slow pace. Finally, my ears registered the command for which I had been listening so intently.

"GO!" yelled the jumpmaster. Tehan disappeared out the door in a flash. It was my turn. I advanced toward the door to occupy the spot that Tehan had just vacated. My right hand protected my reserve chute's deployment handle. My left hand guided my static line hook down the overheard cable. I made momentary eye contact with the jump master as I shoved the hook in his direction. With my left leg extended, I made ninety-degree pivot and stepped toward the open door. I extended my arms out and grabbed both sides the fuselage. For a brief moment I locked my gaze firmly on the horizon. Once my brain registered the cold aluminum of the C-47's outer skin in my hands, I extended my left leg and launched myself through the door and into thin air.

The 120mph wind shear coming over Placid Lassie's left wing caught my left leg like a wind vein and instantly rotated me ninety degrees so that my legs were parallel to the fuselage. In a split second, I found my reserve chute handle once again with my right hand. I slammed my feet and knees together and formed a right angle with my body, tucking my chin to my chest. Like a kid jumping into a swimming pool from a high dive, I felt the momentary terror of being in free-fall. My stomach floated up into my throat as I experience a few fleeting seconds of weightlessness.

Time came to a standstill.

Frame by frame, my brain registered the drop zone rushing up at me. I noticed the toes of my leather jump boots out of focus in the foreground. My heart skipped a beat as my body tried to register the shock of what had just happened. Just as I had been taught at the parachute school, I began to count: *One one-thousand, two one-thousand, three one-thousand.* In the event I made it to four one-thousand, I would assume that my parachute had experienced a high-speed malfunction and deploy my reserve chute. My count was interrupted by the force of my static line going taut, the first step in a successful chute deployment. The static line pulled a small, miniature parachute known as a pilot chute from my pack. The pilot chute immediately caught the wind and deployed my much larger main chute with a jolt. I felt myself quickly decelerate from the momentary free fall. My body whipped 180 degrees back toward Placid Lassie's direction of travel.

The sound of a nylon whoosh met my ears. I looked up and saw the most beautiful sight in the world: a well-deployed, intact canopy in the air above me. Thirty paracord suspension lines, each evenly-spaced around the circumference of the canopy, met at the apex of my green nylon chute. I registered the geometric symmetry of the round parachute. It was a blessed signpost of order in the midst of chaos and terror, and a deeply pleasing one at that.

"Yeah!" I yelled involuntarily at the top of my lungs. "Airborne!"

I was still alive. I survived my exit and my chute had deployed flawlessly. *Fantastic.* Gathering my wits, my eyes took in a thoroughly surreal scene. Jumpers and their parachutes filled the air like locusts, practically blotting out the sky. There were more chutes in the air than I had ever seen before in one place. Wave after wave of C-47s passed overhead in formation, depositing their jumpers over the drop zone. Above me I saw my teammates exiting from another C-47 in quick succession. The rumble of dozens and dozens of radial engines combined to produce a low-frequency chorus in my ears. Approximately 180 jumpers and their chutes crowded the airspace above Sannerville.

"Holy shit," I blurted out involuntarily. "It's raining men!"

Snapping out of my blissful stupor, I quickly reached for a khaki pouch slung over my right shoulder. Originally designed to carry spare magazines for a Thompson Submachine gun, my Canon SLR fit perfectly inside the fabric container. I ripped open the top, brought my camera to my face and mashed the shutter button. The first few images popped up on my camera's rear LCD screen. The photos were too bright. In my haste to start taking pictures, I had failed to check my exposure and subsequently blown out all my highlights.

"Shit!" I yelled.

I corrected the error and fired off a handful more photos. This time my exposure was right on the money. The photos depicted my teammates silhouetted against the overcast sky as they drifted down toward the lush Norman countryside. Once more I turned my attention upward and took a quick photo of my fully inflated canopy. *That's what I like to see.* Out of the corner of my eye, I noticed the ground begin rushing up toward me at an alarming rate. It was almost time to land. I slung my camera back over my shoulder with a hope and prayer that it would survive the next 15 seconds.

"OK, it's time to land. Feet and knees together. Land on the balls of your feet and prepare to PLF," I recited. "Here we go!" With eyes fixed on the horizon once again, I awaited impact.

The next thing I knew, I felt my boots touch down on the soft, French soil. I performed a textbook PLF. Clumps of mud flew up into the air as I impacted the ground and watched the horizon line spin counter-clockwise. I leapt to my feet and surveyed the gorgeous drop zone. My parachute canopy descended lazily overhead as I did a quick inventory of my feet, knees, hip, and upper back. Overjoyed at my uninjured state, another involuntarily expression of pure joy escaped my lungs.

"Airborne!" I yelled with gusto.

All around me tall sheathes of green wheat swayed in the gentle breeze. Across the vast farm field, the rest of my teammates were coming in for their own landings. I unbuckled my helmet from my head, wiped the sweat from brow, and began gathering up my parachute. My hands were trembling from excitement. I shakily stuffed armfuls of the green nylon canopy into a repurposed aviator's kit bag that I had tucked beneath my parachute harness back in Duxford. Next, I clipped my reserve chute to the kit bag's two cloth handles and slung the contraption over my head like a sandwich board. Before exiting the drop zone, I paused to pray for a moment. It was hard to focus with everything going on, but I managed to string a few sentences together. I thanked the Lord for bringing me safely to the ground and asked that I might have the fortitude to live a life marked by virtue, selflessness and courage like the men whose jump I had just re-enacted. *Amen.*

I reached down to grab my helmet and noticed the photograph that I tucked inside its liner before the jump. There was my maternal Grandmother, Doris Valentine Beechwood, looking up at me in admiration. In the picture she was still a young woman, her smooth skin yet unwrinkled. Her flowing golden hair not yet gray as I had known it to be ever since I was a child. She was dressed to the nines in a full-length fur-collared coat. The bright white kerchief tied around her neck contrasted perfectly with her red lipstick. Doris, or "Amah" as my siblings and I called her, was a member of the greatest generation who had herself lived through World War II. After Pearl Harbor, her male high school classmates did what practically every other able-bodied male did: They volunteered for the armed services and shipped out to boot camp. With most of the young men gone from her small town of Ivyland, Pennsylvania, she worked as a freight dispatcher for the Reading Railroad. Under her watch countless freight trains loaded with coal, steel, and other materials deemed vital for the war effort, passed safely over the rails en route to the U.S. Naval Shipyard in Philadelphia. It was a point of pride to have commemorated her service on the home front during my jump.

My grandfather, her husband of seventy years, missed serving in World War II by just a few months due to his age. He joined the U.S. Army Air Corps in 1945 and was slated to begin pilot training at an airbase in Utah when news of the Japanese surrender broke.

With my grandmother's photo still inside, I threw the helmet back on my head and hustled off the drop zone to make room for the next wave of jumpers who were already on their way down. A small, single-lane road bisected the drop zone some thirty yards from where I landed. Thousands of locals and tourists came out to watch the jump. As I stepped up onto the dirt lane, I was greeted by a dozen or so spectators who stood nearby.

"Vive la America," one man called out jubilantly.

"Vive la France," I responded with equal jubilation.

A few of the onlookers asked to take a photo with me and I happily obliged. It was a small taste of what I imagine it must feel like to be a celebrity. Seeing a group of young children approach, I dug into my musette bag and pulled out a handful of miniature Hershey's chocolate bars which I had packed for this very occasion. I passed out the candy, mimicking what so many American G.I.'s had done for children across the European continent during the war. After passing out the candy, I bid the group "au revoir" and began the long hike back toward the rally point.

I felt so much pride as I walked off the drop zone. It was such an honor to be able to act as an unofficial ambassador for the United States. I was so thankful to be there. The welcome I received blew me away. In the same way our World War II veterans had been greeted as liberators by the people of France, so to had the people on the drop zone welcomed me. Of course, I was not a hero. But I did know some men who were. Before I had covered much ground, a restored Willy's Jeep pulled up behind me on the dirt road.

"Do you need a lift?" the driver asked with a thick Dutch accent.

Delighted by the opportunity to hitch ride off the DZ, (and an historically accurate one at that) I responded in the affirmative and jumped onboard. I squeezed into the Jeep with a handful of other guys dressed in World War II uniforms. Being a fellow Jeep owner and re-enactor myself, I felt a kinship with these men. After a short ride to the main road, the Jeep dropped me off near a line of vehicles parked on the shoulder. I left my parachute in one of the team rental vans and then proceeded to meet up with my teammates who were waiting to greet us on the drop zone. We gathered in a large circle and offered up a prayer of thanksgiving. We thanked God for having allowed us to safely accomplish our mission and for the men who did the same 75 years earlier. I pulled a vintage 48-star American flag from one of my trouser pockets and unfurled it for a team photo on the edge of the wheat field.

Several spectators came over to talk with the team after we had taken our photos. One of them, a tall man with two young boys in tow, approached me.

"Excuse me sir, would you take a photo with my two boys?" He asked with an American accent. I readily agreed and knelt down for the photo. As I stood up and turned to shake his hand, I suddenly realized that I had seen the man before. Though he was wearing civilian clothes I recognized him immediately from my time covering the White House. He was a member of the U.S. Secret Service's Uniformed Division.

"Hey, I know you," I blurted out. "You're a UD guy." Not remembering that President Trump was scheduled to be in Normandy the following day, I was blown away that I would run into someone I knew from the States. He pulled a Secret Service challenge coin from his pocket and placed it in my hand. The gold coin featured the Uniformed Division badge crest on one side, and the silhouette of a short-barreled rifle on the other. The coin read "Secret Service Open Carry Sector" in reference to the armed Uniformed Division officers who stand guard on Pennsylvania Avenue in front of the White House. I dug a WWIIADT team coin out of my musette bag and returned the favor.

I bid farewell to my Secret Service friend and jumped into a team van for the trip back to our home base at the Château de Plain-Marais. Located five miles southwest of Sainte-Mère-Église along the Douve River, the château was originally the site of a Roman garrison. In the 1300's stone fortifications were erected on the site. Some 400 years later in the 1700s the château in its current form was constructed. During the German occupation of France, a Nazi general attempted to take up residence in the picturesque dwelling. The resident at the time, a pregnant woman who happened to be very close to her due date, refused the German officer's demands and insisted that he and his staff leave the property. The Germans decided to continue their search for a suitable residence to requisition, apparently unwilling to evict the very pregnant woman from her home.

Our van crossed the serene Douve River and took a sharp right turn onto a long gravel driveway that led to the front of the historic residence. Neatly-manicured grass flanked the drive on either side for a distance of about 600 yards. A stone bridge transported us across a wide moat and through the towering front gate. The "U" shaped château was surrounded by mature trees and a formidable stone wall some fifteen feet tall. As we pulled into the gravel courtyard, a vintage Peugeot sedan from the 1930's greeted us in the driveway. Stepping out of the van was like stepping back in time. The brick walls of the three-story structure towered overhead. An American flag displayed proudly by the château's French owners flapped gently in the breeze from the sill of a second story window. I grabbed my parachute from the trunk of the van and dropped it outside the front entrance of the grand structure. The next day would be spent re-packing chutes in anticipation of additional jumps on the 7th and 8th of June at Caen airport in Normandy.

I stepped inside our wing of the château and looked around the large room. Cots, sleeping bags, and parachute gear lined the walls of the room beneath its ancient, vaulted wood beam ceiling. A massive Norman coat of arms was displayed on one of the walls. A pair of embroidered golden lions with mouths agape and claws in the air greeted me on the red cloth flag. I found an open cot outside on the lawn underneath a large tent and settled in for the night. With the adrenaline of the day's events finally wearing off I drifted off to sleep with a deep sense of satisfaction in my bones.

The team spent the next day packing parachutes on the château's pristine lawns. During our lunch break, I took the opportunity to explore the grounds of the enchanting property. Château de Plain-Marais' owner, Guillaume Daigneaux, was a veteran of the French Army's 13 Régiment de Dragon Parachutistes and a most gracious and accommodating host to our team. He gave me directions to an outbuilding on the edge of the property where an English language inscription had recently been discovered. Guillaume believed that it could have been left behind by an American soldier during the invasion. I set off toward the northwest corner of the grounds and quickly found the outbuilding. Once a small stable for visiting guest's horses, the dilapidated rectangular brick structure was now in a state of disrepair and completely missing its roof. I entered the outbuilding's remains and began my search where Guillaume had suggested along the door frame. Shortly thereafter, I spotted what I was looking for. There, scrawled in pencil on a piece of brick, was a faint inscription that read "Holstein, Oak Hill, West Virginia."

A quick internet search led me to the obituary for a World War II veteran named Corbett Dempsey Holstein. According to the online register, he was born in Coalburg, West Virginia in 1924 and buried in Oak Hill, West Virginia some seventy years later in 1994. Accompanying the obituary was a portrait of a serviceman and a beautiful woman with dark hair. The man wore a khaki uniform with his garrison cap tilted drastically to the left side of his skull. Flaunting Army uniform regulations in this way was the practice of many an airborne trooper during the Second World War. The tilted cap paired with the soldier's steely expression of cool confidence led me to believe the late Mr. Holstein had quite possibly been a paratrooper. The château was not far from Sainte-Mère-Église, a main objective of the Army's 82nd Airborne division on D-day. I framed up a photo of the inscription on the brick for posterity.

In my imagination I pictured Holstein sneaking through the darkness on June 6th, laden down with combat equipment and cradling an M1 Garand rifle. Perhaps not knowing if he would survive the night, he decided to scrawl his name and hometown inside the stable before continuing on his way across the French countryside. I lingered in the old stable replaying this possible scenario in my mind for a few minutes.

Something as simple as some pencil markings on an old brick was enough to provide me a powerful connection to the past.

That afternoon, the team set out on a battlefield tour led by our team's resident historian, Mark Bando. Mark led our team to little-known points of interest far from the popular tourist spots frequented by crowds and tour busses in Normandy. Our first stop was outside a small dairy farm not far from the château. Early on the morning of June 6th, 1944, a U.S. C-47 Skytrain crash-landed on the farm after being blown out of the sky by German anti-aircraft fire. In recent years, locals pooled their resources and installed a bronze plaque in memory of the crew members who perished there. Mark read aloud their names one by one and called for a moment of silence. I bowed my head to remember the sacrifice of these valiant airmen. After a few seconds had passed, I cracked an eyelid and peeked at the rest of my teammates. Some 4 dozen Americans dressed in khaki jump fatigues filled the narrow country lane with their heads bowed in reverent silence.

Our caravan continued on its way. We snaked through a maze of single-lane roads boxed in on both sides by towering hedgerows. A distinctive feature of the countryside in Normandy, the dense hedgerows proved to be a formidable defensive position for the German army. Airborne troops experienced this first hand on D-Day. Through no fault of their own, many men parachuted into open farm fields bordered on all sides by hedgerows. German soldiers could control these open spaces with a single well-placed machine-gun nest. Scores of Allied paratroopers met their fate and were cut down upon landing in the midst of these devastating fields of fire.

In the days following D-Day, the hedgerows also frustrated the advance of Sherman tanks that had rolled off the beaches and were trying to push inland. Tankers from Patton's Third Army quickly found a solution to their hedgerow problem by welding sharpened metal tusks to the front of their armored vehicles. My great uncle on my mother's side of the family, John C. Valentine, was one of the innovating Pennsylvania farm boys who came up with and implemented the idea. The "rhino tanks," as the soldiers called them, helped U.S. armored units slice their way through the thick vegetation that checkered the countryside.

Exiting the maze of hedgerows, we pulled into a farm and parked in-between a pair of humble livestock barns made of earth and wood. Our group gathered around Mark as he told us the story of a paratrooper from Cleveland, Ohio who became separated from his unit on D-Day and took up residence in one of the old barns. The trooper spent the next couple days doing his best to avoid roving German patrols as he attempted to link up with fellow American paratroopers. Despite his best efforts to escape and evade the enemy, a group of German soldiers eventually tracked him and another American paratrooper back to his hiding spot. The Germans surrounded the barn and opened fire with automatic weapons, peppering the walls with machine-gun fire. The paratroopers inside took cover in the barn's hay loft until the onslaught of hot lead finally ceased. Content that anyone inside had been turned to Swiss cheese, the Germans left the area. Inexplicably, the Americans inside emerged without scratch. A short time later, they abandoned the barn and finally managed to find their way to the U.S. front line. As Mark finished recounting the story, he turned our attention to the outside of the barn. The mud facade was still pock-marked with more bullet holes than I could count.

An afternoon thunderstorm cut our tour short, but not before we managed to visit a half dozen other sites of lesser-known battles during the Normandy invasion. There was, and remains, no better tour guide in Normandy than Mark Bando. His knowledge of airborne history on the Cotentin Peninsula is thanks, in large part, to the many personal friendships he cultivated over the years with the veterans of the 101st and 82nd. These veterans had all seen combat in Normandy during June of 1944 and shared their experiences in detail with Mark for posterity.

While our caravan made our way back to the château, I marveled at the scale of the airborne invasion we were commemorating. Tens of thousands of men, parachutes, weapons, and bundles of combat equipment rained down from the sky in the course of a few hours. Entire divisions of fighting men were inserted behind enemy lines via parachute and glider. To this day, amateur historians and treasure seekers still pull battlefield artifacts from forests, creeks, and meadows that have lain undisturbed for more than seven decades. It's not uncommon for farmers tilling their fields or gardeners working in their backyards to pull rust-covered war relics like rifles and helmets from the ground. For the rest of the drive back to the château, I daydreamed about returning with a metal detector and a shovel to unearth treasures of my own.

That evening, our team hosted a banquet on the grounds of the château. A pair of 101st Airborne veterans, Norwood Thomas and Dan McBride, both of whom had jumped on D-Day, were among the guests of honor. These two vets were also frequent visitors to our team's parachute school graduations over the years. A half dozen other D-Day vets joined us for the evening celebration. Throughout the night we feasted on a hearty meal and toasted our guests with copious amounts of French wine. Though they will deny it until the cows come home, these men are heroes. What is a hero? A hero is someone who leaves safety, descends into the underworld, faces down the dragon of chaos, restores order, and returns with a treasure of great value. Norwood, Dan, and the other veterans in attendance that night had done exactly that. They left the safety of their homes to confront evil. They endured the hell of war as they fought across Europe, driving out occupying armies and restoring order. They were exposed to the horrors of combat and sustained terrible wounds on the battlefield. When it was all said and done, they returned home having brought peace and freedom to Western civilization.

With the sun setting and the dinner party wrapping up, our veteran guests and their caretakers bid the team farewell. Before they departed, we gathered for a big team photo in the courtyard of the château. I shook Dan McBride's hand and relayed a message of gratitude for his presence.

"Don't do anything I wouldn't do," he replied as the two of us parted ways.

I watched as Dan and Norwood, the two 101st veterans, walked toward their vehicles. The two aging paratroopers cautiously traversed the château's gravel driveway with the help of their walking canes. Now in their nineties, both men had once been fearsome, combat-tested soldiers in the ranks of America's airborne elite. They both jumped from C-47s on D-Day and fought toe to toe with the Nazis. Old age, however, had taken a terrible toll on the pair of old warfighters. Their mobility, strength, and vitality were not what they used to be. This would likely be the last trip to Normandy of their lifetimes. One day each man would pass their torch of masculine courage, honor, and commitment down to the next generation of American men. I hoped that I would be a worthy recipient of that mantle. I hoped that as an old man I would be able to look back on my own life and know that I embodied those same masculine virtues wherever my life's mission might have taken me.

While things at the château wound down for the evening, I found out that a group of my teammates were preparing to sneak away for a clandestine trip to Sainte-Mère-Église. This was one secret mission I couldn't miss out on. Donning my worn M42 jump jacket and trousers, I grabbed my olive drab garrison cap and ran to catch up with my teammates.

Steeped in history and airborne folklore, the small village of Sainte-Mère-Église was the scene of brutal urban combat between 82nd Airborne paratroopers and crack German troops on D-Day. As the first Americans began to descend toward their drop zones around the village, a number of soldiers were blown off course into the middle of the town. Earlier that evening a fire had broken out in the downtown square. Subsequently, the town's streets were filled with local residents and German soldiers working to extinguish the blaze. A fierce firefight broke out between the Germans and the unlucky souls whose slow descent under canopy was illuminated by the flames of the fire. One of these men, Pvt. John Steele of the 82nd Airborne's 505th Parachute Infantry Regiment, famously snagged his chute on the steeple of the Catholic church at the center of the village. He hung there out of sight as he watched his brothers cut down in the streets of Sainte-Mère-Église some forty feet below him. Miraculously, Steele defied the odds and survived the treacherous night, suffering only a shrapnel wound to his foot. Eventually he was spotted by the Germans, cut down from the steeple, and taken prisoner for a short time. He later escaped his captors during an American counter-attack and eventually linked up with fellow paratroopers from the 82nd. By daybreak the unit had wrested control of the village from the Germans. To this day, a life-sized mannequin dressed in paratrooper gear stills hangs from a white silk parachute on the church's steeple in honor of Pvt. Steele.

My teammates and I found a parking spot on a side street and made our way toward the center of town. Turning the corner, downtown Sainte-Mère-Église came into full view. Historic three-story homes, taverns, and souvenir shops built from stone lined the square. Their charming grey shingled roofs and ornate chimneys pointed to the sky from which the town's liberators had descended all those years ago. Small American and French flags were strung proudly across the streets between stately cast iron lamp posts. World War II helmets, belts, knives, patches and flags were displayed for sale in storefront windows. A throng of soldiers, re-enactors, tourists, and locals filled the streets. The atmosphere of the giant block party was akin to Mardi Gras, minus the beads, Cajun music, and debauchery of Bourbon Street.

My teammate Andrea and I squeezed our way into one of the packed bars and ordered shots of calvados. The French liquor is made from fermented apples that have been grown in the region's orchards since the seventeenth century. Andrea was a thirty-something marketing executive from Dallas with an infectious, upbeat energy and a generous heart. We met the previous October during 2018's fall jump school in Frederick. Despite being far from the picture of a stereotypical paratrooper, Andrea had been voted class leader by her fellow classmates during jump school and proved herself fearless under canopy. We shared a mutual fascination for World War II history and a deep admiration for our country's veterans. With drinks in hand, we made our way back outside to take in the scene.

The atmosphere was electric. Groups of active-duty soldiers from the U.S. Army's elite Ranger battalions walked the streets wearing their coveted tan berets and distinctive ranger scroll patches proudly displayed on their shoulders. Earlier that morning the Rangers had re-enacted the D-Day landings by climbing a cargo net that hung down the face of the cliffs at nearby Pointe Du Hoc.

The party continued into the night as my teammates, and I wandered the square. We looked like reincarnated ghosts of the paratroopers whose boots had graced the very same cobblestones 75 years earlier. It was a point of pride to be there with my fellow teammates. We had come to remember, honor, and serve our World War II veterans, and we had accomplished that mission. To raise a drink in celebration of their victory was exactly what those vets would have wanted. I finished the last of my calvados and watched as sharp-dressed American servicemen strolled down the streets of Sainte-Mère-Église arm-in-arm with adoring French women. Some things never change.

Before we left to drive back to the château, I wandered off from my teammates to soak in the scene on my own for a few minutes. As I had done many times on my trip, I envisioned what things must have looked like back during the war. I imagined the volleys of German machine gun fire echoing across the town square as the bells of the Catholic Church clanged again and again. I pictured the flames of the burning building illuminating the parachutes of the Americans who were descending down through the darkness into the chaos. I thought about the casualties the 82nd took as they fought hard to wrest control of the village from the occupying Germans. I pondered what downtown must have looked like the next morning: silk parachutes caught on tree branches flapping in the breeze, spent shell casings littering the ground, and the cold bodies of American paratroopers still in their harnesses who never had a chance to fight back. I was on hallowed ground.

The following day, our team woke before sunrise and started prepping for an exhibition jump at the Caen airport in Normandy. I felt there would be no topping the experience of my cross-channel jump, so I decided to scratch my name from the manifest list at the last minute. Instead of jumping, I opted to spend my last day in Normandy sightseeing with a handful of other teammates who had come to a similar conclusion. I wished my jumping friends well as they departed the château under gloomy skies. Those of us who had decided to play hooky from the day's jump loaded into a van and set course for the coast.

Our first stop was Pointe Du Hoc. Located between Utah and Omaha beach, the rocky outcropping was a heavily fortified German coastal artillery battery with a commanding view of the English Channel. During the war, thick concrete bunkers housed German gun emplacements that had the potential to wreak havoc on Allied troops landing on Utah Beach. On the morning of D-Day, soldiers from the U.S. Army's 2nd and 5th Ranger Battalions secured their place in the halls of valor as they scaled the pointe's rocky cliffs with ropes and ladders while under heavy fire. Despite concentrated mortar, machine gun, and small arms fire, the Rangers captured and held Pointe Du Hoc against multiple German counterattacks over the course of D-Day. A number of partially destroyed German bunkers remain scattered around the pointe. Indeed, the landscape still bears the scars of the battle to this day. Some 75 years later, the ground remains pockmarked with massive craters courtesy of the Allied bombardment that pounded the area on the morning of June 6th, 1944.

A light rain started to fall as we wandered Pointe du Hoc. Busloads of tourists crowded all around one of the few intact German bunkers on the pointe. I descended a narrow concrete staircase into the belly of one such brutalist structure. As my eyes adjusted to the darkness inside the bunker, I ran my hand over one of its interior walls. Evidence of the fierce battle that had taken place there on D-Day was still visible. The concrete walls of the bunker were pock marked with bullet holes and charred to a dark crisp by American flame-throwers. I moved intentionally from to room, all the while imagining the brave Rangers who engaged in ferocious close-quarters combat in these very rooms and hallways. I peered out toward the English Channel through a narrow slit in the command bunker's main room. Standing in that spot I tried to imagine what it must have felt like to be in a German soldier's boots that day.

The next stop on our tour was Omaha Beach. Famously depicted in the opening scenes of the 1997 movie *Saving Private Ryan*, Omaha was the site of D-Day's bloodiest beach landing. Roughly 2,000 casualties would result from the landing at Omaha alone. I stepped out onto the serene beach and wandered toward the waterline by myself. It was low tide and the sand seemed to stretch more than a hundred yards between the edge of the English Channel and the beach's sea wall. A ceiling of gloomy grey clouds hung low over the beachhead, mimicking the weather on that fateful morning in history. I took some time to quietly reflect on the gravity of the events that had unfolded there: The staggering heroism. The unspeakable carnage. The sons, fathers, husbands, and brothers who had lost their lives that day. The grief so many mothers and wives felt back on the home front upon receiving their dreaded telegrams from the War Department. I imagined the soaked infantrymen huddling behind steel obstacles as German machine-gun rounds cracked through the air and ricocheted around them. I pictured the tide turned red with the blood of young American soldiers. What else could I feel in that moment other than gratitude? I stood alone on the beach as the salt water washed around the soles of my leather jump boots. Kneeling down, I scooped up a handful of sand to take with me back to the States. I never wanted to forget this place.

Later that day I bid farewell to my teammates and hitched a ride to the nearest train station in Caen. Dressed in my team leather jacket, khaki trousers, and trusty garrison cap, I spent the next 3 hours reflecting on the trip of a lifetime as my train sped toward Paris.

The following day, I checked out of my hotel and spent the morning walking along the Seine. I thoroughly enjoyed myself as I took in the sights of downtown Paris for the first time. Eventually I could no longer ignore my growling stomach, so I stopped for breakfast at a picturesque Parisian cafe near the Eiffel Tower. I found a seat outside at a table for two and savored a café au lait and chocolaté croissant. A few tables over, a cute girl with blonde shoulder-length hair caught my eye. I introduced myself and again quickly exhausted the extent of my French vocabulary. As fate would have it, she spoke excellent English. We spoke about the hostel she ran in the Czech Republic and her experiences on a recent road trip she had taken through the American West. I shared about the cross-channel jump and surprised myself with how naturally I embraced the role of cocky American in Paris. With my breakfast plate now devoid of food, I bid my cute European friend "au revoir" and rose to pay my bill. My waiter, a handsome young fellow with a muscular build and inviting smile, happened to be a former paratrooper in the French Army. I emptied my pockets and left him a hefty tip with the last of my Euros. We took a photo together and I handed him one of our team challenges that I had jumped with me into Normandy.

"Airborne!" He exclaimed with a thick French accent.

"Airborne!" I replied.

As morning bled into afternoon, I grudgingly left Paris behind and made my way to the airport. Upon my arrival back at JFK in New York City I was pulled aside by U.S. Customs and Border Protection officials. They had discovered my bag of sand from Omaha Beach in my luggage. A female customs agent approached me and delivered the bad news.

"Possession of foreign soil is prohibited," she informed me in a dispassionate monotone.

My sand was to be confiscated by the Department of Homeland Security and destroyed. The scowl that she wore across her face did not inspire confidence that I would be recovering my bag of contraband from her possession. I determined, however, that I was unwilling to part with my beloved sand without putting up a fight. I asked to speak with her supervisor. The annoyed customs agent rolled her eyes and lead me into a back room. A man I assumed to be the ranking agent sat at a desk in the windowless, fluorescent-lit office. He typed loudly on his computer as I entered the cramped space.

"Sir," the annoyed female officer began. "This traveler is attempting to bring foreign soil into the country." Her words hung in the air as the supervisor continued to bang away at his computer.

"What kind of soil is it, exactly?" He asked as his fingers kept dancing over his keyboard. I cleared my throat and mustered the deepest voice I could manage.

"Sand." I interjected. "Sand from Omaha Beach."

His typing ceased as he looked up from his computer for the first time. I locked eyes with the pale computer-bound supervisor. His gaze darted between my eyes and the bag of sand in his still-scowling subordinate's hand. I held my breath as seconds of silence ticked by. Finally, he announced his decision.

"You're free to go."

My annoyed escort handed me the bag of sand and returned to her post in the customs screening area. Thanking the man, I exited the supervisor's office before he could change his mind. I walked away with both a sense of victory and my sand from Omaha Beach in hand.

I continued to make my way through security and presented my passport at the next customs checkpoint. Suddenly, it dawned on me. In my haste to reunite with my teammates back at the drop zone in Sannerville on June 5th, I had neglected to seek out the French Gendarmerie and have my passport stamped. It seemed that the pair of border police who were present on the drop zone had departed shortly after the last of the jumpers had emerged from the wheat field. Lacking a re-entry stamp in my passport, I technically had spent the last 4 days in France illegally. I began to construct an impromptu legal defense in my head if the authorities confronted me about the apparent diplomatic discrepancy.

"Mr. Sharrett," the customs official interrupted my train of thought. "Welcome home." He stamped my passport and handed it back to me with a nod. *Phew.* As I strolled toward baggage claim a thought popped into my head. You know, the American paratroopers who jumped into France on that fateful night 75 years ago never got their passports stamped either.

On my flight back home to Kentucky I reflected back upon the once-in-a-lifetime trip. I thought about my cross-channel jump. I thought about the photos I had taken. I thought about my bag of sand from Omaha Beach, and I thought about the U.S. Army patch I was carrying in my pants pocket.

During my visit to downtown Sainte-Mère-Église, I struck up a conversation with a group of American soldiers from the 101st Airborne Division. For half an hour we stood around the cobblestone streets swapping stories about all we had seen and experienced during the anniversary. There was something comforting about running into a group of my countrymen so far from home. Upon hearing the details of my team's cross-channel jump, a sergeant ripped the unit patch from the shoulder of his uniform and handed it to me.

The recognizable insignia features the head of a bald eagle centered on a black shield. The bird's eyes are pointed ever-so-slightly skyward with its yellow beak open wide mid-scream. A scroll bearing the word "airborne" spans the top of the crest. The iconic patch has been worn by the 101st since the unit's formation as an airborne division in World War II.

For many decades the patch featured a handful of bright colors not necessarily conducive to remaining undetected on the battlefield. There were white feathers, a yellow beak, and red tongue. This one, however, was different. It was subdued, utilizing various shades of green for the eagle's head. The stitching around the edge of the patch was slightly fuzzy, denoting months of use. It was well-worn. This was the patch of a warrior.

I ran my thumb across the eagle, feeling the soft texture of the embroidery. On the rear of the patch was a small sea of prickly Velcro hooks. I thought about my late cousin Dave, who had worn the same insignia as he patrolled deserts and villages in Iraq with the 101st. I was proud of him. I hoped he was proud of me for having made the trip to Normandy.

As I stood for a moment cherishing the feeling of that patch, I felt the familiar twinge of regret for never having enlisted in the military. Then, it occurred to me. Despite our differences, this soldier and I had something in common. We were both here in Normandy to make sure that the world remembered what took place 75 years ago. We were united in an effort to accomplish the same mission. In a way, we were teammates. We may have only crossed paths for a few minutes in the midst of a raucous street party, but we were teammates, nonetheless. I was moved in the same manner that I had been a decade earlier when that U.S. Marine crew chief gave me his HMX-1 squadron patch. The 101st sergeant and I shared a prolonged handshake.

"Thank you," I said in a low voice.

The sergeant had no idea how meaningful his gift was to me. It was more than just a piece of Velcro-backed embroidered cloth. It was a symbol of belonging to one of the U.S. Army's most storied units. His gesture, simple as it was, communicated to me a message that I longed to hear: you belong.

Scan this code for photos from Chapter 10

ACKNOWLEDGMENTS

To mom and dad, thank you for your enduring love and support. To my sons, thank you for being my biggest fans and for asking to hear each chapter read out loud as a bedtime story. To Daniel Houghton, thank you for the inspiration to write a book of my own. To Bryan Lemon, thank you for your faithful friendship, brotherhood, and advice as I figured out the narrative arc of my last ten years. To my editor Robin Mozer, I am grateful for your keen eye and sage advice. Your expertise took this project to the next level. Thanks are also due to Marlene Merwarth for helping me bring my front and rear cover designs to life. To Doug Mills and Steve Crowley, thank you for mentoring me and shepherding me over the course of two years in the *New York Times* Washington bureau. To my photo editors, thank you for trusting me to report the news accurately over the years. My appreciation is also owed to the crews of Amtrak's *California Zephyr*, *Southwest Chief*, *Empire Builder*, *Lakeshore Limited*, and *City of New Orleans*. It was aboard these trains that most of this book was written and edited. Thanks also to the team at Quills Coffee on Baxter Ave. in Louisville where I sat for many hours putting words down on paper. Thank you, reader, for purchasing this book. Cover and author photos by Bryan Lemon.

ABOUT THE AUTHOR

Luke Sharrett is a photographer based in Louisville, Kentucky. Thought to be the youngest member of the press to have traveled aboard Air Force One, he is as comfortable in the eye of a category 4 hurricane as he is in the Oval Office. When not wrestling with his two sons, he can be found re-enacting World War II battles and parachuting from vintage warbirds in his spare time. This memoir is his first foray into the world of publishing.

Made in United States
Orlando, FL
14 April 2022

16851861R00134